ORDINARY DOGS

Born in California, Eileen Battersby studied English and History at University College Dublin followed by an MA on the writer Thomas Wolfe. An *Irish Times* staff journalist and literary critic, she has written on all aspects of the arts including classical music, the visual arts, cinema and theatre as well as history, archaeology, architectural history, historical geography and horses. She has won the Irish National Arts Journalist of the Year award four times. Her first book, *Second Readings: From Beckett to Black Beauty*, was published in 2009.

Eileen Battersby is, in the words of novelist John Banville, 'the finest fiction critic we have'. Eileen has been reviewing fiction since 1984, the year J. G. Ballard was expected to win the then Booker Prize with *Empire of the Sun* – but didn't.

ORDINARY DOGS

A Story of Two Lives

EILEEN BATTERSBY

faber and faber

First published in 2011
by Faber and Faber Limited
Bloomsbury House
74–77 Great Russell Street
London WC1B 3DA
This paperback edition published in 2012

Typeset by Palindrome
Printed and bound by CPI Group (UK) Ltd, Croydon, CR0 4YY

A CIP record for this book
is available from the British Library

ISBN 978-0-571-27784-1

2 4 6 8 10 9 7 5 3 1

For Bilbo and Frodo, and for Nadia,
who joined us on our journey

. . . Love is not love

Which alters when it alteration finds,
Or bends with the remover to remove:
Oh no! it is an ever fixed mark
That looks on tempests and is never shaken . . .

SHAKESPEARE, Sonnet 116

Contents

CONTENTS

Acknowledgements

Heartfelt thanks are due to Neil Belton of Faber who believed this book should be written; to Paula Turner of Palindrome whose skill, perception, humour, sympathy and love of animals transformed a working experience into what became for me, a privilege; to my friend and colleague Brian Kilmartin, a dog-sensitive cat person, whose insights were, as ever, invaluable; to my generous friends Seamus and Mary Cassidy for their technological support; to Kate Murray-Browne of Faber for her subtle motivation; to Trudi Kiang for being with me when I first met Bilbo; to my friend Sophie Kiang; to my best book buddy Cormac Kinsella; to Caroline Walsh and Professor Anngret Simms for their ongoing encouragement; to poet Gerard Smyth of *The Irish Times*, the finest arts editor I ever worked under; to my wonderful and adored daughter Nadia for everything and to my magnificent, courageous and determined mare, Kate, and the rest of the Katesfield horses, including Katesfield Mozart 'Josh'; his mother Sophie (the horse, not the girl see above); her daughter Katesfield Isabella Esme 'Izzie'; Can I; Ginny; Lady Spec; Katesfield Mary Glen; Katesfield Ariadne and her son Katesfield Hermes Nijinsky 'Hero'; to my beautiful Nala cat and her feline colleagues including Mimi and her little family and always, always to the dogs, the life-enhancing dogs: Ashley and Arhus, her tenacious children, Bilfro, Paddington, Alice and Ruth; to Mitzi and to gentle, loving Kingsley. To the sweet spirits who left too soon, such as Sebastian, Treefrog and Pippi; the mighty collie siblings Nathan and Loveheart; to brave little Holly and to the enigmatic Sox. Most of all, thank you to my beloved Bilbo and Frodo, who opened the world, yet have left it so much smaller.

Prologue

When I think back on those days, as I often do, as I always will, I know now that they were the happiest times. Although, even then, I was already certain of that. I recall the feeling of absolute content and I remember the wonderful open skies, and, most of all, the light, always that changing light: purple yielding to silver-grey, followed by a pink that somehow became pale yellow before it turned to warm gold. All of these colours seeped in from the east, as if in an ordered sequence, various and elusive, only to vanish abruptly. Suddenly the heavens were blue. The other pigments had gone but the light remained luminous beneath a delicate azure that made the sea appear mottled green. Early morning tends to make the world seem better, renewed, more hopeful. There is an energy that lasts for a couple of hours and everything seems possible. I often imagine myself on one such morning when the breeze blew grains of sand across my face, scouring my skin and stinging my eyes. I would have squinted towards the rising sun, confused by the pulsing circles, more like ripples, of red that teased me as I strained to locate the two dark shapes that were moving in exuberant patterns as the tide edged in.

All I could see were wild splashes, frenzied, exploding into spurts of spray, high against the sky. It had been cold and still; the sea was calm, but then it was bright and almost warm, then it was warm. I shook off my old duffel coat and left it on the dry sand, well aware of the coat's insistent, penetrating smell whenever it got wet. Dry, the coat had a nerdy, scholarly respectability, but moisture released hidden odours, a dull stink reminiscent of mice and ancient newspapers. I had learned to stand well away from people in shops or train stations if the coat became damp.

There wasn't much point in trying to run in my heavy rubber boots. Several sizes too large, they thudded with each step, hitting the ground a second before my feet. So I kicked free of them and ran on in my socks, in pursuit of my dogs, invariably called 'The Guys' by me and by anyone who knew me well. They had raced into the small dunes behind the giant rock formations and were gone from sight. I ran down into the surf, knowing that I would feel their paws against my legs before I ran much further. I had fallen from a roof and broken my ankle in three places some months earlier, so I was happy to be able to run again, happier still as it didn't hurt, at least not enough to notice.

We had come back to the beach, 'our beach', in Connemara as we had so many times before. The beach was bewitched, I was certain of that, I knew – as early as the fourth time I had been here – that it was somehow haunted. It was Halloween, and the moon was huge, white, shimmering, diseased; as bright as stadium floodlights across the shining sand. I had hitched a ride with friends who were driving to Galway but had decided to drive on and take us to Claddaghduff and Omey Beach, as I had, apparently, made the area sound intriguing. I was grateful for the lift but not too thrilled about having to share 'our' place. When their car pulled in to the village, it was almost eleven, and my friends thought they might make last drinks at the small pub and left me to walk the dogs. I was pleased. I didn't want anyone to intrude on us. We went exploring. The tide had not come in fully.

It is a tidal beach, so that it disappears regularly. Sometimes you might see an open expanse of damp sand; then again, you might just see the Atlantic overlooked by a small island, also called Omey. The landscape there is always changing: the light transforms it, while the sea glistens and heaves, concealing the beach and causing the island to appear in relief. For the guys, Bilbo and Frodo, it was one of their many places that we returned to again and again, but this was their most special place and I made sure that they were never challenged here by any other dog. But if another dog meant a potential fight, humans were even more unwelcome; I came to resent the sight of any one walking on 'our' beach.

That Halloween night even the tall posts that had been driven into the sand at spaced intervals leading to the island appeared to have acquired an ominous significance. On cue a gull rasped, other sea birds called, shrieking in response. By day there is always, or so it seems, a line of cormorants at rest along the high banks of stone drying their limp wings, which they hitch up over their shoulders as if they were wet garments. But I wasn't thinking about them that night. The sea was moving faster; there was an urgency suggested by its heaving motion, the ghosts were on the move. I remembered the old graves on the island, the bodies buried in shifting sands that frequently exposed bleached thigh bones and yellowing skulls. Omey Island was again almost cut off from the mainland by the tide; the beach was smaller than usual. We ran along in the moonlight. Suddenly I ran into what felt like a heavy, wet blanket, yet I knew there was nothing there. I made a feeble attempt to call the dogs with barely more than a whisper. My teeth were actually chattering. My face was cold. I ran back up the beach, splashing through pools of water and over sand, and reached the small road where I stopped. The guys halted on either side of me. I knelt and stared down the beach to the icy spot where I had encountered that eerie wall.

Stretching both arms out, a dog on each side, leaning in towards me, I closed my arms around them. They were solid, part of me. My dogs, young and fit. They were wet and panting, excited but wary. Both stared at the spot we had raced back from; they looked as shocked as I felt. The moon was reflected in their eyes that had become black glass in the night. Their expressions were uneasy. I don't know what was there, but the dogs saw something.

Several times, during the twenty years and the many journeys the three of us made together, I could only sense what their sharper eyes could *see*. They opened the world to me; I learned to touch, to look closely, to read gestures, even the faintest facial tensing, a shrug. I discovered the pleasure of an hour spent in a wood or down by a lake shore. Even an impromptu canal walk became an entry to another country. Life became more intense, precise, immediate and real.

There were many days on many beaches, in woods, farmland, hillsides, ancient churchyards, expeditions to old ruins; but the place I most vividly remember is Connemara, in all weathers, throughout the seasons, beneath a sun that might be bright in a clear, blue sky or obscured by racing clouds, or those evenings at brooding dusk, as the light finally ebbed away. And once in a wind so strong that it lifted both dogs off balance, tossing them about like the tumbleweeds I used to count in the desert in Palm Springs when I was a child.

I remember how once, late in the afternoon in early August when we were exploring Omey Island, Bilbo ran ahead, only to begin barking, but not quite barking – he was producing more of a sharp, sudden yap. He began to howl and walked slowly towards me, pausing to look back, at intervals turning completely; he would take a few paces as if to obey, then hesitate. He seemed torn between joining me and Frodo, and this new thing he had spotted. He stopped and looked directly at me. There was a sense of purpose about his antics. At first I laughed and reminded him that I was the boss and put my arms out, expecting him to race towards me. But that time he didn't.

Instead he kept running towards me, then away, very agitated, and then he dropped down low to the ground, only to bound back up and at me, and then, just as quickly, wheel around. I ran towards him with Frodo at my side, but Bilbo hurried away, back towards the cliff edge. I was worried in case it was a nest with an angry sea bird. Once, when we were in a small boat, we chugged into a low cave that opened out as we passed through the narrow entry channel into a higher-ceilinged chamber and suddenly, from nowhere, an explosion of movement revealed a cormorant guarding her nest, her open mouth and throat red in the dull light. Her shrieks echoed against the roof of the cave. It seemed as though she was preparing to fight. This was what I feared finding as I followed Bilbo.

He came to halt, his head cocked to one side, eyes bright, focused. I saw what he had found. A dog lay at the cliff's edge; black and white, a kind of sheepdog, big, shaggy, motionless in the scrub grass. The wind was blowing the dog's dull coat into tufts, exposing the grey skin. The dog was dead. My dogs stared, sniffing tentatively, but hesitated, observing me. I knelt down and touched the broad head, fingering the crusted, scarred ears. There was no sign of a house, nothing. The sea was bright blue and vast under a clear sky. Not another soul in sight. Only gulls soaring across the heavens then diving down towards the sea. The big sheepdog had picked a wonderful place to die.

Was there an owner searching for him? Where had the dog lived? What kind of a life had the dog had? A working life by the look of him, never a pet; he'd been out in all weathers and had earned his keep. The soft muzzle was grey and the eyes open but clouded; the black lip curled back over a sharp, white tooth. Ancient scars marked his face and ears, a bare patch under the left eye; the legacy of disputes long ago. I looked at my dogs, the guys, pampered, young, loved, and wondered how their lives would end – in an accident? Through disease? Old age? Would they be alone like this? I left the aged dog, lying peacefully in the secluded spot he had selected. There was nothing to cover him, no driftwood, no stones with which to build a cairn. Only sand, and the wind would have soon blown that away.

Part 1

I

The Puppy in the Pound

The only dogs I knew when I was small belonged to other people.

The first dog I became close to was an old yellow hound that lived in the mountain village near Lake Arrowhead in California, where we had a cabin. He was self-possessed and had long, flat ears and was lean, rangy and sinewy, respected by all. If I ever knew his name I have long since forgotten it. But he should have been called Colonel: he ambled about like a Southern gent, stiff in his quarters, and probably had his own views on how the Civil War had been fought and lost. I see him now in my mind's eye, sauntering slowly, struggling for balance as he cocks a leg against a tree or a rock, or that intrusive automobile there, the one with the out-of-state plates, a car that had no right to be cluttering up the pine-forest path where the clearing extended beyond the tree line to the mountains.

He may have been born there, or perhaps he just fetched up one fine day and decided he liked the lake view and the sharp, clean mountain air. He would stretch out in the sun on the porch of his owner's large clapboard house with the flaking blue paint and sigh at regular intervals. His calm eyes were the colour of pewter. There's a photograph of a young child on his back; I like to think it's me. With age the yellow of his coat faded to pale, dirty grey, his jaw became slacker and his teeth deserted him. Together we'd watched a skunk browsing through the undergrowth on a high bank veined by the roots of ancient trees, always making sure they *were* roots and not one of those swift-moving mountain snakes. He'd come counting squirrels with me and understood not to scare them. He must have known by heart long passages from *The Incredible Journey*, that classic story about two dogs and a Siamese cat who crossed Canada together to return home. I used to read it aloud to him.

One summer he wasn't there any more. A first loss; but he was never my dog – a friend, but not *my* dog. I had had no rights over him. He had not been allowed to sleep by my bed in the attic room with the sharply pitched roof. I wasn't even allowed to bring him into the kitchen downstairs. But at least I could mourn him, and I missed him. Even now, I often think of his flat-footed gait and his habit of leaning against me for support.

There were other dogs. The dogs on leashes in the park, the ones you could pet without the owners becoming tense; the dogs who raided picnics and upended beach baskets. I remember a skinny collie that once ran into a bakery while we all watched. The dog was frantic and intent as he tore an iced birthday cake apart, gulping down huge bits, choking and spitting in desperation. It happened in La Jolla, a trendy enclave beside San Diego, near the US–Mexico border. The baker's wife, who was perhaps Austrian or possibly Swiss, shouted in German and threw an order book at the dog; her face was red, and the people who had ordered the cake for a party later that day gazed mutely at the debris and shrugged the way naturally resigned people do.

Years passed, and I always liked dogs, worrying about the fate of hungry strays, but never having a dog of my own, always having to decline the offer of puppies. I was the product of an ultra-clean home and was neurotically tidy, the sort of kid who wouldn't sleep on pillows in case I creased them. I used to vacuum my bedroom before I went to school. My books and music were filed according to subject as if in a library.

Somehow the timing was never right. But then one day it was. I was no longer living in a rented room, or staying in someone else's house. I had just completed writing a thesis about Thomas Wolfe, a restless, troubled individual from Asheville, North Carolina. When he moved to New York to become a writer, he often wandered the streets at night, arguing with himself. I reckoned that my life would be very different from his – and far quieter. I had a cottage, small and bare except for books, so many books. Sheets of brown paper covered most of the windows. There was no heating and the cottage was isolated, but it was my first house. Then strange things started happening during the night. Laundry was stolen off the line and a tracksuit top was found lying on the doorstep in the morning, folded neatly but cut in two. Clay pots would be smashed, the plants trampled. My bike was stolen, as was its replacement. I needed a dog.

One bright winter morning in early December, a Tuesday, I set off to get a dog. I wanted a big German Shepherd; I would call him Ludwig in honour of Beethoven and take him for runs. My friend Sophie's mother, Trudi, was going to drive me to the dogs' home. She had told me that it was all very well buying a dog from a breeder but, if I went to a pound, I would be saving a dog's life. Such a dog would have superior intelligence, a stronger character and an intuitive understanding of the most important things.

On the drive there I felt a surge of happiness. I didn't have to ask anyone's permission; this would be my dog.

At the pound, the first thing I noticed was the noise: the

barking, the howling, the communal despair and, above all, the smells. There was the harsh, medicinal aroma, intended to mask the animal odours. Buckets of undiluted disinfectant must have been poured neat on to the ground and into the cages, under all that newspaper. But the strongest, most penetrating scent that asserted itself was cat pee. The animals endured that in confined spaces, inhaling that burning smell all day long. No wonder the staff all appeared to be smokers.

A man turned round when he heard us near the first of the kennels. He was holding a sweeping brush and regarded us with a sour glance, as if we had arrived at a prison outside visiting hours. 'I want a big dog, a German Shepherd,' I announced, quickly adding, 'or a kind of German Shepherd,' for fear the man would think I was a snob intent on a pedigree. 'A big dog who likes running, I'm a runner.' I realised I was sounding like a ten-year-old – I've always babbled when I'm nervous. And I *was* nervous, I wanted a dog, I didn't want to leave that dreadful, sad place without a dog, the dog that I had been waiting for all my life.

'There's a fella there,' said the man, half lifting his brush to point at a cage, and he asked if I considered the dog big enough for me. But it wasn't a question; it was more like a challenge. A lone dog prowled a space that seemed too big for one, considering that in several of the nearby kennels eight or ten dogs were tumbling over each other in their desperation to catch a saviour's eye, as if each stray knew they were trapped by a ticking clock. Five days to get a home or die. The solitary dog was medium-sized; black, a kind of skinny Labrador with small, mean eyes. He was cross-bred with something else, possibly a greyhound or a whippet. Whatever his origins, he was wary, suspicious. He looked fit, and was perhaps three or four years of age.

Not what I had had in mind, but then appearance isn't everything. I went over to the cage, 'Hi, boy,' I said, thinking, 'So this is it, the moment.' It could have gone better. The dog snarled, threw his weight against the mesh and made sure I knew he was ready to rip my fingers off. 'He's a bit vicious,' said the man, enjoying his little joke, 'but, sure, when you get him out running with you, he'll be grand.' The dog no doubt had a story but there was no one to tell it.

I said that I was thinking of something younger, more of a puppy and obviously not quite as aggressive, and oh, yes, a dog, not a female. I would have liked to shout at the cynical old son of a bitch, but Sophie's kind, consummately civilised mother was standing beside me. The man pointed to some young pups, but assured me that they were all female. I don't know why I was so intent on a male dog. The kennel they were in was overcrowded and soiled: no one could have kept the floor clean, as the puppies were falling over each other, playing, fighting, peeing. Two of them were very quiet, disturbingly subdued. A pretty, fox-coloured one with big white socks and a thick, black, fawn-and-white tail looked right at me and thrust a paw through the bars. The fur was soft but damp with urine; the puppy stared at me with large amber eyes. The black muzzle followed the paws through the bars. A girl in a white lab coat arrived with a small trolley holding several large metal dishes of food.

All the puppies dashed to the side of the kennel as the girl opened the door and pushed her trolley through. The little dog also joined the others, but quickly left the food and returned to where I was standing. I've never had any interest in jewellery but I noticed that the puppy's black-ringed, burnished eyes were exactly the same colour as the smooth stone in Trudi's silver ring. The puppy appeared to be wearing eyeliner and had delicate black eyebrows and beguiling ears that often stood to attention but also flopped over neatly. A very cute creature; a teddy bear of a dog, with a thick shawl of fur coming down from the back of the head, and over the neck to taper off halfway down the back.

The puppy jumped up and down as if she was trying to tell me something. She wanted me and it was decided. I would take her. I told the horrible little man that I had found a dog and went to open the cage. He stopped me, explaining that I had to go into the office and pay for her, then come back to him, but only if they agreed. There was a formal process. He seemed to enjoy his power. His eyes glittered when he looked at me and said that if I got approval – which he referred to as 'the all clear' – then he would fetch the pup. He also reiterated, 'It's not a dog, it's a bitch. Are you clear about that? Would you not be better off with the lad in the cage? If all you want is something to go running with, he'll keep ye on your toes. Sure, he might even bite them off.' His spluttering guffaw became a wheeze before collapsing into a wet coughing fit. I stalked off to the office. Two women sat at a wooden counter. There was a third one on the phone, advising the caller to contact the police. 'That level of cruelty, you know . . . when there are beatings involved and it most likely will go to court . . .' One of the pair at the counter announced she was going to make tea, but there was no milk. A debate began about whose turn it was to buy the morning biscuits. They were oblivious to me. I excused myself and said that I'd like to take one of the puppies and began to describe her. I remember saying 'a vaguely German Shepherd-ish type', not wishing to sound more interested in the breed than in the puppy. The most senior of the three pounced. 'Give me your details. You can't take a dog just like that. This isn't a shop, you know. There is a procedure: we have to decide if you are suitable, a suitable owner. Are you capable of looking after a dog? Have you ever had a dog?' Each condition was despatched in a quick-fire tone of reprimand.

Her attitude came as a surprise. I had expected communal goodwill and happy smiles. Instead I felt as if I had been caught stealing candy and was awaiting my punishment. 'We have to see when we can send an inspector out. It might take a week, or more, or maybe not until after Christmas. Do you have a garden? Does it have ten-foot walls? Can you afford to keep a dog?' I tried to keep calm.

For the first time in my life I asserted myself – and improvised. Lied, in other words. 'I'm very experienced. My father's a vet.' – Dad had been dead for several years and had never been a vet – 'We have a large garden,' – I didn't – 'and the walls are easily ten foot high.' I lied with a fluency and confidence born of my determination to claim the little dog as mine. There was also the fact that my friend's mother couldn't hear me: she found the place upsetting and had gone outside. 'I'm very serious, I'm a postgrad, I'm writing my research up at home. I never go out. I'm actually reclusive.' I wanted them to think that the puppy would have a full-time carer. The woman asking the questions peered at me. The ideal dog owner had materialised and was standing before her wearing a huge duffel coat and a trustworthy smile. The woman had been won over – almost. 'Even so,' she began, 'we can't just say yes on the spot, we have a policy here.' Diplomacy was now clearly the best ploy. 'I understand. I just want go back and take another look at her. I wish I had my camera,' I added casually, and walked back to the kennel area, intent on getting the puppy.

My nemesis was standing there, smoking away, his half-hearted sweeping on hold. 'They won't let you take it today. There has to be an inspection, you know, of your house and the garden and all,' he said gleefully. The new me was ready. 'Actually it's OK, they know my father, McHale Robinson' – the invented name sounded so convincing. I said that dad was a famous vet, 'A professor of veterinary medicine. You've probably read his books.' I paused for effect. 'I'll just take her with me now. They said that it's fine, it will free up some space for the others.' Sweat was coursing down my back. I wanted to sneeze and shout, run out with the dog. Nervous laughter was bubbling up my throat as I repeated that I would just take her with me. The kennel man was small, about six or seven inches shorter than me, thin and, by the sound of him, suffering from a complicated range of respiratory problems, hopefully serious. It gave me quite a physical advantage and I was ready to hit him if he was stupid enough to intervene. But he was impressed by my famous father and was now eager to assist me.

He fumbled with the bolt. 'Stay here,' he commanded. I pushed by him and reached down for the tiny dog, lifted her up and discovered that 'she' was in fact a male dog. 'Come on, Bilbo,' I said. I don't even know why I said that, but so much for Ludwig – I named him Bilbo the first time I held him. He may have been eight or nine weeks old, with a fat little hobbit belly; he was fluffy, determined and confident that he had caught me. The name seemed right. I swept out of the compound, with Bilbo under my coat and heard the gate rattling behind me as the man closed it and slid the bolt back.

Back in the office, the women looked up. I was going to walk out without stopping, but paused instead to hand in a donation, £20, and, smiling happily, announced I'd be on my way, reminding them that they had my details. One woman hesitated, but steadied herself and told me to put the dog back. She then asked me if Larry had not informed me about the rules. So the old man was called Larry. 'He knows Dad,' I enthused, nodding knowingly. 'My father, the vet – Larry, he's a friend of Dad's, and he thinks I should bring the puppy to Dad straight away for an examination. So I'll just go now,' I offered brightly, edging towards the door. Bilbo had shifted down into the sleeve of the coat. By way of proving how blameless and helpful I was, I mentioned that Bilbo was in fact a he, expecting them to be grateful to me for being able to solve at least one dog's problems.

By then Bilbo was so far down the sleeve of the coat that I had my arm outstretched, straight in front of me, in a type of salute. I acted as if this was a completely normal gesture. 'Oh look, he's really settled in my sleeve. Larry said it was the one who came in late yesterday from Monastery Road, the one the lady with the red car brought in.' The woman at the counter knew which puppy I meant, and said, 'That tawny-reddish one with the big blackish tail?' I reached into the sleeve. He had lodged himself firmly down in it, so my arm was now pointing like a gun at the woman. I could feel the small weight of him, a pressure on the bend of my arm, and said that he seemed comfortable in there and that I wouldn't disturb him.

The woman behind the counter was beginning to lose interest; she wanted her tea and biscuits. She expanded on Larry's comment: 'That lady in the Golf? She'd only had him a day or so. She'd picked him up on the road but she wasn't able to deal with the peeing and the vomiting. Lots of people like the idea of having a dog but they aren't up to the reality. It's a lot of work.' I smiled sympathetically and hurried out before dear old Larry, unaware he was such a close buddy of my father's, arrived and all my lies began to unravel.

Out in the street, away from the fetid smell of the rescue centre, the cold air hit my face, which felt blotchy from the stress of lying. Triumphant, I walked on. My arm was still stretched out before me, showing the way. It looked as though it had been broken and placed in a wired support. The bright daylight welcomed us. Bilbo wriggled back up my sleeve and emerged from the duffel coat to nestle his head under my chin. He arched his back and put his full weight against me, forcing my head up. He would have twenty years and a day to perfect the habit, but he got it right that very first time.

The coat closed around him. I ran up to the car and we drove off. I glanced back at the door of the pound. No angry faces were peering at the departing car. 'What a pretty puppy,' said Trudi, and she drove us off towards her house. She had once had a Pyrenean Mountain dog, an immense animal, and she wanted to give me his bed. His dog basket, however, could have accommodated the average adult, and I had reckoned that Bilbo would be sleeping on my bed. It was time to relinquish my hyper-tidiness. Bilbo would never need a basket that size. As we stood in the porch at Trudi's house, Bilbo ran into the flower beds. Then we went into the kitchen. She took something off the counter, a steel comb with a fine, carved bone handle. It had been bought long ago for her big dog and now it would be Bilbo's. I am looking at it as I write.

On cue Bilbo ran across the kitchen to the bin and pulled

a bread wrapper out, shaking it over his head. 'That's what they do, puppies are such fun,' she said. Then he squatted and peed on the floor, before vomiting. It must have been the car trip and the excitement. I cleaned up the messes. Trudi drove me home. On the way we stopped at a supermarket and she stayed in the car with Bilbo as I went in to buy the first of what would be mountains of dog food. The young girl at the checkout noticed that I had bought nothing else and she asked if I had just got a new dog. 'Yes, my first dog, a puppy,' I replied, aware I was sounding like a new parent and felt self-conscious. 'That's lovely,' she smiled. 'I've a cat, well, he's not mine, he's the family cat but he's not very friendly. He's just the cat.' I carried my gourmet dog food outside, a variety of flavours, and a selection of dog treats. Bilbo was sitting in the passenger seat. Trudi smiled at him and told me that he had just sat in my seat, watching, waiting for me to come back. She had had a lot of pets over the years and said that Bilbo was probably feeling a bit bewildered, so many new things were happening to him all at once. She said that he would settle as soon as I got him home. Her words made me feel better.

He sat in my lap and we drove to my house up the long, windy road, the one I hated cycling on because, regardless of the weather elsewhere, a vicious wind invariably gusted along it, pulling at your hair, your clothes, the skin on your face. After Trudi's car disappeared from sight, I stood in the front garden, alone with my first dog. We couldn't go for a walk; there was a risk of infection, as he needed vaccinations, so our first outing together would have to wait. I opened the door and carried in the dog food. He ran in with me. Reaching up to the cupboard I took down a dark brown ceramic bowl and opened the can. I lifted him on to the table and looked into his eyes, said, 'You are my dog,' and blew in his ear. Then I hugged him and gave him his food. He ate some of it and vomited. I gave him water. Within minutes he was retching it up all over the wooden floor. His nose was dry. He seemed more resigned than anxious. Perhaps he just wanted to sleep and calm his stomach? I gave him my sweater to lie on and left him to rest in the kitchen while I went for a run.

*

The run was not a success. A light shower became heavier and the rain was soon bouncing off the already muddy road. I had intended running up to the main road where there was a long stretch of sandy track under an endless series of yellow lights. All the way in the dark I was wondering what was wrong, how come Bilbo seemed so listless. He was really the equivalent of a human baby, I reasoned, drained from the excitement of the day. Of course, he would be exhausted. But even then I knew that an eight- or nine-week-old puppy is far more developed than its human counterpart.

I turned back and hit the only stone for miles and twisted my ankle. I ran on and got back to the house, realising that I had forgotten to lock the door. That was putting a heavy responsibility on a weak, possibly dangerously sick puppy. Kicking free of my wet runners and socks, my bare feet made damp patches on the wooden floor. Back in the kitchen, Bilbo was lying on my sweater; his food was untouched. There was more vomit, and more puddles of watery diarrhoea and his nose was not just dry, now it was alarmingly hot. He groaned when I tried to lift him. His body was burning. I began to panic. It was about 6.30 in the evening, perhaps later. And there was no one to help. I needed a vet and help from someone with a car.

The fourth front door I knocked at opened, and a young woman, obviously a new mother (as I deduced, wrongly) stood looking at me. Her hair was wild and she looked very tired, her pink dressing gown was short and not too clean, and her chunky legs were bare and grey-white. 'Yes, what do you want?' She looked ready to slam the door. 'I'm so sorry to bother you, but my dog is not well . . .' She stiffened with irritation, and told me that she was a nurse, not a vet, and paused for a moment before adding that she had been having the first sleep she had had in days. Instead of telling her how sorry I was to disturb her, I thought, what luck, perhaps she could help us. I looked into her eyes. I begged her to do something. I must have reminded her of people she had seen at the hospital, not the sick ones, the others, the ones who waited in the corridors or by bedsides, hoping for miracles.

*

'Who's your vet?' asked the nurse, her irritated expression changing to one of resignation, asking for information in which she had little or no interest. I told her that I didn't have one, that I'd only got the puppy that day. The woman was not exactly sympathetic, but her professional conscience had been aroused and it seemed that she would rather help me out of a sense of duty than feign neighbourliness. I wasn't complaining. She took control, telling me to get a vet. She went to fetch the phone book for me, while she had a shower. I began looking up numbers. Each call was met with an answering machine and strings of out-of-hours numbers I was too flustered to take down correctly. Finally a voice answered and the man on the other end told me I was in luck and if I arrived within the next half hour he'd have a look at my dog. His address meant nothing to me, but the nurse said it was near 'her' hospital. 'Come on, I'm ready,' she said. 'I don't even like dogs.' We went out to her car. It was small, very clean, complete with a box of pink tissues and an overpowering scent of sharp musk: a single woman's tidy car. I hoped Bilbo wouldn't vomit in it and I hurried to fetch him.

Back at my cottage, I opened the door and hurried into the kitchen. He was lying there, very still, face to the wall. His ear lifted on hearing movement, and he turned his head towards me. I bent down to lift him, wrapping him in the tartan car blanket I had been given as a present, even though I didn't have a car. I pulled the kitchen curtains and put on the ceiling light, then ran out, closing the door, and hurried to where the car waited, engine running. 'You'd better sit in the back, odds on the dog will be sick. I grew up on a farm and the dogs were always sick. They get into all kinds of dirt and they're great for heaving it all up. Was it poison? It looks like poison.' On she drove, angry, bothered by life. I didn't care. I just wanted to get to the vet. Bilbo was very weak. She broke the silence by switching on the radio.

A play was being broadcast. Two female characters were arguing; they had been friends but one of them had got involved with the other's husband. The man had just been killed in a car accident and the wife had phoned her friend for support. But the friend, now the bereaved mistress, was too upset to help. The voices were shrill, vindictive.

The script was clichéd and the dialogue was being batted back and forth between the two actors but both had opted for the same sneering tone, and neither seemed truly engaged by the thin storyline. I hated listening to it. The nurse, however, was captivated; her face seemed younger, hungry. 'That happened to me, but the guy, total bastard, didn't die – he just got sick and went back to his wife, leaving me as if it were my fault. My friend hasn't spoken to me since. People . . .' She sighed in disgust and asked me if that was why I got the dog – revealing the first sign of interest in me or Bilbo and apparently assuming that I had a history of bad relationships. I said I had simply wanted one, I'd always wanted a dog, and my voice faltered. I began to cry. It made me think though – had she decided that lonely people saw dogs as substitutes for human companionship? In the years to come I would often think back on that conversation, admittedly with increasing irony. But at that time I was fairly open-minded; I had seen good relationships as well as bad ones and certainly believed in the possibility of the Great Romance. She had obviously had a bad experience. My sobbing made her uncomfortable. The subject was dropped and she drove on, eyes fixed in the road. Bilbo chose that moment to vomit on my lap. It was hot, runny and somehow also got on my hands. She asked when I had last fed him and she seemed more kindly. I said that I had given him food but that he had barely touched it. The car slowed to a stop. I thought she was going to tell us to get out. 'It should be there, see the gates. He has a flash Range Rover, no ball hitch though . . . Like I said, I'm a farmer's daughter, I notice things. You want me to wait?'

I wanted to be on my own. If Bilbo died there, I was going to bring him home with me. I would carry him back to the house. I thanked her and apologised again for waking her. She got out and said she was going to the shop and waved. 'Good luck, the world is full of dogs.' She meant it to be kindly.

*

A loud ticking came from somewhere yet there was no clock. The vet's surgery was quiet. It was late in the evening, and the lights were off. He had opened the front door of his house and nodded towards the extension at the side, mostly of reinforced glass with strong double doors. He told me that it was unlocked and to go and wait, the waiting room was on the left, and that I was to keep 'that dog' in my arms as he didn't want infection being spread about the floor. As curt as that, he turned and went back to his television and sat down, I could see him through the gap in the curtain. I walked over to the surgery. The waiting room was decorated with friendly wall charts, each offering advice about flea control and vaccinations.

After about twenty minutes, the vet appeared, having finished whatever it was he had been watching. 'In here,' he motioned, and I followed him into an examination room. He told me to put Bilbo on the table and began to address me in a detached, almost formal way. 'As I said on the phone,' he began, 'it's probably distemper and there's little I can do.' I looked at this stout, middle-aged man, with his broad face and his perfect garden. On the phone he had sounded interested, almost keen and had told me to bring my dog to him immediately. Now he seemed indifferent, dismissive. The vet took Bilbo's temperature. He frowned and said that he hadn't a hope, it was 'far too high' and he would 'sort it out, now'. He avoided my gaze as he spoke. I thought I should sound involved so I tried to speak although my eyes were sore from crying. I asked about the medication. Would Bilbo need injections and antibiotics? This time the vet actually looked at me and explained what he meant, that he was going to put him down, that there was nothing to be done. He said that it was about as bad as distemper gets before death and seemed rather irritated as he remarked that the puppy had already been ill with it before I had taken him from the dog's home where he had no doubt contracted it. He mentioned a cardboard box that was out in the passage and told me to fetch it, adding that Bilbo would 'be gone' before I got back.

A queasy sensation surged up my throat, that and a rage. I pleaded with him to give my dog something, to give him a chance. I said that he was young and could fight. Give him medicine, I cajoled, assuring him that I could pay. The vet was firm and described the condition as too advanced, explaining that it compromises the nervous system and that Bilbo, even if he recovered, might never be right. Again he stressed that he should never have been released from the animal shelter; that his symptoms would have been obvious.

This was happening because of all the lies I had told at the pound, all my clever lies. I had caused this. The vomiting, the thirst, the lack of appetite, the signs had been there. Squeezing Bilbo's tartan car rug between my fingers, I kept on, badgering the vet, insisting that he give him some medication, and that if he refused to help him, I would tell the police. Even at the time I realised this was extreme and I knew I was out of control as I stood there. Bilbo suddenly seemed more alert. The vet looked mildly shocked, and then became interested. 'All right, I'll give him this shot now, it may help.' He more or less said that, if Bilbo survived, I was to bring him back the next evening at about the same time. He stressed that it had to be after hours, as he couldn't risk the spread of infection. 'Bring Bilbo back,' he announced, 'and we'll see what happens.' I turned to walk home; it was about five miles. There was no lift waiting. I had often run five miles but had never walked that far, carrying a dog. The vet switched off the lights, the garden disappeared into the darkness. He hadn't even asked my name, but he knew Bilbo's; he'd heard me talking to him.

Leaving the vet's surgery with Bilbo in my arms, I had to kick the gate shut. The nurse's car, as expected, was gone. It was better this way. Bilbo seemed brighter, a little more alert. I walked on, holding him close to me, wrapped in his tartan blanket, under the duffel coat. He wasn't trying to climb inside the sleeve now, he was very quiet. Then I realised that I didn't know where I was. The small shop that the nurse had walked over to was now shuttered.

There was a pub. Into the smoke-filled darkness I went. The frantic outcasts, who now stand outside pubs defiantly sucking their cigarettes, were all inside, holding court. I was an easy target, with my swollen eyes and my strange bundle. 'You're not going to start begging in here,' said the barman, motioning towards the door. 'It's not fair on the child, never mind the customers.' What child? I wondered and looked around. Then I realised he thought I had a baby in my arms and was about to ask for money. I tried to stay calm and began explaining that Bilbo was ill and that I had been given a lift to the vet, that I had never been there before, and in fact had only got the puppy that day and was lost and didn't know where I was in relation to my house. All of this was shouted at the barman as the bar was so busy, full of voices. I began to cough, my voice faltering. The barman took control; he called a younger man, who looked like a student, and snapped orders at him, telling him to find out where I was trying to get to. 'She's lost,' he announced, adding, mistakenly, that my dog had been hit by a car. The younger man took charge. 'You need a vet to take a look at that, sometimes they can get them going with a shot to the heart, if, like, it's not too late.' I wanted to scream

We went out to the street. 'The vet's over there,' the barman told me, pointing out that the surgery would be closed. I felt so tired from no one appearing to hear what I was saying, as I explained my every need and action. My arms were aching. Bilbo was shifting about; I didn't want him to jump down. All I wanted to find out was where I was and how I could get home. The young man was shivering; the cold street was very different from the sauna-like atmosphere of the pub. 'It's miles. You need a taxi, but they won't take the dog in case it shits or pukes . . . don't you know anyone? Haven't you a friend?' He acted as if I were an alien. I assured him that I did have friends, just not nearby. 'Not here; not around here.' I wanted to sleep on the spot. Most of all I wanted to get away from him and I said it was OK and that I would walk as it wasn't raining. Two men and a girl came out of the pub. The barman knew them. 'It's your chance to do a good deed,' he said to one of the men, slapping him on the back. The man eyed the back-slapper. He seemed not too steady on his feet and I thought of dying, crashing into a wall beside a drunken driver. But the girl announced that it was her car and she was driving.

Confident that he had solved my problem, the young barman waved and jogged back towards the pub. The two men, the girl and me walked in single file to an old saloon car, sloppily parked half up on the kerb. 'Give me the keys,' the girl demanded of the second man, who could have been her boyfriend. 'Where exactly are we going?' With a vicious squeal of the clutch we set off into the night. She was sober but she drove in spasms, slowly at first, then accelerating abruptly, only to slow down and stall, without changing gear. The car heaved and bounced.

*

'What's wrong with the dog? Did you find him on the road?' The other man, the tipsy one, asked me without a glance in my direction. It seemed as if weeks had passed since that morning at the animal shelter. I had not eaten and felt sick and dirty. Bilbo's vomit was on my clothes, in my hair. There was dog pee on my jeans. It didn't matter. I began to explain about Bilbo's illness but the three had begun speaking among themselves, no one was listening to me. What with their drinking and smoking, they probably couldn't even smell us. I smirked to myself and looked down at Bilbo. His eyes were on me. He put his head in close under my chin and sighed. He was my dog, I was his person.

'This is as far as I can go, I'm low on petrol and I don't want to get us all stuck out here and I still have a bit of difficulty reversing.' The rest of her driving was not so hot either. 'You know the way from here,' coaxed the girl, 'I think that's the long road you mentioned. Hope he gets better; dogs are tough – they've great attitude.' She said goodbye and the car lurched off into the darkness.

*

All the way up the road I spoke to Bilbo, telling him that he would get better. It was dark, no moon, just the familiar cutting wind that always tore up that wasteland road. Back at the house in the bright light of the kitchen he looked smaller, less fluffy, drained. His bowl was on the floor. The food in it had dried out. I washed the bowl and put some tuna in it. He sniffed at it, seemed interested . . . but no, he left it and went to the corner, peed. And then walked back to me, putting his head in my hands. His nose was still dry, not quite as hot, but it was alarmingly dry. I noticed he had one of those black birth marks on his cheek, just like a real German Shepherd. I picked up his bowl and rinsed it and held it under the faucet. He drank all the water, and immediately looked up for more. He walked back to the tuna and ate some. I muttered my thanks to God. 'I'll be back,' I said to Bilbo, and went off to fetch my sleeping bag and the book I was reading. I would keep my vigil with Bilbo in the kitchen. The smell of the pub lingered on me; it seemed to fill the room. That night I was to read Canetti's *Auto da Fé* for the first time, smiling at the idea of the solitary lunatic in his house full of books.

The wooden floor was hard; I needed pillows and went to the bedroom, a dark little space at the rear of the cottage. Back in the kitchen Bilbo had moved. He was now sitting on top of the sleeping bag, his front legs stretched out before him, his expression contemplative, but his food still untouched. I tried to unfold the sleeping bag without disturbing him but it was bunched up under him, leaving just enough space for me to kneel on it. I edged the material out from under him but he began to groan. I went back to the bedroom for more blankets and the bedside lamp. It was going to be a long night.

Reading proved difficult: the words kept running into each other and the print was small. Instead I studied Bilbo. What kind of character did he have? Was he a fighter? Or would he simply give up? He seemed intelligent but, as I have come to realise, I have yet to meet a stupid dog. Dogs are reactors, deliberate, astute and aware that life is for the moment. My face was sore from crying, pleading, trying to explain his situation to other people. So much tension with the lies, the pleading and now the incredible importance that this puppy had assumed, at least to me. I was prepared to make demands on his behalf, even to the extent of threatening the vet.

Not being able to concentrate on a book was a new experience. Until that night, a bomb could have exploded, a riot could have been going on outside in the street yet I would continue reading. Once, when camping in Greece, I sat reading in a tent while a rat, having chewed a hole in the back wall, methodically ate the bread and cakes stored in a basket a couple of feet from where I was sitting, propped up against a pile of rucksacks. 'He must have been a very quiet eater,' I explained to my friends who had looked at me with a hint of revulsion, horrified by my casual attitude. (At school I had been in charge of the white mice that lived in the science lab. I was considered 'rodent friendly'.)

That night, with Bilbo, I was his protector. I watched his every twitch, monitored his groans and whimpers. There was a packet of fig rolls in the cupboard, and as I began to eat one, Bilbo became interested. I gave him one too. He took it in his mouth; then let it fall. He came closer to me, stood on my leg and sniffed at my mouth; I took mushy, chewed biscuit out and dropped it into my hand. He ate it, swallowed and looked for more. As fast as I could chew it and transfer it to my hand, he was eating the fig-roll paste. I felt elated. By the sixth biscuit I decided to stop, for fear his delicate stomach had had enough. He sighed and began to settle down; he released more of the sleeping bag. I finished off a jar of sauerkraut and ate an orange and a banana, then took up my book again. It was late; the bulb in the reading lamp began to flicker. Perhaps it was my eyes that were tired.

I was being held down, but fought back against the pressure on my chest. Dull light seeped in from the edges of the curtains. Bilbo was sitting on me. I rolled over to check if he had vomited the fig rolls. No. He looked better;

but he was still listless, his nose was still dry. It was just nine o'clock in the morning and the entire day had to pass before we made our return to the vet. All I could remember was that the pub had been called the Marco Polo, and that the vet's name was Whitford or Whitfall – something like that. The visit to the vet had to be planned; I didn't want to ask the nurse for another lift.

A very small shop, useful only for urgent supplies such as milk and logs for the fire, was about 800 metres from my cottage beyond a vacant field rutted with paths hacked out by the cows that used to be kept in it. I ran to the shop, just for milk, noting that the nurse's car wasn't outside her house. On the way I noticed a man with a dog, a cocker spaniel wearing a tiny Superman vest. A man who would put a Superman vest on his dog must be approachable, I thought. The dog bounded up to me as if I were an old friend. The man was impressed and told me that I must be special as Tessa, the cocker, hated most people and barely tolerated the man's wife. He asked me if I had a dog. I sensed he would give me a lift, providing he had a car. I explained about my new puppy and Bilbo's dilemma, attempting, poorly, to keep my desperation at bay. The man looked sympathetic as I explained about the visit to the vet, the bleak prognosis and the need to return to the surgery that evening. His name was Robert, a teacher who had retired early. 'My nerves,' he said. 'Well, really, the kids – boys of sixteen and seventeen, look like men and act like girls.' He said that he would drive me to the vet and that it would be fine. There would be no fear of infection as Tessa hated the car and rarely travelled in it.

I ran back with the milk, and intended to make a large bowl of comforting hot chocolate. I didn't want to eat.

Yellow diarrhoea had formed a patch on the sleeping bag. Bilbo was sitting under the table, his face to the wall. But there was no trace of vomit. After I cleaned the floor, the air smelt of pine. It seemed a good time to bake some bread, as a way of improving the smell in the kitchen. Then I remembered I had a jar of cinnamon and left it open on the counter, hoping its spicy aroma would overpower the stench of illness.

*

Time passed slowly. Bilbo looked at me now and then as if he didn't know who I was. Having made such a point of selecting me as his person, he no longer cared. Aside from the milk there was nothing edible in the house. A cycle-ride to the big supermarket would use up some time. Before I left, I mashed up another fig roll, but now Bilbo didn't want it. Off into the wind I rode, sensing he had lost interest, not only in me but in life.

Food for fat dogs; for thin dogs; for puppies; for young adult dogs, for active dogs and older dogs, 'senior' food intended for the elderly (a stage of life which begins, apparently, for dogs at the age of seven), gourmet food, economy food; choice cuts in sealed foil, dry food known as 'complete'. Biscuits, bones, chocolate drops. Dog food comes in all shapes and sizes, from tiny trays for the discerning Yorkie to massive sacks for hounds the size of small ponies. I didn't look at the dog food that afternoon, there was no point. Instead I stood before the baby-food section and wondered if any of the tiny meals for three-month-old infants would tempt Bilbo. I reached for the chicken vegetable stew, three jars, and for me, some chocolate yogurt, chocolate bars and orange juice. Only the first week of December and already Christmas music was blasting through the store, as a creepily knowing voice crooned, 'I Saw Mommy Kissing Santa Claus'. 'Big deal,' I muttered, making my bitter way to the checkout.

'No dog food this time?' a young voice asked. It was the girl who had told me about the aloof cat that had barely tolerated her or the rest of her family. 'How's your puppy? Is he settling in?' she asked. The girl had soft, reddish-brown eyes; she was thin and looked about eighteen. She had probably left school at fifteen and was destined for a tough life. I imagined her with six children before she reached thirty. Her face was kind, and so was she, but I just looked at her. I couldn't speak, overcome by a sensation of being underwater. I felt foolish but realised that the girl was probably thinking that I had forgotten her. I said something about him being really sick and that I thought he was dying and began to tell her what the vet had said but stopped abruptly, murmuring something about how unfair it all was. The girl looked devastated. Her eyes filled and she said she was 'awful sorry', that 'awful' seemed so right, and she said how happy I had seemed the day before. I *had* been happy. The woman behind me in the queue was busy emptying two trolley-loads of food on to the counter. I remember she had about twenty loaves of thinly sliced white bread wrapped in bright yellow and blue plastic.

One of my yogurt pots hit the ground with a plop. 'Go and get another one,' the girl had said. 'It doesn't matter.' She smiled her gentle, weary smile, watching me put the baby-food jars into my sagging pockets, as if she already knew that life was all about disappointment, and I went out, hoping my bike was still there. I had forgotten to take the lock with me.

*

The wind drove the dust on the road into my face. It caused the plastic bag to twist round and round, the orange-juice bottle kept time, rotating, striking the bike frame before bouncing off my leg. I stopped and thumbed the wrapper off a chocolate bar. My hands were cold. Perhaps I was never meant to have a dog? It seemed ironic that for all my neurotic tidiness, and my irritating habit of reading paperbacks without ever bending the spines, here I was now heading back to a kitchen with a floor greasy with sick and urine, the atmosphere thick with illness and an animal that was miserable. I decided then it wasn't fair. If the vet recommended putting Bilbo to sleep this time, I would let him. It would be a kindness for the little guy. It had been a painful interlude. At that time I had not even begun my sequence of disastrous human relationships and had already failed my dog.

The front wheel skidded to the left, the tyre sighed: a puncture. It didn't matter. Cycling into the vicious wind was no fun, all I had needed to dismount was a good excuse. I walked on. Apart from Trudi, none of my friends knew about Bilbo, which was just was well. This would be a secret grief.

But in the kitchen, Bilbo seemed slightly better. He looked up at me and his tail wagged briefly. I took a small plate off the rack but on reading the label on the baby-food jar I realised that the Traditional French Farmhouse Chicken and Vegetable Casserole required gentle heating. There was a small, red ironware pot in the cupboard. Emptying the contents of the jar into the pot I looked at Bilbo: I told him the food was for babies and advised him to eat it. He cocked his ears, with his head tilted at an angle as if to say, 'Are you an expert on dog care now?' I put the plate down on the floor and stepped back. He began to investigate.

I braced myself expecting him to sniff and reject. But he didn't. He ate it all with a determination I had not seen in him before, aside from that moment when he chose me in the dogs' home, which seemed a lifetime ago. The plate was cleared; I reached for the second jar to prepare it, just as he vomited up the first plateful. I began to cry. But after a moment's pause, he went to the vomit and ate it. Then he came up to me, stood on my foot, and looked as if he was asking for more.

Why not? I heated the contents of a second jar of food and gave it to him, waiting for him to eject it again. But he didn't. He licked the plate and settled down. Within seconds he was back on his feet and I expected him to begin that retching action. Instead he came over to me. I was sitting on the floor, my back against the dresser, and he laid down, his head on my lap.

The sharp tang of steaming urine woke me some three hours later. Urine, but no vomit. There was another six hours to go before we left for the vet. Sleeping on the hard floor was not exactly comfortable. 'Come on,' I said. 'Follow me.' And I went to the bedroom, knowing he would make a mess, but I wanted to sleep in my bed. Bilbo walked into the bedroom and began sniffing my three pairs of trainers. Each shoe intrigued him. I put a blanket beside the bed and collapsed on to the mattress. When I woke this time, he was on the bed beside me, as were all three pairs of runners, and one shoe had been pulled apart. This was a good sign. Better still, no vomit. Only a neat pat of strongly scented mustard-coloured waste. His nose was still dry but he looked at me with interest. His coat smelt of the vet's surgery, vomit and baby food. Time perhaps for another jar.

But first, a bath. In the excitement of Bilbo's arrival and

subsequent crisis, the immersion heater had been ignored and had been simmering away for more than two days. If ever there would be sufficient hot water for a deep bath, this was the moment. Bilbo sat dozing as the steam filled the room. I felt like Wile. E. Coyote, beaten and dejected after losing out yet again to the Road Runner. Just as I began to relax in the bath, I sat up, thinking Bilbo would get cold on the tiled floor. I picked up a towel for him from the bedroom, and ran back into the bathroom. Still more than an hour before we needed to leave for the vet's; there would be enough time to warm him up before going out into the cold of the winter night. He didn't need a chill on top of a fever.

This drive to the vet's was very different from the edgy journey with the pragmatic nurse. Robert the dog owner spoke at length about his Tessa, a creature of rare cunning. Her days were dominated by her quest for food, by her obsessive devotion to him, and by a series of nasty pranks including the savaging of his mother-in-law's antique handbag. Tessa sounded like a difficult child. 'She's much more interesting than my children were at that age,' announced Robert. Both his sons, he told me, were now working in banks. I had begun to feel that perhaps Bilbo would make it; the second serving of Traditional French Farmhouse Chicken and Vegetable Casserole had stayed down. Before we had reached the end of the wind-blasted stretch of road I realised that Tessa sounded like a pampered horror and vowed, if Bilbo got better, never to regale anyone with stories that invariably confirm that some owners get the dogs they deserve. Bilbo, I liked to think, would be above petty theft. If he ever committed such offences, I would keep them secret.

Robert said he would wait outside and seemed subdued

because Bilbo had vomited about a mile from the vet's surgery. Most of it had landed on my duffel coat. But Robert was determined to show that he didn't mind.

Inside the surgery, I again noticed the ticking of an unseen clock again, and the humming of the small refrigerator in which the drugs and serums were stored. A faint crying began, low, regular. It may have been the sound of a cat regaining consciousness, perhaps after a spaying. The vet – was he Mr or Dr? It didn't matter, I didn't much like him – made a clicking noise with his teeth. He told me to put Bilbo up on the examination table and he fetched a thermometer. He said nothing, just looked and prodded at Bilbo. He opened the puppy's mouth, felt his stomach. 'Stools? Still runny? Vomiting? Keeping anything down? Any whimpering?' The questions were fired off in sequence without giving me a chance to respond.

Mr/Dr was stout and as complacent as a high-court judge; he rocked back and forth on his heels as if deliberating. Was he debating Bilbo's right to live, or his need to die? He began by stating that cross-breds were very tough, 'hardy and intelligent'. Then he addressed Bilbo's case. 'This lad is tough; you might still lose him over the next forty-eight hours, but he has a chance. Is he keeping anything down?' It was the first time he had waited for an answer. I told him about the baby food. The vet said nothing. He enjoyed playing God. I hated him for his silence. Then he gave his summing up. I was pleased. 'If this dog does live, it will have more to do with you than any drug I can give him.' He told me to return the next night and to keep him warm and continue with the baby food. 'Baby food,' he laughed a great booming laugh, pronouncing it as a good idea and one he would never have thought of.

Robert was waiting in his car, listening to Johnny Cash at full volume. The car smelt of cleaning fluid and I noticed he had spread a large plastic sheet over the back seat. He looked sheepish. 'Just in case he wets or something. You were very quick. So he's still with us, ready to fight another day. He looks better.' Bilbo squatted and peed beside the vet's flower bed.

*

During the next two days Bilbo took to yapping a lot and ate a carton of banana yogurt, then showed interest in custard and drank half my mug of coffee. I didn't care. On the way back in the car from his fifth nightly visit to the vet, he began to struggle and pulled at my hair. The vet had given him a cautious all clear, offering me some hope, only to say then that while he *seemed* better, he in fact might not be. It was going to take time. The course of antibiotics was finished; nothing else could be done for the moment. He explained that the virus often affected the nervous system, but perhaps we had been lucky. He concluded by telling me to phone if there were signs of a relapse. My face must have fallen. The vet paused and said, 'Good luck, Bilbo.' Perhaps I had been wrong about the vet. If I had been older or a lot younger I might have felt differently, but at the time I felt that the vet had turned our encounters into a battle of wits. Aware of having acted like a spoilt child, again I wondered how had I become so attached to a little animal who probably viewed all humans as fools.

Back in the kitchen Bilbo jumped up and down. He began to snap and bare his tiny pin-like teeth. They stung as he nipped at my ankles. He was hungry; I was delighted with these demands for food. All I had left for us to eat was an entire apple pie and he ate it all.

How quickly I became an authority on his bowel movements, the amount of water he drank and his range of facial
expressions. Shortly before Christmas I had to leave him
for a few hours a day to dig a garden for a newly married
working couple. Times were bad and there was no work
for an over-qualified postgraduate with no experience. The
woman's husband, a languid man with the tapering hands
of a model, seemed slightly embarrassed when he paid me.
She noticed and laughed, 'Ian is useless, he hates dirt.' I felt
like replying, 'While I, for one, simply love it.' 'Hold on a
second,' she said, and ran into the house, returning with a
box swathed in Christmas wrapping. 'That's for you! It's not
a book,' and she made a funny face and bowed, warning me
not to drop the box.

I walked away, closing the little gate, convinced that they
had decided I was a misfit, an over-educated social outcast.
Conscious that they might have been watching me I didn't
rip open the parcel but waited, wondering what on earth
she could have bought for me; hopefully, not a pair of high-
heeled leopard-skin slippers similar to the ones she was
wearing.

It was the day before Christmas Eve and I had been a
dog owner for twenty hectic and often hysteria-filled days.
I opened the box; it was a bottle of cream liqueur. My first
thought was that I would re-wrap it and give it to someone
who drank alcohol. Curiosity then took over. What was it
like? Probably very sweet; I remembered being told once
that drinks like that would make you sick long before there
was any risk of becoming drunk. I would wait until the
evening and sample it, celebrating the end of the gardening
job and the beginning of Bilbo's recovery.

Two small glasses bearing the name Baileys came with

the smart brown bottle of liqueur. I filled one, or thought I had, placing it by the fire. Then the phone rang. Each time I thought I was ready for my experimental celebration drink the phone summoned me back to the kitchen. Then back to the fire, and still I had forgotten to fill the glass. Bilbo had had enough of the fire and had wandered away from the rug, over to a cooler place on the varnished wooden floorboards. As I walked back to the fire for the fourth or fifth attempt, he staggered over to me and collapsed. The vet had been right, he was suffering from delayed nerve damage. He appeared to be paralysed, quickly slipping into a coma. I went back to the kitchen to call the surgery, aware that it was almost Christmas.

But I needed that vet, not a stranger, not an emergency locum unaware of the puppy's history. I had never been fully confident that Bilbo was completely cured, yet I had allowed myself to believe that he was getting stronger and even growing. The vet's phone kept ringing, no answer. Then I noticed the level of liquid in the bottle was lower than it should have been, perhaps five glasses lower. I had filled the glass and gone on refilling it because Bilbo had been drinking it. Then weighing no more than six or seven pounds, he had licked clean five glasses of rich liqueur and passed out. He slept for four hours and woke up thirsty, demanding only water.

2

Dog's Day Out

Freedom is seldom experienced by the modern dog. Consummate browsers, dogs are patient and methodical, alert to the mysterious potential of every trace of scent. To watch a relaxed dog investigating a hedgerow or a ditch is a privilege: you are observing an uninhibited natural scientist of rare insight at work. It requires patience on the part of the human and sufficient time for the dog to assess the immense variety of scents. But most dogs don't get those chances, not now. The city dog has long been living a life of confinement. An acquaintance once assured me that her large Old English Sheepdog was 'completely content', living as he did in her suburban garage with no light and a five-minute toilet break in the morning and at night. 'It's easier to keep him clean,' she added. It was a tragic existence, but it is not that uncommon, although one more usually endured by small dogs. People still aspire to own the large breeds as trophy pets; the pedigree of a dog is often treated with more respect than the actual animal.

The truth is that the best a city dog can hope for are those inadequate morning and evening walks, with perhaps a secure garden to patrol. Roaming the city streets carries more risks than being hit by a car. In the city a stray dog can become the enemy, resorting to theft and, at times, to attack – usually in self-defence. For the urban dog owner, walking his or her confined pet ironically creates a pleasant release for both parties through the dog's need to be exercised, and this duty can offer a lifeline to the human, who also benefits from the walk, although the dog would prefer to explore, to improvise. Being attached by a leash to a human programmed to walk in a straight line can be very frustrating for a dog more inclined to a zigzag approach to exploration. It confuses rivals as well as enemies; only the very best sniffer dog could possibly follow another's browsing trail.

So the city dog gets a regimented walk, is denied any chance of imaginative variation and is accompanied by a human with no appreciation of the wonders of smell and little inclination for meandering digressions. Dogs are improvisers; they don't plan routes. Yet the all-forgiving dog has a flair for adapting to human limitations. If treated well, they invariably understand or at least accept the life that is given to them. Not that a dog's life is all that much better in today's countryside. Many farmers consider dogs as much a menace as the fox. A farmer near where I live recently bragged about shooting local domestic pets, including a big Labrador who had dared stray about a hundred metres from his owner's gate.

All of this was in my mind as I anticipated the life to come when we began our walks. Eventually Bilbo was fully vaccinated and prepared to experience the world. Then it all began. A leash was attached to his collar, by me, aware that it was the first time I had ever done such a thing, and off we went on a bright, cold, late January morning. Bilbo tugged like a small husky. As for me, I was not a natural walker: I had always run, cycled or ridden horses, other people's until I had my own. Running with Bilbo was never going to work; a runner is a poor dog walker. We like to run onwards – with no diversions. The dog has other ideas.

The combination of runner and browsing dog can work in an open field or on an empty beach, but not where there is a chance of a car appearing from the shadows. Bilbo that morning had his head down, and he tugged and gasped, a pack pony on a mission. I followed, careful not to step on him. He had grown bigger; the walking was like a workout for him and it was developing his shoulders. If I tried to jog along with him, he became excited, wheeling about and wrapping the leash around my legs. It was better to walk sedately; I could go running later, alone.

A housewife called to me from her garden. 'She's so cute, like a cuddly toy, what's its name?' It? Cuddly toy? I told her his name and said I was hoping that he would become less toy-like and more of a German Shepherd. I was aware of sounding like an idiot and softened my priggish reply with a smile. Bilbo had other plans, though, and he marched on, neck bizarrely elongated, paws clawing at the ground. I wondered, should I get him a harness? Did they come in such small sizes? He pulled on and there was a ping – his collar snapped and he was gone. Now we *were* running. He darted here and there, enjoying the chase; I ran after him, not as taken as he was with the game because I feared the sudden arrival of a car. Now tired, Bilbo sat down in the middle of the road. He was still a baby and not yet the fluent, powerful athlete he would become. He panted, wagging his tail, and then crouched down, tail and bum in the air.

I lifted him up and jogged back to the verge just as a car appeared. I tried looping the leash around his neck but his sled-dog pulling caused the leash to tighten like a noose. He gagged. Back in my arms, he coughed as I carried him home; dog walking was clearly more complicated than it looked.

A new collar, more walking, still the relentless pulling: Bilbo believed in resistance work and the more he pulled, the stronger his body became. He seemed more interested in hauling at speed than in sniffing; it was as if he saw the walk as a test of his strength. Other dog owners disapproved of our frenetic approach to exercise. There are always people ready with an opinion. 'You should give that dog some time,' a neighbour announced. 'It's not fair to be racing along like that. He needs to lift his leg and have a good squirt.'

Restraint was the shrewdest tactic to these unsolicited observations. But he didn't 'squirt' yet, he still squatted like a female; and I wasn't rushing him, he was setting the pace. The woman who had given me her advice had a garden that resembled a bomb-site, complete with a burnt-out car lodged in the ditch to the side of the house. She told me that he had feelings and that I was not allowing him to develop his senses. 'Do you have a dog?' I asked, assuming my eager-to-please smile. 'Oh no, I'm too busy. It's not fair to have one unless you have time. They need so much attention.' I was protecting him from the world, from illness, from other dogs and the rain, but I smiled and nodded. 'I guess, what with your garden and all, you couldn't spare the time for a dog.' I edged away, wearing what I hoped was a bland expression. 'I spend hours with Bilbo. I'm teaching him German. I read to him at bedtime.'

Our walks continued. One morning we met a woman out with a group of six or seven dogs, all loose and running in circles. They darted on to the road, into the gardens of the scattered houses, leaping up to and down from the varying heights of the little garden walls, barking and yelping. She looked crazy, a kind of hippy wearing several layers of floaty skirts and sweaters. On top of all that fabric was a pale beige cardigan, a man's garment, with long, sagging pockets and on her feet were flat elf boots of faded green suede. 'How can you bear keeping that poor dog on a lead? It's so cruel, he is inhibited, he'll hate you for it.' Thanks, I thought, here we go again, more advice. I told her that he was very young and had had a bad start in life, in the dogs' home; and besides, I wanted to avoid having him run over. I wondered why I was defending myself to another stranger. 'Do they all belong to you?' I asked quickly, nodding to her troupe of dogs. 'No, no, only the brown and white fellow there; the others just team up with us and we hang out. It's fun. No leads. Dogs never get hit by cars, only cats do, because they are so stupid.'

She said that she had taken time off work and added dreamily that she had been having fun walking for the past few months. It turned out she had been working in her boyfriend's restaurant until they broke up. 'I go walking and all these dogs join in; they play on the green there and I keep watch. I'm not paid, but I enjoy it. It suits me.' The 'green' was in fact a large expanse of half-hearted grass. I gazed at it and tried to imagine it alive with tents and stalls and small enclosures housing goats and sheep on Fair Day in the Middle Ages. It remained a dreary, vacant space, the emptiness relieved only by weeds and stones.

Bilbo was pawing the ground, hopping up and down, tugging. The other dogs came over to investigate him. It was like the first day at school: he was the new boy, and they were sniffing him. Low growls began to coalesce into the distinctive clamour of a dog pack. He didn't roll over; he was irritated, and his fur rose off his shoulders. 'That's a good sign,' she said, impressed by his attitude. 'He's a good dog. Dominant. Alpha, a leader. Usually they roll over and submit but he didn't – and the really good thing is that he's on a lead so he is at the disadvantage. What's his name?' Swelling with pride at this acknowledgement of Bilbo's leadership qualities and obvious valour, I said, 'Bilbo,' expecting instant recognition from a person who had selected such amazing boots. She looked pained. 'Biffo? That's a horrible name, couldn't you think of something better?' 'No, not Biffo. Bilbo, as in Tolkien.' She looked blank. So much for the elf boots. 'I'll take Bilbo with us the next time,' she decided, 'It will be good for him to socialise. This is a good crowd for him to be in with. See ya.' Off she drifted on a cloud of floral skirt, vague, yet very self-aware, deliberately taking long, slow strides, possibly in an attempt to offset her below-average height. Bilbo and I went through a small gap and up a lane before returning home. Perhaps she was right. He was getting physically stronger and maybe it was time for some fun with other dogs.

*

A large puppy head. A smiling puppy with big ears and a broad yellow nose. It is white and made of shiny clay. It has painted-on brown eyes and bears no resemblance to Bilbo. It has been placed, by me, on the old dresser in the kitchen. It is a cookie jar and I have now had it for many years. Trudi had bought it for me as a surprise present later in the afternoon on the day I met Bilbo. But when he became so ill, she had kept it. After I announced that he had recovered, she drove out to my house to present it to me. On the day she came, there just happened to be three packets of fig rolls in the cupboard. It took two packets to fill the ceramic puppy's storage area, its square belly. By that stage Bilbo had his exclusive dog-biscuit supply, and

I was already cleaning his teeth with a toothbrush. He appeared to like toothpaste. But at that moment I wasn't contemplating biscuits, I was tense, glancing out the window, and then back to the ceramic dog. I saw it as a kind of Buddha protecting Bilbo. It was a morning of stress; the hippy dog walker had talked me into letting Bilbo have what she referred to as 'a normal dog's life'. Aware of my oddities – my chronic tidiness, my failure to attend parties, my dislike of all large gatherings and my tendency to spend long hours reading when not running in the rain – I had to agree to let my dog experience 'normal' independence, running free with a gang, or should that be pack? 'Pack' – a loaded word associated with marauding sheep-killers. They were merely a bunch of bored or neglected domestic pets, eager for company. I remained uneasy.

I kept watch out the window as the hippy woman wandered about, smoking, oblivious to the number of times the dogs, individually and collectively, narrowly avoided being hit by cars. Months later I discovered that her dog walking was a cover for spying on her erstwhile lover, who often drove down the road beside the green area. Among the dogs there were many skirmishes, sudden feuds that broke out and looked like serious fights to the death only to end happily about thirty seconds later. I rubbed Biscuit Bilbo's head and realised that my dog was suffering from my obsessive protectiveness, and that when I had children I would probably monitor their every movement until they were at least twenty-five years old. They would marry to escape me; I would become the sort of old woman people flee. I was staring at a bleak future. Bilbo needed to be liberated from me. He seemed to enjoy being groomed each morning, but was he only pretending? Did he see me as his jailer? All these doubts ran through my mind, along with the fear that he would be hit by a car or savaged by the other dogs. There was also the risk of his being stolen; he was beautiful, much more attractive than the other dogs. It even occurred to me that the hippy might try to steal him. Had she planned a kidnapping? Perhaps she banked on using Bilbo as a way of winning back her fickle boyfriend? I knew this was extreme and dismissed such irrational notions. Reduced to keeping an eye on the dogs from behind the kitchen curtain, the only one in the house – the brown paper was still taped over the other windows – I attempted to be calm. But it was not enough. There was something I could do.

The dog woman was wandering about, smoking, singing, most likely talking to herself. I had decided that she was beyond eccentric and that her broken romance had left her damaged, detached from reality and possibly delusional. I put on my running gear and jogged by as casually as I could pretend. Bilbo saw me and ran over. 'Hi,' I waved to the woman, and jogged on. My dog followed me. Then I sat down on the grass and began stretching, acting as if I was intending to do some serious sprint training up and down the slight incline with no thought of spying on Bilbo; although I had expressly come to keep watch. As I continued stretching, doing sit-ups and push-ups, Bilbo slowly lost interest and returned to the other dogs. Furtive glances kept me informed of the pack's movements. The dogs played on, gradually moving off. I jogged past, before returning to the green to wait for them, under the guise of more stretching. How much longer could I carry on doing sit-ups? The dogs ran by. They all charged at a stone wall. It was a like a scene from a television commercial for toilet paper. Bilbo slipped, and tumbled back with a yelp. My heart contracted. He got up and began to limp. I had my chance. 'I think he's injured,' I said decisively. 'I'd better take him home. Oh look, his paw is cut. He's bleeding.' I picked him up and ran home. His first day of 'normal' life had lasted just over an hour. It had been exhausting.

Dog Lady still seemed to expect Bilbo to join her on the outings. When possible I managed to avoid her, but often she sought us out and I was obliged to cooperate and prevaricate. My excuses were inventive. 'We are just back from three days' trekking across Connemara. He needs a rest.' But she was persistent. One afternoon I heard her tapping at the kitchen window. 'Where's my favourite boy?' she asked. I tensed, silently festering. There were two new dogs with her. 'Who are they?' I asked. 'I don't know,' she laughed. 'I've only just noticed them.' Immediately I panicked, leaning out of the window. 'But they could be diseased, they could cause a fight, they're big.' Bigger than Bilbo, who still had some growing to do. 'I don't like the one there, he has mean eyes.' My concern caused her – what was her name? Eva, Evanna, something like that – to laugh. She said that she had not asked the dogs for their vaccination records. I could see she considered me too fussy to take seriously. 'I don't even think my fella was ever vaccinated. I didn't get him any shots . . . at least I don't think I did.' For once, she sounded slightly irritated. 'You'll never be able to manage a house full of kids if you don't learn to relax.' She sauntered off. Bilbo yapped and jumped up and down excitedly in the kitchen behind me.

I opened the door; he ran out and hurried to the dogs. I followed, keeping about ten paces behind her. This could not continue; I would have to move house. But I had no job, aside from gardening work and my other speciality, sanding and varnishing wooden floors. But in just under ten minutes my problem was solved.

One of the newcomers, the dog with the mean eyes, launched an attack on a gang member. Evanna began shrieking; she waved her arms. 'Do something!' She screamed at me. 'These skirts will get torn.'

Close up, a dog fight is frightening. The attack that day, begun on one dog, quickly developed into a general riot. 'Here Bilbo,' I called and concentrated on saving my dog. He looked at me and as he trotted towards me he was attacked. Blood splashed into the air; I felt it spray my face. Evanna moaned a couple of feet away, clutching her sides as if in agony. I asked her if she was OK and wondered whether she had been bitten or had just had her clothing ripped. She was hysterical; her shouting was lost in the growling and yelping that seemed to be coming from a hundred dogs. It was the first time I had smelt a dog fight: a bitter scent is released, and the noise is crazed, murderous. I went into the tangle of bodies, kicking for space, making contact with something, and grabbed Bilbo by the back of his neck and heaved him upwards. Something nipped my ankle; a sharp pain shot through me, followed by a really nasty stinging sensation in my left buttock. I kicked out again, held Bilbo close to my chest and ran back to the house.

There was blood on my hands, on his back, and his coat was thick with blood, red turning to black. He would need stitches. We rushed into the bathroom and I put him in the bath. Soaking a face-cloth in warm water I washed away the blood, being careful of the wound. But there was no wound. The blood must have belonged to one of the other dogs. He licked the bath, he was thirsty. Anarchy, I thought. The fury of mass gatherings. Canetti. What caused such explosions of rage? Too many people, or, in this case, too many dogs, too much energy.

*

There were other complications as well. Over the next few days a small black dog, skinny and filthy, took to hurling herself against the front door, howling and yapping. She was insistent; she was in heat and saw Bilbo as her chosen mate. The little dog was giddy and tenacious, the canine equivalent of one of those children exploited by chimney-sweeps in nineteenth-century London. Her ears were tattered, she had a deep scar under one eye, and was inclined to limp. Had she been a stray, human decency would have compelled me to give her a home. But, neglected or not, her skin showing through her dull, matted coat, she did have a home. She belonged to a local family with several children.

The path leading to the family's front door was littered with ruined bikes. Two of the bikes consisted only of frames, the wheels gone. The mother lived in a purple bathrobe; she wore sunglasses on her head and favoured bare feet in all weathers. She controlled her children from the front door. Their father drove a truck – but like the abandoned bikes, it never moved. The immediate area of the homestead smelt of motor fuel. The little dog emitted the same aroma. Her name was Nigger, and having met the truck driver, it made sense. Here was a man who set out to provoke; he had named the dog and made sure that people knew the name had been his idea.

I discovered all this when I went to tell the family that the dog was risking her life on the road on her way to visit us. I thought they would probably be relieved, decide that she would have a better life with me, and we would sit and have the proverbial friendly cup of tea. Bilbo would have a friend and I would have the right to wash her and remove the clumps of matted fur from her spindly body. It would be better for everyone. Leaving Bilbo watching from the kitchen window, I walked Nigger home. I would be non-judgemental and pretend I thought her name was Tigger. Several of the bikes I noticed had moss growing on them; they had become garden fixtures. A decayed yucca tree in a plastic flowerpot filled with earth that had become powdery dust lay slumped over in the porch. I waited. 'Yeah,' said the man who opened the door. 'Yeah.' He looked over my shoulder, at his truck; he then raised his shoulder to scratch his chin. 'What can I do you for?'

Attempting to smile, I told him that I was just bringing little Tigger home. But he was quick. 'Her name's Nigger, you got a problem with that? She's my fucking dog and I'll call her whatever I want.' I began an elaborate explanation, pretending I had misheard the name. I said that I thought that the children meant Tigger, from *Winnie the Pooh*. The man was a sullen individual and far from stupid. He made it clear that he didn't know anything about *Winnie the Pooh* and had less interest in learning the details. 'That dog's mine and I named her.' His stance suggested that he was not about to hand her over to me. This was clearly a territorial issue. He glared at me and asked whether there was anything else on my mind because he was planning on closing the door. Then I mumbled my concerns about her being in heat. I didn't get to finish: he stepped towards me. 'Are you telling me to fix my dog? She's had litters, that's what they do, and she'll have them again.' He told me to get Bilbo fixed, and, while I was at it, to get myself fixed as well. He slammed the door. Nigger/Tigger followed me back to my house.

*

I realised that if I took this unfortunate character in, or if she disappeared, that thug would burn my house down. I closed the door on her. I had tried. Then it began all over again. Her moaning and yapping at the door, with Bilbo becoming excited, clawing and yapping from the inside, as he scratched long grooves down the side of the wood panel and pulled the inside flap off the letter box. The door was soon raw, splinters littering the hall floor. I had been told that dogs would jump through glass to engage with a bitch in heat and now I was watching nature in reverse.

Neutering was the responsible solution. It is the only way to avoid seeing tragic unwanted cats and dogs dying horrible deaths. In the case of Bilbo, I had already been approached by people eager to bring their females to him. He was cross-bred, but his temperament was exceptional and he was beautiful. No wonder the little female was besotted. I was not prepared to let him mate with her, as it was unlikely that she had ever had any vaccinations. Their mutual torment continued through the night. When I brought him to the bedroom, she ran around the house and jumped up on the windowsill. There were no curtains and as she pawed at the glass it clouded and became streaky. We camped in the bathroom for the night.

Until now, convinced that I could protect Bilbo from all the spayed females in the neighbourhood, I had not considered having him neutered, but now I could see the need. I went to consult Tessa's owner. Robert was emphatic. He told me it must be done, and that Tessa had been spayed. His vet was wonderful, he continued, saying that she really understood Tessa. Considering Tessa's repellent personality this suggested that the vet was indeed highly evolved. Robert insisted on driving us.

The night was bright and it was cold outside. The sickly moon suited my dejection. I felt upset. I had not planned on this. Would this surgery affect his confidence? His personality? He was sensitive. Now I had a great excuse not to let him out on Evanna's mad walks; he would be attacked by the unneutered males. He would be regarded as a lesser dog.

It was morning; Bilbo had fasted from midnight, so I had no breakfast. It was impossible to eat toast and not share it with him. At the surgery a nurse in pink scrubs and matching clogs asked me to sign a form.

But what was I signing? 'It's nothing, just a formality covering us if anything happens. It's a permission.' My horror must have been obvious as I was told that the form I needed to sign stated that I was aware of the risks associated with a general anaesthetic but that signing this form was merely routine. I had not considered the potential danger and now I was faced with it. The veterinary nurse's tone became sharper. Clearly she was not used to being questioned. Her heavily made-up eyes rolled ceilingwards. She told me she was busy and that I was making a fuss over nothing. Then she said, 'The odd dog doesn't make it,' conceding that this *could* happen, though rarely. She gave me the official line about my animal receiving the best professional care available and that they did these procedures all the time. I imagined a conveyor belt of dogs in procession, waiting in line to be neutered. She was irritated and gave me the option of leaving. Robert was looking away, reading the various posters. 'See you, Gillian,' he called to her as he waved and walked out, deliberately avoiding my eyes. I felt trapped. Bilbo was already behind the white door marked PRIVATE. I asked if I could say goodbye to him. The nurse tensed her jaw. 'If you have to.' But I turned away. 'Be back here at six,' she said, and without wasting a further glance on me, asked a younger girl if Mrs Rees had collected the kittens yet.

Robert hummed to himself in the car on the way home. Finally he spoke. 'That's the vet Tessa goes to, not the woman you were dealing with but that practice. I have to keep on good terms with them. Tessa is highly bred, very temperamental.' He made it clear that he didn't want to be involved in any arguments there. He was more than happy with the service, and the staff. All I could say in my defence was that I hadn't been expecting the form, and had not realised that there was an actual risk of death. Robert was not appeased. Accidents do happen, he said, and told me about a friend of his who had gone to hospital to have his wisdom teeth extracted. 'He died on the table. It was years ago. He was only young but he had a heart attack and just died. That's life.' Back at the house, I thanked Robert for the lift but didn't ask him to bring me to collect Bilbo that evening.

*

By late afternoon I was determined that I would get driving lessons and become independent. Shortly after four o'clock, a car horn sounded outside. I looked up and saw a battered old station wagon. Robert appeared from the driver's side. 'I've just borrowed this for later, we may need it. I'll be back to help you collect him.' And he drove off, more like his usual friendly self.

At the vet's later I felt sick. Why hadn't I just marched in and taken him back when the nurse snapped at me? I regretted having left him. But now it was over. The same nurse came out and motioned to Robert, not me. He listened and then looked down. The nurse glanced at me and walked out. Robert began to say something about there being a bit of a problem. He stepped back and let me walk in ahead of him, down the narrow corridor beyond the white door. Another door was ajar. Robert called me inside.

Bilbo was lying on a table, his tongue slack, hanging out of the side of his mouth, over his teeth. He was dead. I gasped and looked at Robert. I began to sob. A vet I hadn't seen before, an older woman, came in. 'It's not as bad as it looks. He hasn't come round, yet, but he's not dead, not yet. But . . .' 'But what? What happened?' She said something about a one in a million chance, a bad reaction, that Bilbo had not been able to deal with the sedation. This vet seemed sympathetic, even disappointed, and said that there was still a heartbeat, but that I should take him home and keep him flat on a board. She offered to lend me one. I looked at the vet and she thrust her hands deep in her pockets, and reminded me that I had signed a consent form, as if to caution me. 'This isn't supposed to happen,' she said, 'but it has. All you can do is wait.' Then she walked out of the room, closing the door softly behind her.

I stood looking down at Bilbo, so young, his muzzle so velvet black, his paws so white. So this was what it was like; this is what the end looked like. After the stress of the illness and the dog fights and my attempts to protect him, a simple procedure that I didn't really want had ended like this. I felt limp. Robert took control; he and the nurse carefully lifted Bilbo and slid him on to a board. The nurse stressed the importance of keeping Bilbo's neck level and warned that if his head were to roll, his air passage would be compromised and become blocked and that . . . She didn't finish the sentence and was far more subdued than earlier, when he had been admitted. She didn't look at me. Robert picked up the board and we left.

When we reached the station wagon it occurred to me that Robert had known that the operation had gone badly. That was why he had borrowed the larger car. He knew he would need the extra space. 'They called me earlier. They saw there was a problem.' His voice trailed off. They had given him too much anaesthetic . . . the possibilities churned around in my mind. They had killed him. I should have cancelled the 'procedure' and just brought him back home.

Robert offered to carry him in. I didn't reply, but opened the front door fully and then, lifting the board myself, slowly walked inside, kicking the door back, struck again by how clean Bilbo was, how young. His pads were still pink, barely worn. 'Bye,' said Robert, anxious to be free of my gloom. What happens now? I wondered. Where will I put him? I went straight to the bedroom, nudging the door open, and laid Bilbo's board down on the bed. Then I immediately decided against it: if he did wake, he might fall. I bent down slowly and placed the board on the floor beside the bed. As if in my own trance, I returned to the little hall, locked the front door and came back. Bilbo lay utterly still. I got into the bed with my clothes still on, removing only my runners and pulled the blankets up over my head. I would have to bury him on my own.

It had all been unreal, from the very beginning; he was never intended to live long, he was a beautiful interloper, and I was not meant to keep him. There was no point in trying to read so I lay in the gathering darkness, conscious of my own heartbeat, too upset even to cry. I had only one photograph of him, gazing wide-eyed into the camera; Trudi had taken it the day I first brought him home. 'It's so unfair, so unfair.' I kept saying this to myself over and over. The first vet had been correct in his assessment: he had never recovered from the distemper. I was exhausted, cold and weary, too tired to eat. I pulled the blankets tight in around me. By then it was so dark I could see nothing in the room except the shape of the chest of drawers against the wall by the window.

*

It started tentatively, the scratching. It must have woken me. Rats, I thought. Would they interfere with Bilbo's body? The scratching continued; it became louder, more persistent. I became uneasy. The scratching changed rhythm; it was like a scrabbling, loud. It sounded more frantic. Then whimpering, tones of growing panic. I became more alert. Shock, then hope. Bilbo? Down on my knees, I looked under the bed. He was struggling. Yelping, terrified, but he was trying to move. It was 3.58 a.m., almost ten hours since we had come home. I pulled the board out from under the bed. Bilbo was thrashing about. He had pulled himself on to his stomach and his front legs were trying to haul the rest of his body up. His back legs were paralysed.

How much more would this dog have to endure? Should I call a vet? How long would that take? Should I smother him now with a pillow? He was clawing at the floor, fighting his own body. My college scarf was folded on the chair, under a pile of clean clothes, so I yanked it free, causing the clothing to tumble to the floor. 'Here, Bilbo,' I urged. 'Come on, boy,' and I pulled the scarf around his middle and edged out of the room, shuffling backwards with tiny steps. 'Come on, come on, you can do this.' He was working his front legs, with his rear legs dragging, splayed out behind him. I thought movement, even as crazy as this, might start his body functioning again. All I had to draw on was my own memory of a general anaesthetic and of being paralysed for days after it. I remembered the helplessness. All the while as I looked down on him, I prayed for movement, if only a twitch. I begged him to try.

He needed his circulation to get going again, a kick start. We shuffled through the house to the hall. It was narrow but gave us a clear passage. Up and down the hall I shuffled, pulling him, all the while looking him straight in the eyes, reassuring him, attempting to convince him that this was normal, that his human, me, was helping him and that all this sliding about would help him. Up and down: at last his back legs began to work and his feet were feeling for the ground. He was up, wobbly, but up on his feet. 'Come on, guy, that's the dog, come on, little man.' He was walking like a drunk, unsteady, shaking. The cold air outside, I felt, might shock him into action. It was worth a try. I lifted him and hurried into the bedroom. 4.27 a.m. on the clock; pushing my feet into the nearest trainers, I fetched the duffel coat from the hook on the bedroom door.

It was really cold. Now we were both very awake and I was focused on saving his life. I set him on the grass and walked a few feet away. 'Come on, here, to me, that's it.' He swayed towards me, straightened up, walked, then progressed to a slow jog – he was finding his feet. His balance was returning, the strength was slowly surging through him. I held him, kneeling on the ground. He put his head into the coat. What a dog. We walked on out the gate, down the road. The few houses were in darkness. I laughed aloud, knowing that with my luck someone would be awake and would see us. The eccentric dog owner in her giant coat had taken to walking in the early hours to avoid all other humans, dogs, cars, germs.

We did a short lap of the green. By now, he was bouncing,

having regained his light-footed gait. Bilbo was never earthbound. He was graceful, athletic, a dancer. As we walked back to the house, he kept looking up at me.

In the kitchen, food became all. I had never been so hungry. Slice after slice of toast popped out of the toaster with a wheeze of springs and quickly disappeared. He was matching me, bite for bite. Crumbs scattered across the counter; I hadn't even bothered with a plate. I made tea. Slowly I began to understand that my euphoria was probably a by-product of shock. Meanwhile Bilbo was chasing his tail, a good form of exercise; it was making him bound and leap; twist, turn, luxuriate in his newly revived power of movement. I watched him and realised that I should have named him Lazarus, Lazarus the Miracle Dog. Ten hours of waiting at home, trapped in a state of suspended animation, and a further – what? Six long hours in the vet's surgery. Bilbo's trance had lasted sixteen hours. Sleeping Beauty, saved not by a prince but by raw frenzy. He had returned. Beneath the joy there was disquiet; I had him back by the skin of my teeth, and his, and I knew it.

3

Gathering the Kelp

Seaweed is such a theatrical substance, ideally suited to the darkest fairy tales. It makes me think of a mermaid's hair, but more particularly of despairingly rejected girls who, stricken by impossible love, choose death by drowning. It conjures images of seahorses draped in its tangled fronds. The Californian beaches I knew as a child extended for miles of dry, clean, pale sand, flanked by the Pacific Ocean and were strewn with seaweed. In the sea it was thick, oily organic material floating in great dark browny-green masses, heaving and sighing, thick ropes of it, with its clean, fishy smell and its healing powers.

When washed up and land-locked it became home to various creatures, particularly armies of busy crabs, flexing their claws as they scuttled about. The salt in the seaweed became visible only after the fronds had been cast up out of the water on to the sand, where it shrivelled under the sun. I had not given much thought to seaweed for years until I read J. M. Synge's wonderful book, *The Aran Islands*. It made me think differently about fantastical, serpent-like seaweed. Suddenly the glamour and mystery vanished. Seaweed was a life-saving crop for starving fishermen. Synge wrote as a reporter, observing a culture concerned with survival. He watched the islanders, desperate for food, collecting the seaweed they called sea rods while patient donkeys, coarse baskets slung over their backs, waited. Today there are seaweed baths and shampoos and it is eaten as a health-food delicacy, but for those Aran islanders it meant survival.

Seaweed also enriched the poor soil on the islands. In order to showcase my gardening skills, and attract more commissions, I decided to transform my small patch into a subtle work of art, worthy of the Chelsea Flower Show. What better preparation for barren earth than the rich tonic of seaweed? It needed to be dug in and turned with patience – one quality I always had in abundance – and I was in luck: my boyfriend had a car and an outing to the coast pleased him, as usually it was an effort to get me to go anywhere. He was less enthusiastic about the idea of bringing Bilbo with us as he seemed to associate him with drama – I could not imagine why. Off we went, and as we neared the sea the smell as always made me think of the world made clean.

It was Bilbo's first glimpse of the sea and he appeared to be intrigued. The drive to the coast had also seen his first encounter with motorbikes. One pulled up right beside us at the traffic lights; for once Bilbo dropped his cool, graceful demeanour and turned into a fierce, snarling wild animal, saliva streaming down the window as he clawed the glass, barking at the helmeted head and at the humming machine. His nails tore into my thighs. The lights changed; the motorbike roared off. Bilbo was once more his usual collected self. A strange interlude but one that had introduced me to an unexpected side of Bilbo: his fury.

We parked at the yacht club and walked along the promenade of Dun Laoghaire, a polite nineteenth-century seaside town, shabby yet still bearing traces of a weary elegance. Yeats had often strolled here, as had Joyce and, of course, Beckett, who was given to pondering the hopelessness of all that water and of everything else. We would walk further out, beyond the rocks, and – at least this was my plan – fill four large buckets and several builders- grade sacks with a harvest of richly fertilising seaweed.

Anticipating a vista of heavy floating seaweed masses, I led the way down the beach. It didn't take long to discover that seaweed didn't undulate freely here; instead it clung, fiercely, to the rocks. We wouldn't be dealing with oozing armloads, we would have to pick and scrape it off the wet slimy stone. It was not what I was expecting and the romance quickly ebbed out of the project. Our labour would produce very little but, having come all this way, we, or rather, I, true to my Calvinist nature, persisted. If not ropes of seaweed, I would gather enough to nourish my small patch of soil. After all it was still seaweed, just of a more labour-intensive variety than the one I remembered.

Bilbo was browsing. The sun was shining, a gentle breeze softened the heat and sails were billowing in the distance against blue skies; all was well, at least in my little universe. This was the dream, the dream of having a dog; a silent, highly intelligent, responsive companion who could read your mind with a glance and make sure you looked closely at everything. I felt a pleasant surge of contentment. To look at Bilbo was a joy. His bright fox's coat was shining. He would be with me as I dug all this stuff into the garden: he would be there. Not for the first time was I wishing that it was just my dog and me; the effort that went into a human relationship made me wonder if it was worth the trouble. It seemed so natural to be there with Bilbo. Since I was a child I had always been watching humans, trying to read their mood through their expressions and edit my conversation to suit. My then boyfriend never seemed to be all that interested in anything. It wasn't that he didn't say much, it was more that he could simply switch off. It made me uncomfortable. He always ruined our walks because he treated them as a chore. Bilbo, I decided, was not only better company, he seemed to *want* to understand me; he was always engaged with whatever was going on.

Then Bilbo darted away. By then, I knew he would rarely go far, even when he set off on one of his wild runs, his 'crazy feet' sessions, which consisted of doing laps around me as if he were a horse on an invisible lunge rope. He invariably kept his amber eyes focused on me and stayed close.

He barked somewhere behind me and his bark became frantic. Had he seen a gull? Would it attack him? That familiar feeling of panic, the one I by now associated exclusively with Bilbo, began building in my chest. I turned just as a flash of black was disappearing: a cat, with Bilbo right behind. A yowl, the cat's, a bark, Bilbo's. He raced across the road. I heard a scream, and saw an elderly man with a stick, more screaming; a scream so loud, so shrill, that the sound was shocking. It was such a sharp shriek, accompanied by the words, 'The dog, the dog, over the wall.' I realised he meant Bilbo, but the wall didn't look that high. Then I looked over it: it was such a long fall, down on to the railway track. A drop of thirty feet? Forty feet? and on to hard, solid stone. I couldn't see Bilbo, but he was down there, somewhere.

No, no, I thought, not this. The man was still standing, looking down; two women had stopped and were comforting him. I knew that the railway line was not in regular use but that test trains were running on it; an engine could appear at any minute. Bilbo's body would be mangled. I was barefoot. How to get down on to the track? I needed shoes. 'Leave it, leave it,' urged my boyfriend. He advised me not to look, that it would upset me. He kept saying, 'Leave it, leave it,' and that Bilbo wouldn't have had a hope. I ignored him and ran off. I ran back to the little inlet where we had been picking seaweed and grabbed at his pair of huge rubber boots, the ones that I had been wearing, several sizes too big for me, and clumped off. My boyfriend didn't follow, even though he was wearing trainers. He seemed more irritated than sad at what had happened, and he made no attempt to help me.

But then, Bilbo was my dog, mine alone. Like most athletes, I suffered from the problem of being too fit to run fast, ironically, unless I had spent about an hour stretching, jogging and building speed through a series of gradual strides. In a short dash to a bus, the unfit office worker usually beats the athlete because the serious runner hovers between supreme fitness and ultra-fragility, the fear of sudden movement and injury to a tendon, a ligament. If I tried to sprint from cold I could pull a muscle, and I did exactly that. A sharp, ripping sensation dulling to a pull meant that yet again my hamstring was torn.

I hobbled on, the immense rubber boots clugging along, banging on the ground. I was groaning and sobbing. People were looking, no doubt assuming that here was a victim of a broken romance. My jeans were sticking to me. And weighing me down, those awful boots, rubbing my bare feet. Sweat – or was it blood? – had gathered in the wellingtons, adding to the swampy sensation of running on the spot, in quicksand. I seemed to be progressing by mere inches. Where was the crossing? When did the wall give way to steps? It had to, but where? The more I ran in my hobbled state, the further I was moving away from the spot where Bilbo had gone over. When was the next test train due? Had he suffered? Had death been instant? Would the train driver see me? Or was it an automated test engine that wouldn't stop?

Never had running been so difficult. My feet were raw, apparently swimming in blood, the boots becoming heavier with each crippled stride. My body was shuddering, my hamstring was screaming. I felt hot, sweat was stinging my eyes, but I hobbled on, conscious of being a spectacle. 'Try getting yourself some running shoes,' sneered a young boy. His pals sniggered and one of them stuck his leg out to trip me, but I clumped around it, too flustered to swear at him.

Gates, white, with lights, signal lights. This was the crossing. I ran to the gates and clambered awkwardly over them, then turned to run back, parallel to where I had just come from, back to Bilbo. I ran on, remembering holding him, his habit of pushing his head under my chin and his scent of warm biscuits, a clean smell. Wood smoke in his fur after an evening by the fire, the sheer physical closeness of him, the way he had begun to anticipate my actions. The verge was stony; the stones were sharp, jagged, too sharp to run on. It may have been more dangerous, but it was easier to run down the middle, between the tracks. It wasn't exactly straight; there was a subtle bend, a curve. Undergrowth of tall weeds with scattered trees became denser, heavier on the side near the sea. I ran on. No sign of him. I looked up and tried to pinpoint the spot where the old man had been standing – it had been near a spire or a clock tower, something tall. I remember thinking that the angle made it seem it was growing out of the man's head. My side began to hurt. What a time to experience the first stitch of my life. I snorted with laughter, mucus plopped out of my nose.

They were up there. People, the women. Heads, all looking down. Arms pointing. A woman shouted. 'There,

there, over there. Keep on, just ahead.' I looked up at her and then braced myself. I saw him, a flash of bright fur. Bilbo was there in the corner, intently looking up. Standing at full stretch, staring up along the wall, quizzical, looking as if he was wondering how he could crawl up it. His front paws were reaching upwards, scratching the stone.

'Bilbo?' I called. He looked, jumped down and trotted over to me, tail wagging. I knelt down. I relaxed, feeling as if I had finished a race. I bent and ran my hands over his sides, felt his legs. Holding his head in both hands and peering into his eyes, I opened his mouth. No blood, no sign of injury. Only a mud patch on his left hip. My hair was wet with sweat; my clothes were stuck to me. The skin of my face felt tight. I became aware of a muffled buzzing in the distance. The small crowd were waving as one. I nodded back, too tired to speak, I didn't have the energy to shout. We walked back along the tracks. 'Bilbo, Bilbo . . . And they called him Lazarus,' I kept repeating over and over again. I couldn't even speak to him. It was as if he was trying to test me, or someone was, intent on finding out exactly how far I was prepared to go with this bond I had formed with a young stray, the dog that had chosen me.

On the drive back, I studied Bilbo and suggested that we stop at a vet's as Bilbo might be in shock or concussed. There might be internal bleeding, brain damage. True to character, the boyfriend said nothing; his eyes stayed on the road, sick of the sideshow and my excessive engagement with this puppy. But I persisted, voicing my fears. 'He's fine. Just get him home,' he said in a neutral voice, turning up the volume of the radio.

4

A Little Death

After a week or so I stopped peering into Bilbo's eyes to see if they were following the direction my finger was taking as it cut slow arcs in the air. No damage had been done; he seemed well, interested in the world that was gradually expanding around him, a world that was becoming his.

Digging the soil, turning it over, enriching it, even without any seaweed, settled into a ritual, and became a way of playing for time while I decided on how and what I would plant. Eventually it was time to sow grass seeds in the area I had marked out for a lawn, but which was more like a clearing. Elsewhere would be flower beds, carefully planned in order to create an impression of random spontaneity, a cottage garden with pretensions to woodland. Would he dig anything up? But Bilbo was patient, as patient as I was. I worked; he watched, monitoring my efforts. I planted potatoes – for conditioning the soil, not for eating – and he was confident that we would soon set off on an outing. Fastidious in his ways, he could, at times, be calm and self-contained. My muddy clothes and boots contrasted with his bright fur and white paws.

When other dogs passed by he was satisfied with jogging to the wall, wagging his tail and greeting them, but he stayed with me, my protector, my companion. Even the busy little love-sick black dog, undulating, wheedling, in season or not, failed to coax him out, unless I went too. We were bonded. I had to stop and think of a time when he had not been with me. He had established himself so completely in his quiet, strangely dignified way. As the bright spring mornings were replaced by spectacular summer dawns, we went out earlier and earlier. Near the end of the lane a large animal moved: it was black and white, a badger, the first live one I had seen. All the others had been corpses, hit by cars. I ran up for a close look and was shocked at the reaction; the badger spun around with surprising speed and rage, baring its yellow teeth, ready to attack. I retreated, holding Bilbo by the collar, and ran back down the lane, waiting for the badger to trundle off.

It was on one of those early morning walks that we found the little black dog. She had been crushed. Her face was distorted; her jaw had been broken, as had her back. Her matted coat was even dirtier than in life, wet and crusted with dried blood. She was a character, at times a nuisance. She used to drag trash on to my doorstep, from where she kept vigil for her prince, Bilbo, while he was sleeping in the bedroom or sitting by the fire. Her manic, dancing courage and innocent optimism made her oddly heroic.

That morning, as Bilbo stood looking down at her body, he whined and looked up at me as if I could do something, work some miracle: fix her. All that stuff about animals being philosophical in the face of death is not true. He was bewildered; so was I. I recalled the evening several weeks earlier when I had so confidently, and mistakenly, approached her owner, the thug with the truck and his hillbilly squalor of ruined bikes and abandoned shoes. It would have been so easy, so kind, to have simply handed her over; I would have looked after her and Bilbo would have had a companion. She had been small, less than a quarter his size; her electric frenzy had made her appear larger.

It was early, not quite six o'clock, but the sun was already bright. I bent to lift her but her stomach had burst out on the dusty road. Unzipping my tracksuit top, I thought of scooping her into it. It would be messy. But first I had to bring Bilbo back home. He stood stiffly at my side, tense and uncertain. She had been a happy little creature; desperate to please, crazed when petted. Looking at her, dead on the road, I felt guilty about the times I had described her as a cartoon character. I always laughed as she scuttled towards me on her spindly legs, invariably limping. Her knobby spine was sharp beneath the matted fur, and she remained hopeful in the face of whatever disaster had most recently happened. Her first litter of pups had been drowned by the owner; his children informed me of this when they stopped me on my bike, asking, 'Can we have Bilbo for Nigger to make new puppies?'

Before turning to go back to the house with Bilbo, I paused to put my tracksuit top over the small body, but then hesitated. It made it look as if I had done this to her. We ran back to the house, and leaving Bilbo in the kitchen I set off again. A van had arrived. It was parked on the side of the road; a man came out from behind it. 'There's a dog there, hope it's not yours? I just kicked it into the ditch, I think the crows were at it, it's in bits.' The van driver was chewing gum. It made a snapping sound. He had bright green eyes, unnaturally green, with deep, dark circles under them and a thin face. If he was as exhausted as he looked, he must have been bone-tired, yet he was cheerful, utterly oblivious to the dog that had been killed. 'I think I should bury her,' I said, 'I wouldn't if I were you,' he announced. 'You could get any amount of diseases, and there's bits of it all over the shop. I got to head. See ya.' He drove off, leaving me wondering aloud what an odd turn of phrase 'all over the shop' was.

His kick must have been vigorous; it was difficult to find her. When I did, she was half submerged in muddy water. I felt sick and ashamed, as if I had let her down. I blamed myself for not bringing her body with me when I brought Bilbo back to the house. What if the owner had seen me? I realised that the family would never know what had happened. There would be no farewell. I walked back home, too dejected even to jog. Bilbo was waiting in the hall, pacing, I could see his shape through the glass side pane. It had begun to rain, but that wasn't the reason I stayed in. There would be no walk that day.

*

Would those children come to me looking for her? Would their loutish father try to comfort them? All I knew of the mother was the figure in the purple bathrobe directing her domestic empire from the doorstep. Bilbo was sitting on the kitchen floor, his paws neatly folded. He seemed contemplative, very quiet, glancing at me briefly, before looking back down at his paws and beyond them.

She had been a loyal pet; she followed the children and endured their rough play, games that consisted of screams and fights. I could remember smiling when the children seemed astonished that Bilbo was allowed in the house. They had seen him standing at the kitchen window. 'But is he often let in the house like that?' For them it must have been a special occasion. 'Bilbo lives in the house,' I assured them. 'He sleeps in the bed, well, on it, unless it's really cold and it seldom is, as he usually gets too hot under the blankets.' The children recoiled and I laughed outright when the boy, he might have been nine or ten, declared,

'Ma would never allow that, it's dirty. Nigger doesn't get in the house at all, in case she dirties it.' I told them that Bilbo was super-clean and that my house was the cleanest house they could hope to find. 'You', I said with emphasis, 'could eat off my floors . . . If Bilbo's paws are wet, I dry them, in the bathroom.' For further effect, I told them that Bilbo had bubble baths – he didn't, even I would not go that far. The children were mightily impressed and I had a fair idea of how dirty the house that had been deemed too clean for a dog really was. The pot of tea sat untouched for hours in the kitchen. Without realising it, I was waiting for the children. I expected them to call on me and ask my help in searching for their dog.

The rain was heavier but I needed to fetch some food before it became too wild. Halfway down the short lane that led to the long windswept road, I saw three small figures; one orange hooded rain jacket and two pink ones. It was the children. I never knew their names. I braced myself for the tears and said hello without asking about her. 'Nigger's dead,' said the boy, the family spokesman. His sisters nodded. They seemed almost excited by their news. 'She was hit by a car sometime yesterday and was dead when we found her. Da said to leave her, she was too messy to bring home. We're gonna get rabbits, they'll stay in cages.' Not a damp eye between them. She had been with them and now she was gone. It was the first time I had spoken to them without their asking about Bilbo. It was as if a common bond was broken and they had no further interest in my buddy, or, it seemed, in me.

*

We didn't forget the little black dog. When we walked past the house to which she had belonged, Bilbo, pulling on his leash like a husky in a sled team, invariably slowed and turned his head to look at me. And whenever we were on the patch of road where we found her body, he stopped and peered into the ditch as if he were continuing a search. I was his person, he had decided that and the bond was real for both of us. But I felt he needed his own kind as well. Dogs like people, but male dogs in particular also need a canine peer. Finding Bilbo a partner would not be easy; he was immensely self-contained. He had played with the local dogs but never had any difficulty in detaching himself from them. He was not a pack member; it was as if he had decided that the house was his exclusive territory. The little black dog had imposed herself on him, he was happy to play with her in our garden, or when we were out walking, although he never sought her out. She always came to him.

As for the rabbits, they didn't last long. They may have been content to stay in cages, but the children quickly got bored with them and placed the rabbits out on the road. Within hours both rabbits were dead, savaged by the dog owned by their next-door neighbours. The boy saw one of them die. 'The dog just flipped it over and broke its neck and ran off with it, pulling it to bits.' Those rabbits were pet-shop models, black and white, drowsy, placid. The rabbits in the fields were dun-coloured and darted about. Pretty but commonplace, not like the hare – serene and quixotic, a creature from myth. Coiled for action, his sinewy legs folded into a crouch, the hare has a singular allure, intelligence and, always, a hint of menace. One of my prized possessions is a framed print of Dürer's famous hare. Far more than even the sharpest photograph, it conveys unsettling magic. I hoped Bilbo wouldn't chase rabbits, but I prayed he would never harm a hare. Then one calm

June morning, just as I was about to let him off his leash, I noticed a hare, as still as a statue, only a couple of feet from us. Its long, bony face looked thoughtful. It was composed, taking the measure of my young dog. Bilbo, even then, was very fast. But the hare knew no dog could outrun it. I closed the clip on Bilbo's leash. He lunged towards the hare, but I held him tightly, with both hands. The hare took off, sprays of earth scattering in its wake and was gone.

5

That Shadow on the Wall

It was a harsh and angry fight. No doubt about it. This was no game. The bigger one was dirty white, with a pink nose and a coarse, stupid expression. The other one was smaller but compact, well muscled; he was definitely a male and was mahogany brown. He had a small star, more of a fleck of white, on his forehead. He had large, floppy ears and somehow, despite the fury and the blood and the bits of fur littering the scene and the vicious yaps, these ears added an element of comedy to the proceedings, horrible to watch, but it was also peculiarly funny. I found myself laughing at the sight of the Mighty Mouse of a beagle type crossed with a dachshund who was gradually taking control. The bigger dog seemed surprised as if he could not understand how he had been overpowered by the squat character who should really have been wearing a bowler hat. What on earth had they been fighting about? There was nothing else in sight. It was a dull morning and I had jogged to the deserted green area with the intention of sprinting up the slight hill, which was a stretch of about 300 metres or so. I would do this ten times with a slow-jog recovery each time before sprinting back up. Then I would have earned my breakfast. I could not have done it had Bilbo accompanied me, which was just as well as he might have been drawn into the brawl and those pugilists, particularly the tough little quasi-beagle, were serious fighters.

The bigger dog skulked off; he had conceded defeat. The

victor came over to me. His right ear was torn and there was a gash under his left eye. When not engaged in combat he had a sweet expression with bright, very dark, brown eyes. He was standing square on short, thick legs with big, flat paws. I noticed he had a tartan collar. A stocky, small dog, he was somebody's pet, adult and confident; yet here he was, wandering about and getting into fights. I sprinted back up the hill. On the way down, I noticed that the white dog had returned and the hair on the beagle's back had risen in a long ridge along its length. He began to bark: a loud, flat, honking kind of yelp, almost goose-like. A true hound's bark. He ran after the other dog. The fight seemed set to continue. I ran back up the hill, conscious that I still had four of these 300-metre sprints left to do and that I was more hungry than tired. As I jogged back that time, by now interested in the war, both dogs had disappeared from sight.

The next day I was walking with Bilbo. Our outing began in bright sunshine and suddenly we were being beaten by sharp hailstones. We walked on, heads down, but then Bilbo sounded his low growl, the warning that indicated possible trouble. There, directly ahead of us, was the white dog, now looking even worse than on the previous day. His flank was torn; there were other smaller, fresh gashes. He was limping and, on seeing Bilbo, he simply stopped and glanced dully at us. There was no challenge in his eyes. Then the beagle appeared. It struck me that perhaps he was the bully, ever on the lookout for a scrap. His eye was slightly swollen but he seemed fine. He trotted over, wagging his tail, a straightforward, businesslike tail, nowhere near as plush as Bilbo's thick multicoloured plume. I waited for Bilbo to tense, as he was on a leash and therefore more vulnerable. Would the beagle attack?

Bilbo was bigger, possibly as heavy, but he was still only nine or ten months old and this other dog was at least four years of age, mature, confident, a proven fighter and he had not been neutered. He was also calm, but whereas Bilbo's calmness was a dreamy kind of absent-minded intelligence, the beagle seemed practical, streetwise and patient. A dog who could plan a successful bank robbery. Bilbo's would be far more ingenious but it would collapse under the weight of detail. The tartan collar was faded but sufficiently vibrant to make me fantasise that the quasi-beagle was a Scot. 'Hey, Mac, where are your people?' I asked and he wagged his tail and kept on following us at a friendly, if polite, distance.

*

Standing at the kitchen window, I kept watch to see in which direction Mac would go. Where did he live? If he was a local dog, he was one I had not seen before and that was surprising, as he appeared confident and well used to solo expeditions. He could look after himself, that was obvious. He settled down on the grass verge just beyond my gate, and was staring at my front door, willing it to open. His ears lay long, down by the sides of his face; his chest was broad. He looked solid, dependable, independent, a dog that could be trusted to get home in one piece. He was also, as I had already seen, the one to put your money on in a fight. It was time to settle down to reading. A friend had given me a three-volume edition of Robert Musil's *The Man Without Qualities*. I hadn't read it before. The title made me smile; the little dog outside certainly had many qualities. Whoever had given him that tartan collar already knew that.

*

It was cold, too cold to read in the living room where the light coming through the long narrow windows was all that an overcast sky had to offer. I decided to read in bed, something I usually avoided doing during the day as it seemed such an idle thing to do. But I wanted to read the Musil, so I could justify decamping to the bedroom and Bilbo was pleased to join me. We nestled down in bed and I made my acquaintance with the God-free Ulrich: I liked to think of Musil writing in a Viennese cafe at the same time as his great rival, and another one of my heroes, Joseph Roth, was apparently equally busy at work mere streets away. The rain returned, thundering down on the slates. Reading in bed was a good idea. After a few hours, I went into the kitchen, intending to eat something. The little dog was still outside; he was sheltering under an old blue pick-up truck that I recognised. It appeared from time to time, I never saw it arrive, or leave. The mystery pick-up was useful that day, it was keeping a dog dry. I stood at the window, not sure if Mac could see me; I washed an apple and took it back with me to my book.

Later I set off to the local shop. It was almost dark and the rain was lighter, but heavy enough to soak through my fleece. There was no sign of Mac: he was smart, and must have gone home. I smiled to myself, thinking of how he had looked as he waited; his big, broad, white paws, with flecks of brown showing through the white, folded primly in front of him. What kind of home did he have? And where had he come from? Again I wondered why, in all my outings with Bilbo over the previous eight or nine months or so, we had never come across him. I couldn't quite decide if he was aggressive or merely able to look after himself.

Leaving the harsh lights of the shop, where the floor was slippery from so many wet feet and dripping umbrellas, I went back out into a darkness that was by now complete.

I walked towards the field and into a blind area. I sensed movement but couldn't see anything and walked on, slightly wary. The 'grass' had long since turned into mud and I was conscious of how thoroughly wet my feet were. On approaching the road that led to the houses, the light from various kitchens illuminated the lane. I saw where the sound had come from; Mac was back. He peered into my face as if he were trying to remember something. For a moment I felt a rush of concern and didn't like the idea of him standing outside in the dark on a wet night in late September. I looked around and saw no one. As soon as I went inside he would go home and, though I felt mean-minded about it, he was somebody else's dog and they were waiting for him.

Everything seemed cleaner the next morning, rain-washed. Steam drifted slowly upwards from the wet ground; the sky was blue. I had continued reading until after 3 a.m., and had almost reached the end of volume one of *The Man Without Qualities*. Half hoping Mac wouldn't be there, I pulled open the kitchen curtain. The blue pick-up had gone, and so had Mac. Dogs have a wonderful flair for making us feel guilty.

*

Since I had met him, I had been imagining Bilbo in the various situations in which I was now seeing other dogs. I had tried to help the little black dog, now dead; I felt I could have saved her. And there had been another incident, a few months earlier. I still have a dent on the top of my finger as a reminder. On that morning it was more like a flattened pea. In the days leading up to the Fourth of July, a big black dog had taken to patrolling the green area leading to the small shop.

He was a heavy Labrador, grey at the muzzle, plain enough to look at, but he had presence. He had the eyes of a stoic, one who has come to terms with life. I knew enough to keep Bilbo away from him; he would lunge at such a dog and come off worst. Bilbo was benign to any dog smaller than him but once a dog was at least twice his size, he would strike. The big dog, about four times Bilbo's weight, lumbered over to me and I patted his heavy head, noting the thick shoulders. I had seen him several times. Once he had made eye contact when Bilbo was with me and I quickly looked away, lifted Bilbo and ran home. But this time, it was different. The dog was distracted, preoccupied. He had a purpose. He gazed up at me, seemed satisfied, and then set off, glancing over his shoulder at me, willing me to follow. He appeared to have decided that I could help him.

His breathing resembled that of an overweight jogger. He was authoritative, in charge, leading the way towards the shop, as though he were about to stride in and stage a hold-up. If he was hungry, he was showing me where I could buy food. But he walked past the entrance and then slowed, looking back at me. Against the side of the shop wall, the side I never walked past as it was in the opposite direction to my house, there was a huddle of black. A young black dog was lying on her side: five puppies, all black, were feeding from her. The mother was exhausted; bone-thin and so weary that she seemed detached from her pups. A couple of feet away there was a small, dark mound, a dead puppy, and slightly further away again lay another one. The old dog stood close to me, watching my face, hopeful that I understood. I moved closer to the bitch, but she didn't react. It was a bad sign that she didn't seem to care. Family dogs don't always allow even their owners to stand too close to new puppies, and these pups were tiny, possibly only a day old, and I was a stranger. I went into the shop to get a couple of cans of dog food but instead decided on slices of cooked chicken from the deli counter. At least I would know what she was eating.

I asked the woman at the counter for some paper plates; she also handed me plastic knives and forks, not knowing that the food was for dogs, not me. I thanked her and bought two bottles of water and a large plastic mixing bowl. The shop assistant gazed at the bowl but said nothing. The old male was standing at the shop door, waiting for me. I came out; he stared at the bag with the chicken. He was hungry, so I decided to feed him first, then buy more for the mother. He sniffed at the meat and moved towards it but stopped and looked away, back towards the family. Despite his bullish head and menacing expression he was a kind dog and somehow, before I had even seen the puppies, I had guessed he was not their father. At some time in the past, by some owner, he had been neutered. It made his concern even more touching. I offered the chicken to him. He paused, studied it, glanced back to the family, and looked briefly at me before turning to jog over to the puppies. I followed him and opened the bag, placing the chicken slices on one of the plates and slid it towards the bitch. She could smell it and slowly she hauled herself to her feet. She was surprisingly big: underweight but tall, with a small head and a matted tail. She gulped down the chicken and watched as I poured the two bottles of water into the bowl. Down went the water. I felt she could eat more chicken but decided to feed the other dog first.

In the shop I asked for more chicken. The woman half-smiled at me: she knew exactly what I was doing and asked me directly if I was feeding the dogs. I had barely admitted to it when she warned me that the manager was furious about the dogs and had called the dog warden to collect them, but no one had appeared. I asked her for the same again, telling her that the mother was very thin. The woman sighed as she opened a large foil bag and told me that I could take the rest of the meat. 'I'd an old dog myself; she used to watch the telly with me.' Although I had been in the shop many times, I realised that the woman had never spoken to me before. She was severe-looking and rarely smiled but she had seemed genuinely moved by the strays. The big dog was waiting outside. I bent down and fed him by hand. He was hungry but ate slowly. I noticed he had lost three or four teeth and made a whistling sound as he ate. He was even older than I had first thought but he was strong; a tough and wise dog.

After checking the mother, who had settled down again with her pups, I walked home thinking about the lives of dogs and how they varied, from pampered to destitute. The old male ambled at my side until I came to the path leading to the houses; he stopped, looked at me and then turned and lumbered back across the field, to stand guard over the family. The dogs needed help. I could get them food, but they also had to have shelter.

I had noticed a wrecked car, a once flashy white saloon, low-slung to the ground with leather seats, now burst at the seams. Left abandoned at the far end of the so-called green area, it had probably been stolen and used in a fast getaway. The driver's door was dented, as if by crazed kicks. Best of all, the car was closer to my house than the shop was and far more private. If it were possible to lead the dog and her puppies to the car, they would be safer and at least dry. This plan went through my mind as I looked at Bilbo, knowing he was waiting to go out. But it was still raining. I opened the back door and walked out into the small garden, which was long and tapered into a grove of trees, the only ones that had survived the building of the houses. He walked behind me, carefully avoiding the puddles. I wanted to prevent his encountering the persistent old Lab.

*

How to move five puppies? Would the mother permit me to handle them? How would either of the dogs react? There was also the problem of having seven dogs who would consider me their provider camping in such close proximity to Bilbo, knowing his views on larger dogs. It was a mess but I was already more than halfway in. Early the next day I scanned the immediate area, hoping that I could get Bilbo out for a walk so that the resettlement could begin in the hour before the shop opened. The fewer spectators, the better. Barely ten metres from my gate, Bilbo's low growl made me glance back at the green area from which the old Lab was charging towards us. I picked Bilbo up and ran back to the house, opened the front door and shoved him through it and pulled the door closed. The Lab lumbered closer, barking. He was agitated as I ran towards him; he turned and ran back to the shop. The dog family must be in trouble, I thought, and ran on. But then I heard Bilbo's bark.

Looking back towards the house I saw him racing towards me and realised he must have jumped through the bedroom window. I panicked. He barged past me and raced directly for the Labrador, who stood his ground, an expression of surprise on his face. It lasted until Bilbo's first charge; then the Labrador responded. The heavier dog quickly took control. Why hadn't I kept out of it? 'Bilbo's going to get killed' was my first thought. I pushed my way into the tangle of limbs, kicking and shouting. Somehow I grabbed Bilbo, but the old dog's jaws had closed on his neck. I watched in horror, expecting to see his throat being ripped open but I pulled and forced the wet jaws back. It felt like opening a bear trap. A sharp, stabbing pain went through me. I felt I was about to vomit. The little finger of my left hand was torn; I kicked at the old dog. He was so surprised by my suddenly turning on him that he stepped back, despair on his face. I ran back to the house, holding Bilbo above my head, wriggling and snarling, his saliva dropping down my arms and on to my face.

Just at the gate the big dog lurched up against me, clawing at Bilbo. I felt a tearing sensation down my back. Kicking at the old dog I got the key in the door, opened it and pushed through, slamming the door shut. I ran into the kitchen, then rushed out to close the inside hall door to prevent Bilbo escaping through the bedroom window to continue the fight. But he had lost interest in it and instead was watching me, as I held my injured hand. Turning on the faucet I put my finger under it but the water stung. There was a first-aid kit in one of the cupboards. Tearing open the new box of plasters, I wrapped a big, gauzy thing around my finger. The pain was sickening, and there was blood and water all over the sink. I felt I was losing my balance. But at least the blood was contained within the dressing. I looked at Bilbo, who was serene, oblivious of the way his coat was standing up in tufts, sticky with saliva. There was blood on him, but it was mine. I laughed wildly. He had caused the fight and I was the one that got hurt. I ran my good hand over his body; there were no bites, but I reckoned he was badly bruised and would be sore the next day. I gave him water and watched as he lapped at it. Perhaps he had learned a lesson, I muttered, before walking out of the kitchen. The door closed with a soft clunk and I turned the key, just to make sure.

Outside, I glanced at the kitchen window. It was open only an inch or two. The keys were still in the front door. The old dog was lumbering back. I called to him. He stopped and spun round, looked at me, and charged on, towards the shop. I followed, my hand throbbing, blood seeping through the dirty gauze.

*

The bitch was gone, so were two of the pups; the remaining three lay in a cluster, dead. Someone had placed a newspaper over the dead puppy from the day before. The second corpse from the previous day was also still there but not covered. The old dog was distraught, confused and howling. A man came out of the shop; he had a black plastic sack and asked me if I knew the old dog. 'No, not really, he seemed to be minding the mother and the pups.' The man grunted. 'The dog warden took it and the live ones, took his time getting here. I better get him back for that one,' he said, waving the sack at the Labrador. He looked at my wounded hand and asked had the dog bitten me. When I said no, he then asked would I put the Lab into the storeroom behind the shop. The man was direct and admitted to not liking dogs. He was irritated by the warden. 'Don't know why he didn't take these three here,' he said gesturing towards the dead puppies. 'Does he think I'm going to bury them?'

My hand was sore, I was tired. The old dog stood at a distance from me. I walked towards the open shed; it was a storeroom full of crates of empty bottles, bits of display units and a bike. Every storeroom always seems to have a bike, just as every stretch of deserted road always seems to have a lone shoe, usually a man's. I called to the dog. He could read my mind. I had been his collaborator in a rescue that had failed. We walked towards each other. I hadn't realised how stiff he was. Being in the storeroom meant that he would end up in the pound, and, at his age, be put down. 'Come on,' I said, 'here, come with me.' He followed me, wagging his tail, hope lighting up his big, plain face. I thought I could secure the garden shed and he could live in there; I would keep him well away from Bilbo. He could live outside; Bilbo would be the house dog. It would be tricky. At that time, I had a commission. I was writing a textbook on industrial relations. It was extremely boring, but paid very well and it was a break from digging other people's gardens. I had gone to tea in a smart city restaurant with a man who worked in an office. He wore a suit, his nails were perfect. He had told me that I had nice eyes, but couldn't help noticing that I had the hands of a labourer.

As I neared the house, I realised the dog could spend the night in the old getaway car. I could bring him food and he would be safe, as would Bilbo. He followed me over and I opened the door. 'Now just wait here. I'll be back.' The dog knew all about waiting in cars. He jumped into the passenger seat. It was a good plan. After a couple of strides I looked back, and he was sitting in the driver's seat, ready for me to return and drive us away.

Before I bought dog food, I had to examine my finger. The gauze was now stuck to it. I peeled it away and realised I was looking at bone. A door opened a few houses away. It was the nurse. She waved. I held up my hand and hurried over to her. 'Jesus, did your dog bite you, the bastard. You'll need stitches. Whatever about the stitches, you need a tetanus shot. You'll lose the top of your finger. But you're in luck, I'm going to work. Get in; just don't bleed on my car.'

*

The nurse made sure her colleagues realised that I was a weirdo. 'She collects strays dogs and then wonders why she gets bitten.' My suffering gave her enough material for a comic routine, particularly the part when I was having the injection. The first needle broke on contact with my hip. More laughter. I was aware that my boots smelt, as did the rest of me. When I was leaving one of the nurses remarked with some surprise, 'Oh, you speak English. I thought you were Russian.'

Back in the kitchen a now righteous Bilbo was suspicious. He checked me over, sniffing at my boots, my jeans, my hands. Perhaps it was the hospital smell? But I think he could smell the black dog. Meanwhile, back at the car, the old guy was nicely settled. As I approached, the car began to rock from side to side, it was shuddering. Inside he was wagging his tail. I smiled at his trust. 'Hey, fella, have some supper.' I opened the door and he bounded out, so happy he knocked me over. He was a heavy dog. Bilbo was no match for him. As the dog gulped down the food, I realised that I was watching real hunger, but a hunger that had lost the additional sting of desperation. Unease began to cut through the satisfaction; this arrangement was going to be impossible. Bilbo was never going to accept this dog and, even if he did, he would only do it in a mood of submission. It wasn't fair to Bilbo; he would be undermined and I was the one who was going to cause him hurt. I surveyed the empty green area. Not a car or person in sight. On cue, a lone magpie darted into view, a bad omen. The Lab had finished his food and was watching me with a soft, contented gaze. He had needed help, and I had tried to save the mother with the litter. They were gone, but now he had me. As far as he was concerned I had passed some kind of test: I wasn't all-powerful, but he knew he could trust me and that was enough for him.

*

We did a lap of the field, the big dog and me. He was thrilled, lumbering along, glancing back at me, his broad face happy. It was touching, yet I felt like a traitor, knowing my little guy was facing the loss of his world, the kingdom that he had established with me, the kingdom of which he was the centre and which had already more or less killed off my struggling relationship with a likeable man who nevertheless believed animals should live outdoors and who was losing patience with my solitary ways. The Lab was amiable but domineering, as was Bilbo. Bilbo was lighter, smaller, and he would start fights that were bound to end badly for him. This old dog had already had a life that I would know nothing about. Judging by the way he was acting with me, he knew all about moulding a human to suit his needs. Bilbo was working off instinct, but the black dog knew about bonding. I didn't know what I was doing. Now it was almost dark. I motioned him to hop back into the car and gave him a large bone, the size of a small dumb-bell. I reckoned it would keep him occupied for a few hours. I tried not to think about my problem.

I woke with a start. Bilbo was frantic, barking, jumping up and down, his hair in a ridge along his back. I saw a shadow on the bedroom wall, a bulky shape magnified by the moonlight; someone was trying to get into the house. I knew the back door was locked. There seemed to be only one intruder; my hockey stick was in the hall, not much use to me. The bedroom window was big by any standards and ridiculous for the size of the room. Bilbo leapt up on to the wooden chest of drawers, an old pine one that I had bought in a junk shop. It had taken many hours to strip it, plane it down and apply Danish oil. All my work was being destroyed as Bilbo, jumping up and down, clawed at the wood in his rage. The ungainly shape was moving further along the garden wall, slowly and unsteadily, tottering, not too agile. A burglar would need to be a bit fitter than this. I felt angry that anyone so incompetent fancied his chances of breaking in. I climbed up on the chest and reached for the window latch. I roared at the shape and discovered to my relief that it was the old Lab, eyes soft, his big thick tail began to wag with a force that was bound to upset his balance; he would fall off the wall. Bilbo barged by me and was preparing to launch himself into the garden. I grabbed him around his middle and hauled him back in, pushing him on to the bed before slamming the window. He bounced down on to the floor, preparing for battle, but instead he found himself being ordered into the bathroom. I pulled my dressing gown off the door and placed it on the floor. I ordered him to sit there and, looking into his worried eyes, told him that I would be back.

It was after one o'clock on a still night; the moon was huge and resembled a platter of beaten silver. My surprise visitor was happy, waiting for me at the back door. This had become a serious mess. Bilbo was feeling threatened by a huge newcomer with an iron will but the old guy was also a sweet character, with no options. If he went to the dogs' home, he would be dead in four or five days. Who would listen while I made a case for the homeless Lab? The only person I could think of was the acquaintance with the trophy pet, the Old English Sheepdog who lived in a suburban garage and spent his days waiting for the brief toilet breaks that passed for walks. The black dog didn't have a hope. I sat with him on the little step, gazing at a small group of conifers I had intended to plant into the flower beds. They stood like tiny sentries in plastic pots. It was very cold and still; the only sound was his breathing. Suddenly I felt very hungry and wanted to sleep. Meanwhile I could sense Bilbo fretting in the bathroom, angry and bewildered, far too intelligent to be sitting meekly on my dressing gown.

Back at the getaway car, it was obvious that it was no longer working as a secure kennel – the door lock was broken. The old dog's weight had buckled it; he had tired of waiting, ripped the car seats apart, burst through the driver's door and blustered over to the house, my house, now his house, our house. That was that. I ran home. Bilbo was barking, but now there was a forlorn element to his protest, more of a desolate yap. The black dog was investigating the garden of his new home. On hearing movement inside, he jumped up at the back door, his blunt head casting a shadow the size of a basketball. He began barking: the sound was deep and resonant. I felt trapped and went into the kitchen to make hot chocolate and devise a plan, hopefully an improvement on my more recent efforts.

The milk in the pot came to the boil and I thought again of that woman I knew and her passive Old English Sheepdog in its suburban garage; perhaps he would like a companion? But the black dog was domineering; I could see him taking over. This was a dog intent on being the boss. He had probably come between a husband and wife, threatened the marriage; perhaps that was why he was homeless at his age. He certainly knew all about sitting in cars, and now he was working on shaping another human, me. I liked him: his concern for the bitch and her pups had been remarkable – and heartbreaking – to observe, a further, complex insight into the minds of dogs. But he couldn't join us; here were two dogs who would never be friends, two dominant personalities – it was impossible. Bilbo was trapped in the house; there would be no more walks for him until the bigger dog had an alternative home.

And the chocolate tin was almost empty. I put the last of the powder into a mug and drank a cup of what amounted to hot milk flavoured with sugar and, with a box of breakfast cereal that I often ate dry, went in to sit on the bathroom floor with Bilbo. His expression was solemn; he flopped across my lap. It was chilly on the tiled floor. Condensation streamed down the window. It was almost five o'clock in the morning; I must have dozed off. The subdued dawn light suited the mood. The big dog was now clawing at the back door. He had decided that the garden was fine, if somewhat limited, but that inside the house was more interesting, and his next challenge. I took a heavy blanket from the linen closet – a modest cupboard with the beginnings of the vast collection of sheets, blankets and towels I would amass, a *Hausfrau* in the making – and placed the blanket on the bathroom floor for Bilbo. I told him to lie there and have a nap, and that I would sort out the mess. But first I had to sleep. I went to bed, deliberately not looking at the chest of drawers Bilbo had scratched in his fury. Within moments, the Lab was back at the window, barking, demanding entry, while in the bathroom Bilbo had begun howling as if all his dreams had been shattered.

*

It hadn't been sleep; it was more like collapsing after a dull blow to the head. I came to with a groan and wished I could drift back into unconsciousness. This was the first time since I had met Bilbo, aside from when he was terribly ill, that I hadn't woken up to see him watching me. He was still in the bathroom. I went to fetch him. He was huddled against the wall, camped on my dressing gown as if it were a small island, which it was, as he had wet the floor and the outer edges of the robe were soaked. He had ignored the big blanket. He looked at me with an accusatory expression. Bilbo then walked carefully to the kitchen, ignoring me.

In the hope of avoiding the sight of the big dog's endearing face at the kitchen window, I kept the curtain closed, although I did peek out. Toast was the only thing that would draw Bilbo out of his mood. 'Hey, come on,' I fawned, hating myself and my creepy, pleading voice. He looked away, refusing to engage, the way a mare will when she has had enough human company for the moment, and wants to eat without an audience. I wanted him to grasp that I was only trying to help another dog and I put my arms around Bilbo, saying his name over and over in an attempt to comfort him. He stood rigid, intent on ignoring me, as I rocked back and forth and, when the toaster popped, I kept on rocking. The smell of the toasted bread made me hungry. On I rocked, talking to Bilbo, rubbing the side of my face against his head. He began to relent; finally, he jammed his head under my chin. I began buttering the toast. As long as the big guy didn't appear outside the kitchen window, there would be a peace or at least a ceasefire between us.

Bilbo was busy at his water bowl when I took two cans of dog food from a cupboard and crept out of the kitchen, with a large, lightweight mixing bowl, closing the door behind me. At the back door, the big guy was sitting stretched out in the sun. He had pulled several of the conifer plants out of their plastic containers. It was now unlikely that any of them would ever be planted, since most of them were crushed and he had also broken the pots they had come in. The mess was impressive, a giant infant bored and anticipating the next instalment of his new life. His face lit up and he came over to me.

Holding his head between my hands, I realised that he was about the size of an adult sheep. Had the situation been reversed, I reckoned that the older dog would have eventually tolerated Bilbo. But Bilbo would never accept a newcomer. There was no point in trying the neighbours; the Lab needed a home miles away from Bilbo. I bent down and began clearing up the mess. Who would take on a large, intelligent and obviously experienced dog? Then I realised the only person I knew who would even listen to the story of this most recent entanglement was Robert, the long-suffering owner of obnoxious Tessa.

By then, it was almost nine o'clock on a brightening morning. I glanced in a window and saw my reflection. My hair was standing on end. I looked crazed and, well, I was. My little life was getting very complicated. I only had four days to complete the industrial relations project. The history sections had been easy to write, but now I was faced with the Theory of Work; it needed to be convincing and I knew nothing about the subject. I would have to make it up as I went along; and here I was trying to settle a conflict between two dogs. Tessa, mistress of all she surveyed, wouldn't want a second dog moving into her house either; that was obvious, so Robert would understand why I needed the tenacious Lab to move to a home, miles away, preferably abroad. I stood up and emptied both cans of dog food into the mixing bowl, and then presented it to my lodger; the smell of the dog food was not nearly as strong in the open air as it always was in the kitchen.

Bilbo was sitting in the kitchen, ready to be friends with me, his graceful, fluffy tail, so unlike the big dog's club-like stump, wagging happily. He was content in his kingdom. I gave him my sweater to sit on. He had had enough of the bathroom for the moment, so I left him in the kitchen while I had a quick bath. Robert would listen to my tale and come up with something, I hoped. Something, most likely desperation, made me remember a friend's brother back in the States, who was a banker. Perhaps I could phone him in Manhattan, telling him I had found the perfect dog for his dacha in upstate New York.

Robert never seemed to sit still; he was already busy that morning, painting the low wall that ran along the footpath in front of his house. He seemed to paint the wall every few weeks. In the same way he maintained his car, washing it relentlessly. Every other car in the neighbourhood was splattered with mud but Robert's was perpetually shiny. He believed in order. Tessa was glowering at him, through the window, from the back of the sofa. 'She's not allowed out when I'm painting in case she gets paint on her,' he said. Her annoyance immediately turned to outrage: the black dog was at my side. 'Where's Bilbo?' asked Robert, concern flooding his face, 'Who's this?'

Aware that Robert was still slightly embarrassed by the way he had not exactly supported me through Bilbo's bad experience of neutering, I felt I had a small advantage over him: I also knew he loved a crisis. I was sure he would be touched by the black dog's heroic efforts on behalf of the young female and her pups, so I began my plea in the manner of a defence attorney, confident that Robert would appreciate the old dog's valour. He listened, and before I got very far in the telling, he stopped his work, peered at the Lab and then carefully wrapped the brush in a plastic bag and placed it on the front path. Replacing the lid on the paint bucket, he put his hand on the old dog's head. 'I have seen this lad about, I know I have. He's big, you'd notice him, and I did see the dog with the pups, but only once. I meant to help, but when I went back, they were gone.' I filled in the rest of the story; Robert looked upset and for once ignored the yapping Tessa, glowering at us through the window, more than ever resembling a spoilt dowager demanding immediate service in a high-class restaurant.

On I went, extolling the black dog's courage. 'He's terrific,' said Robert, holding the dog's heavy, broad head, staring into his friendly eyes. 'He's lovely, a real, real dog.' No doubt Robert was well aware that Tessa was not a real dog – she was a petulant diva – and he looked at the big dog with a gaze full of longing and asked if Bilbo liked him.

Holding up my damaged finger I spoke about the clash of two strong characters. 'If only Bilbo were older,' I lamented, and said that I knew it would never work and that I was going to phone my friend's wealthy, rich, share-dealing brother, adding that he tended to select dogs on looks, not temperament. Robert was rueful and admitted that if it weren't for Tessa, he would take him, as he knew I would have done had Bilbo not objected. Robert realised that the dog's size would be against him, particularly for any family with small children. It was not going as I had planned.

Robert seemed defeated. I again mentioned approaching my friend's brother. Robert took up his paint brush and resumed painting; there was regret in his every movement. I was so disappointed. As I turned, Robert spoke; I was not in the mood for one of his monologues. But he seemed positive and spoke about his mother. She had had a long succession of dogs; they'd all been named Toby. There had been a great Toby when Robert had been ten or eleven, that Toby could talk – but he stopped his reminiscence and became far more deliberate. If his mother were to take the dog, he would have a big place; the kitchen was, as Robert described it, bigger than his entire house. He paused, knowing that this was the most important factor: she lived hours away.

Hope began to rise in me. But then I wondered if Robert had suspected me of playing him. Why was he so vague about where his mother lived? I didn't care. There was a chance for the dog. Back at my gate, a woman was waiting for me. 'Your dog, that dog there', her voice shrill with accusation and certainty, pointing at the big Lab, 'killed my chickens.'

'Impossible,' I countered, 'this is a house dog, he lives in the kitchen. You must be confusing him with the stray that comes here from time to time. Johannes here is a lamb, he babysits small children,' I enthused in a Maria Von Trapp voice, assuring her of his kindness, his pleasure in watching the wild birds feeding in my garden. I waved and walked quickly to the door. Bilbo began barking in the kitchen. The woman's eyes were on my back but I couldn't go in the front door with the 'house dog' so I opened the side gate leading down towards the back garden, 'Come, Johannes,' I beckoned, singing out his new name, intent on sounding carefree, as the dog heaved his bulk through the passageway, looking unwieldy and awkward, and I called back to the woman that he was expecting me to dry his paws.

*

I liked the black dog, his homely face, his inelegance, his innocence, his hope that his luck had changed. Nor had I forgotten the despair of the pound. The name Johannes suited him; he needed some good person who needed a good dog. I had never been interested in driving but suddenly I realised what a useful thing a car would be. If I had a car, I could have put Bilbo in it and driven him off to a safe space for a run. But instead we were now under siege, trapped between the bathroom and a kitchen running out of food. If we left by the front door there was a very good chance that the big dog, despite his size, would somehow manage to climb over the garden wall – as he had already – or might simply smash the gate, and there would be another fight. I had gone from dog paradise, me with my boy, to a canine nightmare, the circumstances of which would make most people laugh aloud – at me. What to do? More toast. It was impossible to think about industrial relations, harmony in the workplace, or 'Trade Unions in Practice'. One of my friends had just met Mr Wonderful and was going to move to Paris with him. For a moment, only a moment, I wondered would the happy couple like to take Johannes with them. Robert's mother sounded like a long shot; if she was as fussy as her son, could she possibly take on a dog strong enough to smash a car door? I was glad that I hadn't told him about the battered saloon in the field.

Bilbo paced the kitchen floor, agitated and despairing, his glances reproachful. Something had to be done. I went to fetch real comfort food, a volume of Wordsworth. I sat down on the floor with the book, hoping Bilbo would settle beside me, and he did. Relief. After an hour or so, the phone rang. I jumped. My deadline. But it was Robert. This, I thought, is when he gives me a lecture in his retired teacher's tone about 'the tough decisions life presents us with'. He saw himself as an experienced dog person, while I was still a rookie, admittedly a rookie thrown in at the deep end. I decided that I would be calm, mature, acknowledge his wisdom; I would offer him tea. I opened the window and pulled back the curtain. Should the big dog appear in the front garden and begin pawing at the glass panes, I would have to grapple the frenzied Bilbo. Robert would see this and might be sufficiently moved to do something; it was all I could do.

When Robert arrived he bounced into the kitchen on the balls of his feet, like a boy on a first date. I'd never seen him so happy. He had spoken with his mother. He explained that she had sold their old family home, the one he had grown up in, and had gone to live in a vast thatched farmhouse in Wales, with two of her old friends. They all first met at boarding school, but were by then all widows. 'They've created magnificent gardens at the tea rooms they opened.' Was he going to tell me that they wouldn't take the dog for fear he'd dig up the gardens? His mother had had to consult with the others. 'She *knows* Tessa,' said Robert. 'They don't like each other. Tessa is very highly strung.' Visions of Tessa in a Far Side cartoon being strung up by a lynch party of dogs wearing cowboy hats flickered across my mind's eye. One of them, a white hound clad in a leather waistcoat, sports a sheriff's badge. Robert sighed, rocking back on his heels. I kept smiling my fixed smile. Oh God, would he just get to the point? My eyes were beginning to water but I continued looking directly at Robert, willing him to say what I wanted to hear.

He described his relationship with his mother as delicate. He had been the eldest, and she had never liked his wife.

'I'm telling you this', said Robert, 'because the one thing
we have always had between us, like a kind of special bond,
is dogs.' Relief was beginning to wash over me, the smile
on my face felt permanent; Robert deserved a better dog
than Tessa. His mother had loved the sound of the big dog,
'and she trusts me,' said Robert. Tessa had been owned by
another friend and she couldn't manage her. Robert had
taken Tessa as a favour and, well, that explained why he had
her. Robert had borrowed the old station wagon and would
drive the big dog to Wales. He said it was going to be hard
because he knew that by the time he reached his mother's
home, he wouldn't want to part with the dog because he
loved him already. He was right, I thought: Johannes was
one of those dogs. Closing the kitchen window, I pulled
the curtain and told Bilbo to stay. I led Robert through
the house to the garden. The big dog was sitting in the
sun, his eyes squinting into the light, the heavy paws, for
once, neatly arranged under him. He was a study in serene
control, surveying the garden, his garden. He jumped up
and lumbered over to me, before turning, in his new role
as host, to Robert, who was already in love. Content and
relaxed, Johannes followed us out to the station wagon.
Robert remarked that he had been meaning to visit his
mother. The dog lifted his front paws on to the open back
of the station wagon and, feeling both guilty and relieved,
I pushed his behind up into the car, my face squashed up
against his broad, dusty hind quarters.

Ever organised, Robert had a small suitcase and a basket
with dog food, two bowls – for the dog – and a flask for
himself. Wet gear, a first-aid kit, a flash lantern: Robert
knew how to do things properly. In his own way he was a
hero, a man who had always made the best of his lot, even

enduring the neurotic Tessa. As the car pulled away, the big black dog realised I wasn't coming and began thrashing about. Robert slowed down and I could imagine him comforting his distressed passenger. It was upsetting to see Johannes go, but it was an ending so much better than it could have been. Within weeks a pink envelope arrived in the mail, the tea rooms and pretty gardens in a photograph, a glimpse of the hipped roof and whitewashed wall of an atmospheric farmhouse just visible to the side. Standing proud in the foreground was that wonderful dog, now answering, according to the brief note accompanying the photograph, to the name of Toby.

6

A Singular Individual

Rain pattered down tentatively, as if testing the roof of the garden shed. Initially little more than a random tapping, it became louder, more drum-like, falling furiously above my head as I crouched inside repairing the puncture on my bike. The lighting inside the decrepit shed was poor; a dim bulb had been fitted long before, by other hands than mine, into an ancient fitting. It was brittle and suspended from a worn, furry old cable which tended to swing like a hangman's noose, casting weird shadows on the spiders' webs and the dirty window with its two smeared panes of cracked glass. I fiddled about with solution and patches, wondering about the traditional, if charmless, procedure. I knew some seriously cool cyclists; did they actually go through this clumsy routine? Wasn't there some other way?

Hours later, I realised that we needed supplies, and I knew that if I sat down to read more of *The Man Without Qualities* I would do nothing. Bilbo would get hungry, as would I. The worm-eaten door of the shed had begun to sag – the wood around the hinges was rotting – and it fell towards me as I reached in to fetch the bike. I pulled at the handlebars and moved around the frame, preparing to push it down towards the side gate, but it moved sluggishly. Despite my efforts, the tyre was flat again. The local store would have to do instead.

The shop was a capricious place, poorly stocked most of the time, often appearing as if it had just been raided. Yet occasionally exotic wonders would appear: the odd melon, bottles of French blood-orange juice, elegant jars of cherry conserve or bars of fine soap, so beautifully wrapped it seemed a shame to open them. But these gracious wares would quickly vanish from the shop, never to be seen again. That day's luxury offering was black grapes, bursting with sun and possibly chemicals, but they looked wonderful and there, among the standard Danish pastries, were maple doughnuts and small chocolate twists. I stocked up, exiting the shop in triumph. Halfway across the field towards home I heard movement and turned. Mac was following me! As soon as he knew I had seen him, he stopped, ears swinging, to stare back, in his mild, non-committal way. He sniffed the air and walked towards me with a jaunty, jog-like walk.

Although he looked hungry and was underweight, Mac, naturally broad-chested and stocky, looked solid enough, with those dark, liquid eyes that I had already noticed were more like those of a horse. He was calm and had deduced that I presented no threat; I was barely a challenge, in fact. He didn't dive at the cakes; he knew he wouldn't have to exert himself to get something from me and gently accepted the piece I handed to him. We walked back to the house. He was easy company; he had no desperation, no demands, no frantic displays of affection. At the gate I turned and said goodbye. Johannes had been a useful experience in how to complicate matters. Detachment was vital to survival. I noticed Bilbo observing us from the kitchen window; he was relaxed – Mac was outside but Bilbo was comfortably inside, happy that his human was back and that the large black interloper was gone. In the kitchen, Bilbo was far more interested in me than he was in the dog standing at the gate. A rough sketch of a garden design I was working on lay on the table. First, though, I needed to eat. Then I would begin work. Later there would be a run for me and a walk for us. After that I had a birthday party to attend but my bike was temporarily out of action.

The walk went well. Within a hundred metres of the house Mac had appeared, sauntering over to us as if the meeting was purely a chance encounter. He materialised beside us, maintaining his customary polite distance, suggesting that he knew he was engaging with an established unit – human and dog. He stopped only when Bilbo wanted to sniff something interesting and would walk on as soon as Bilbo was ready It was highly civilised: two dogs out for a walk, one on a leash held by a fussy, protective human, the other, unfettered, self-possessed and at ease. Daylight was fading; it was early October. Shadows were pooling and the sullen sky revealed a startling slash of watery pink turning to scarlet as the sun prepared to set with a flourish. We did a long lap. The rain began yet again, and here and there lights went on in the various clusters of houses. I was determined to get to the birthday party. There was an incentive. My horoscope had advised me to 'break out' and 'seize the opportunity of re-establishing contact with one you have admired from afar'. It was all too accurate; there had been a certain rugby player at college. He had messy, dirty blond hair, kindly, sleepy eyes and a good-natured smile. Men liked him, females sighed; he was that type of man. He was not a driven student and had repeated a year. He once asked me whether I had seen a particular film, a Russian movie, *Burnt by the Sun*, to be precise; my reaction had been deranged, or, worse, pathetic.

Instead of saying 'no' I had almost shouted 'yes' in a ringing, triumphant voice. (Why? Why had I reacted like a contestant on *University Challenge*?) Then I went on to analyse it, and, worst of all, place it in the context of Stalinist Soviet literature, talking about *And Quiet Flows the Don* and *The Don Flows Home to the Sea*, clearly confirming that I was a nerd programmed to respond to any chance enquiry as if it were an exam question upon which my future depended. My unofficial beloved had looked perplexed, no, repelled. Blushing now at the sheer horror of the memory, I recall that I wasn't all that surprised when he quietly replied, 'I must go and see it,' before shuffling off. Despite this debacle, there was a chance that he might be at the party and my older, wiser self had acquired, in the intervening period, an element of decorum. It would be nice, I thought, to see him again; particularly as I was not happy in my current relationship and continued to dream about finding a soulmate. I hoped that I was by now sufficiently intelligent to deny having seen any movie he might happen to mention.

Just as well the bike repair had flopped; I would summon a taxi and arrive like an adult dressed for a social occasion, not for a sports meet. If the fantasy figure of my youth happened to be present, and the horoscope had been accurate, I would ask him about the future of rugby as a professional sport and refrain from bombarding him with textual criticism or stories featuring Bilbo as intrepid superhero. While I would mention my garden designing – it had a genteel ring to it – I resolved not to discuss sanding floors in case he realised that my postgraduate qualification had thus far led to a precarious career as a freelance handyman.

The gathering was informative, if depressing. Many of my former college classmates had jobs, mainly in teaching. My fantasy figure was there: he looked just the same, though slightly crumpled and heavier – to be truthful, noticeably fat. He was working in a bank, as an advisor. It sounded very unlikely; I had thought he would have made a sympathetic teacher with his relaxed approach to life. (The last conversation we had had was about *Middlemarch*. He had asked me if I liked it. I was prepared to be calm and measured in my response, but he cut across me and admitted he had not read it, 'but I have these study notes, they're very detailed'. He smiled, and just then two other rugby types thundered over; the library floor groaned beneath their combined bulk and that was that.) A bank, why a bank? I thought to myself while trying to appear interested instead of horrified. 'My father-in-law is high up in one and he got me the job. It's not too demanding, just as well. I've been injured for months, so I just sit around drinking coffee and eating. There's always pastries or biscuits or fancy sandwiches lying about after meetings . . .' Father-in-law? The horoscope hadn't mentioned anything about fathers-in-law; the smile on my face began to ebb. Somehow I asked him what his wife did, and he told me that she was not very well, and that she was expecting a baby. 'How wonderful,' I replied, resenting even more my oddball life sanding floors. I wanted to run. The smoke and the heat closed in around me. The food was a hot curry gloop being ladled out of a large pot. I wasn't interested in waiting for the birthday cake.

*

Stars filled the night sky; it was freezing outside but I walked for a mile or so before attempting to stop a taxi. A late-night shop was open. Inside the lights were bright, almost comforting. I glanced at myself in a mirror and saw my expression of furtive embarrassment which summed up exactly how I felt. I was the person who had come back from

Siberia to discover that life had moved on. I was sanding floors and digging gardens while my fantasy figure had an easy job with his wife's daddy. Bars of Belgian chocolate in elegant white wrappers were stacked on the counter, near the cash register – very expensive, but vital sustenance to me in my dejected mood. I bought several – and then set about finding a cab.

I ate all the way home. The driver was grim, silent and drove with a sense of outrage; he seemed personally insulted by being asked to venture into the outskirts of civilisation where my house happened to be located. The inflated fare suggested that he had added danger money. 'Keep the change,' I growled, handing over the exact amount. My expedition had been disappointing. Mac was on the doorstep, rising to greet me as if he were a professional doorman. 'Hi, guy,' I muttered, opening the door, and closing it behind me. Bilbo was dozing in the kitchen, on a beanbag – one of the assortment I had scattered throughout the house for his comfort. Fetching a bottle of water from the refrigerator, I slunk off to bed, Bilbo at my heels. It could have been worse; I might have been running my own bike repair business and my lost-never-love might have appeared one day with five children and his permanently pregnant wife to buy a better bike than my meagre shop happened to stock.

Morning dawned murky and sombre, perfect for the darkness of my feelings. I didn't feel like running or even eating. 'Come on,' I said to Bilbo, 'let's go, now.' He peered at me as if to say, 'How about breakfast?' but followed me to the hall and then back as I remembered I had left the keys on the bedroom floor. Nothing stirred outside; there was a row of wood pigeons perched on the high telephone wires. Strange, I had never noticed the wires before. Silence. It was Sunday, the air was damp. We set off. Bilbo was off his leash, I felt if we could reach the big green area before a car appeared we would have a good session. In my right hand I gripped Bilbo's multicoloured frisbee, punctured here and there with teethmarks, but it was pretty, a cheerful splash of colour against the leaden sky. I jogged about, spinning it high over Bilbo's head; he darted after it, twisting his body in mid-leap, retrieving the disc and then, head down, bum in the air, daring me to take it from him. I ran towards him, snatched the frisbee and sent it spinning. Bilbo charged off in pursuit and Mac, appearing out of nowhere, had joined the chase

Bilbo lifted his toy and ran back towards me. Mac made no effort to grab the thing; he merely followed Bilbo. The game continued. Every time I sent the plate spinning, Bilbo ran off, followed by the beagle making it clear that he had no interest in the frisbee and was joining in only for the wild sprints. Peace was sustained, there was no tension. It made me recall the outings with the little female, Bilbo's would-be girlfriend, who had ended up dead in a ditch. We went home, Bilbo on the leash, Mac a couple of strides behind us. Back at the house, I opened the gate and the three of us walked in. I unclipped Bilbo's leash. All was well until I opened the door. Bilbo trotted in, tail wagging. I followed. Then Mac placed a cautious front paw on the hall floor, and Bilbo spun round, a low growl contained deep down in his throat. It was a warning that clearly stated, 'No further.' I closed the door on the small dog; he was looking up at me, his bright gaze still confident. There was no pleading in his eyes. But there was something else in his look that I couldn't quite interpret.

*

The temperature dropped abruptly. Heavy frosts slowed everything down. The air hurt, the ground was hard and unforgiving. Everything seemed paler, bleached of life, even the grass was drab. I now kept Bilbo in until late morning when the natural colours were released from their icy frosting. I would go out on my runs, my feet crunching the thin layer of frozen earth. I would often see Mac and by the time I returned to the house he was always there, seated calmly at the gate, waiting for Bilbo. My guy usually bounced out, happy to see this new companion. Together they investigated the world surrounding us; it was like watching Jeeves and Wooster. Mac indulged Bilbo without ever being sycophantic. A pattern emerged; all was highly civilised and companionable until we got home, where Bilbo invariably made it clear he would share his outings, even his garden, with his new friend, but not his house. Three, perhaps four, days passed like this. I never knew where Mac went or who was feeding him. It was time to find out where he lived.

*

Stopping to call in at each house, avoiding the ones where I knew particularly vocal dogs lived, was not that difficult; the dogs regarded it merely as a variation on their walks. They had settled into this routine of being together outdoors, as long as it did not extend to the house. I had even sat on the doorstep reading while the two dogs dozed in the weak autumn sun, taking turns to drink from a bowl of water.

'Why is the bigger one on a lead?' asked a teenage boy who stood barefoot at his front door, shouting at me above the music screaming out of a room behind him. I explained that Bilbo was mine and that the other dog was lost or strayed and that I was trying to find his owners. 'I don't know,' the teenager's voice trailed off as he had obviously used up what tiny amount of attention he was prepared to expend on us. He shrugged, said goodbye and closed the door. I could feel my face turning red as I shuffled down the path and closed the gate behind me.

On we trudged, collecting a cross-section of opinions: 'I'm a cat person', 'I'd never keep a pet', 'I am allergic to animal fur', 'I'm terrified of dogs', 'I'm not here enough', 'I hate dogs', 'Never saw it before, if it's strayed once, it'll stray again' and 'Have you nothing better to do than bother people about a lost dog? Why don't you get a life?' Some doors closed politely; some banged, others never opened. There was the sweet old lady who said she'd love to take him in but she couldn't and who then began to tell me the story of the only dog she had ever had in her life – 'years and years and years ago' – a handsome collie dog that her father named Winston, who had then surprised everyone by having puppies.

We explored roads with rows of houses I didn't know, widening the radius of our search for where Mac could have originated. It was strange; he was rather striking and very confident – who could have lost him? How could he have come to lose himself? The tartan collar he had been wearing when we met had disappeared but someone, obviously an owner, had put it on him. This was no hobo. 'Hobo' – that word had fluttered up out of the back of my mind, reviving a memory from the past.

When I was perhaps six or seven – I'm not sure – there had been a TV show that I used to force myself to watch, not because it was bad, but because it was guaranteed to make me cry. *The Littlest Hobo*: it was about a dog, a confirmed wanderer. Each week he would have adventures, invariably dangerous, often involving villains. The winsome terrier was the hero and always resolved whatever disaster had been threatened by outwitting the evildoers through his superior intelligence. Grateful humans fell in love with him and wanted to give him a home – but he never settled. As the credits rolled each week, he'd be back on the road, walking along to the mournful theme song: 'Travelling along the weary roads / Sometimes I think I'll settle down / But I know I hunger to be free; / Travelling's the only life for me. / A-drifting, the world is my friend. / A-travelling along the weary road . . .' or words to that effect. Each week I would be upset by the sight of the lone hero, battling on, leaving his new friends – and me – devastated, and I resolved never to watch it again. But every time I heard the theme song, I always ended up watching.

Humming the tune to myself, I looked down at Mac. He did not seem to be a stray, willing to follow whoever came along. At none of the many houses we stopped at did he seem eager to move in. We walked on; it was getting dark. Then we came to a large detached house. Expensive, battle-scarred toys were scattered across the neglected but still impressive lawn. I pressed the bell and a chime-like peal sounded. The door was opened by a stocky, smiling man wearing round glasses which magnified his equally round brown eyes and their thick black lashes. He looked surprised, but I soon realised that slight amazement was his usual expression. 'Hello, hello. You have brought your friends to visit me? Is this one the girl?' he asked, pointing to Bilbo, 'She's very pretty.' 'He's my dog, but I'm wondering if you know anything about this one?' The man bent down to pet Mac and one of the four small children who had gathered behind him at the open door climbed on the man's back.

The man told me that he was from Libya and that his wife was out shopping, leaving him 'with all these children, my children,' he gasped, the breath knocked out of him. 'No, your father is now too fat to have people walk on his back,' he said, attempting to stand. The child jumped down, laughing and the family delighted in petting the dogs. 'We want a dog,' the man announced, and told me that he was a paediatrician. 'I love children and animals. Since I came to this country, I have wanted a dog and here he is, he comes to my house and asks for me to share my home with him and I say yes. Walk with me and I will soon be thin. What will we call him?' The children shrieked together in one voice 'Dusty' but their father waved this away and said, 'No, his name shall be Rusty, because he is red. Come, Rusty, welcome to your new home.' He bowed low and beckoned to Mac, now Rusty, inviting me in for tea as well. Bilbo trotted in as if accepting formal invitations were a normal part of his day. Mac looked up at me and carefully made his way in. Bilbo did not react. It wasn't his house.

The kitchen was large, L-shaped, and very modern, full of stainless-steel units and flat tables; a cross between a restaurant kitchen and an operating theatre. The refrigerator was made of chrome and had double doors; our host opened them wide. One of the children, the tallest, a girl in pink, took charge and presented me with a carton of apple juice. 'And you can have a bar; they're there in the big jar, but we can't have any until after supper,' she said. Her father deemed her restraint wonderful but clapped his small, soft hands, announcing, 'No, today there are no rules. Rusty has come to live with us. We celebrate.' The children were very excited and the dogs stood to attention on the white-tiled floor. Car lights swept across the window; it was the mother returning. The children shouted over each other, intent on being the first with the news. Mummy was small, a slight English woman, with pale red hair and a tired smile. Life with her happy doctor husband must have been filled with surprises. Had she arrived home to discover a pet elephant in her kitchen, or Johannes at his most emphatic, her reaction most likely would have been much the same.

She smiled at me, the dogs and her children, and said, 'That's nice. Wherever did you get him?' She continually addressed her husband by his name, something soft and musical, it sounded like Radja. She was delicate-looking; her shoulders were narrow and she had thin, red hands. She looked beaten by the cold weather and seemed to suffer from poor circulation. 'Or did you', meaning me, 'bring him? How kind. I had a dog when I was little; well, not exactly my dog, I think he was there before I was born, so he was really my mum's.' She couldn't remember his name and wasn't sure if he had been black or dark grey, or a muddy brown. Her vagueness horrified the children. 'How could you forget something like that?' asked the girl who had given me the carton of juice. The mother just smiled, saying by way of explanation that it had been a long time ago. Then she became sharper, and said something about Helen having been there as the floor was very clean. Her tone suggested that it wouldn't be for long. Was she hinting that the dogs would mess it up? I became uneasy and glanced quickly down at my shoes; they were sufficiently presentable to pass inspection.

Mac had moved up in the world, living in a big house with a nice doctor, lots of children and a conscientious cleaning lady. It was time for me to go, so I called Bilbo and Mac came too. 'No, no, you're staying here with your new family. Be a great dog.' I held his head in my hands and looked into his eyes; he was such a good character. Whoever had lost him had lost something special. It was all smiles at the hall door. 'Thank you for bringing this wonderful dog to my family,' said Radja. 'He will have a happy life with all of us.' Bilbo glanced back at the door and then up at me before walking on. I wondered if he would miss his playmate. The doctor's children were too young to be out walking dogs and the couple were busy people. Mac/Rusty was going to be spending a lot more time indoors. There was no chance of meeting us while out on walks; he would probably not have any walks for a while – unless the cleaning lady took him out.

It was cold but dry; we walked the long way home. It was fully dark by the time we got back, and as I opened the gate Bilbo stood straight; his ears were pricked and he gave a businesslike bark. Mac, possibly not yet answering to the name of Rusty, trotted up to us. There was a short cut to the doctor's house and I began walking quickly to it.

*

Every light in the house must have been on. Dr Radja answered the door, as jolly as ever and he seemed glad to see the dog, greeting him with affection. I explained that he had been waiting for me back at my house. The doctor said that after he had fed him a couple of cans of tuna fish, because he had not yet bought dog food, he had let him out because the dog had begun barking. 'He has a very loud bark,' the doctor reported. I already knew that: it was actually more of a honk than a bark. 'So I thought he must need to toilet, so I let him out. But he went home to you.' Radja looked slightly disappointed, but his smile soon returned as he decided that the dog just needed time to adjust. He put out his hands in welcome and called to Rusty, telling him that it was now bedtime. We said our goodbyes and I walked back alone. It was a peaceful evening; me and my dog enjoying the comfort of the fire. I read for a while. Mac would settle. Radja was already very attached; Rusty would become his dog. They were both lucky, I told myself.

A new day; I had reached the third volume of *The Man Without Qualities*, and had had little sleep, but it didn't matter; wandering through the streets of Vienna in the company of a self-absorbed character I didn't much like was intriguing. Eventually it was food that called a halt to that marathon reading. On the way to the kitchen I let Bilbo out for a minute before giving him his breakfast. Mac was on the doorstep. He rose to greet us, stretching stiffly but as polite as ever, calm, no frenzy. The top of his head was so cold, as were his paws; he must have been there for hours. I closed the door and went in to get Bilbo some food. It was still and very chilly; I reached for my duffel coat, and stepped outside before pulling it on. 'Come on, guy – home.' We went out of the gate, and as I closed it I saw Bilbo at the kitchen window; he had nosed around the curtain and was watching us, intent. I trudged on, already anticipating the embarrassment I would meet at the doctor's house.

Radja was standing outside, dressed in a smart black suit. He was edgy. 'Hello, I didn't know where to find you and was hoping not to leave until he had come back. Little dog, don't you like me?' The doctor seemed despondent. 'I fed him in my study and told him he could stay with me, away from the noise, the children – they play the television very loud. But as soon as he ate, he wanted to go, and he paced my room as if he had an appointment – he did, with you. I think it will take him time to get used to all the children, and to me as well.' Mac was not a nervous dog; he had all the cool of a bomb-disposal expert. But I agreed with Radja and suggested that they should just keep him indoors until he settled. It might take a day or two and seemed a good plan. 'I will put him in the utility room,' he said, warming to the idea. He felt that the humming of the washing machine would soothe him. The doctor was beginning to draw on his experience with children. He was patient and instinctive; I wanted the arrangement to work both for him and for Mac. I knew that if the dog ever needed anything Radja would provide it.

That evening I was back at the doctor's house, having again returned the dog who was a practised escapee. Before I pressed the door bell, a car pulled up behind me. It was Radja. Having left the dog in the utility room, he was bewildered. 'Come in and have some tea, and thank you for again bringing him home.' And he wondered who had let him out. He could not have done this himself. The window was high, more of a push-out slit, not really a window at all. 'I will find out the sequence of events,' the doctor said. His use of language was always quite formal.

Within minutes he had solved the mystery. The cleaning lady, who was actually more of a hands-on housekeeper, was in the kitchen, cooking the evening meal, and quickly took control. She had heard the scratching and let the dog out. She decided that this was the moment to object to the mess that had been made of the door. If it, meaning the dog, had to stay, she said, a dog kennel was needed. Radja thought her reaction was most amusing and argued that it was only a door: it could be painted. 'But call him Rusty, never please, refer to him as "it". Rusty is coming to terms with his new life; he will be my dog. At the moment, he is exploring all possibilities.' He went on to explain that Rusty would sleep in the doctor's bedroom, on the floor beside their bed. Radja would find a man to paint the door and the dog just needed time to settle. He smiled at me; we were collaborators in helping the little dog adapt to his new home.

Here was this very clever, able man, not intent on dominating a dog that was proving somewhat enigmatic; instead, he was hoping to make a connection. I could understand the emotion. Radja might have been in his late forties; to me at that time he seemed middle-aged, several years older than his wife. Nowadays I would have asked him so many questions about his country, its culture and its literature and music, but back then my tongue was too big for my mouth. I barely spoke, and felt guilty about introducing more chaos into his cluttered life. The simple act of giving a dog a home now seemed very complicated. I could understand, having myself only recently gone through the initiation he was about to begin. Watching Radja's excitement as he tried to enter the world of dogs was touching. I was learning all the time and knew I had a special relationship with Bilbo. Yet whereas he had seemed to pick me, Radja had set his sights on the little newcomer that had arrived by chance at his door. Meeting Radja was fortunate, his kindness would eventually win Mac/Rusty over.

*

All the way home I thought about Radja. The children seemed to have become detached; Rusty was now their father's pet. Or perhaps it was simply that they were waiting for him to complete the finishing touches to a companion that would play a role in their individual histories. In the years to come they would remember the adventures they shared with this dog. This is what happens between dogs and humans; dogs move in and stamp their personalities on their owners. They feature in human family histories. Rusty would always be a mystery – no one knew where he came from or what he had looked like as a puppy. He would be old before any of Radja's children even became teenagers. No doubt I would see him looking out at the world through the window of Radja's shiny black car. Of course, he would be allowed to travel in the front passenger seat. Images of Rusty's new life of privilege made me smile, as did thoughts of Radja and his beaming child-like face.

Reality took over as soon as I reached my gate. There was Mac/Rusty on the doorstep. Again, Radja welcomed back his runaway. This game went on for days, nearly two weeks. Once, while I was walking the fugitive home to the house he wouldn't stay in, Robert drove by and stopped. He thought it a wonderful story and was impressed by the doctor's persistence. 'Most people would have given up; perhaps the little dog is overwhelmed by the children?' I felt like a guard entrusted with a rebellious prisoner – except that he wasn't in the least difficult. On a Saturday afternoon, just before dark, I arrived at the house and was met at the door by Radja's wife. Her expression was neutral but I sensed she had something to say. 'I've been thinking,' she began. 'Perhaps it's all a game? Here's a stray dog that suddenly is the centre of attention and he's loving all this fuss. Instead of walking him back, just leave him. If he wants to be here, he will come back; if he doesn't, well, what did he do before you came along? He's a sweet little lad but he has no interest in being with the children. He won't stay in the house. Next time you see him, ignore him. Please. Walk away.' She seemed to have said what she had to say.

But she wasn't quite finished. She asked me exactly how

long he had lived with us and conceded that it was 'very hard to get rid of a dog after it's lived at your house'. I was shocked; she was accusing me of trying to dump him. I explained that he had never lived with me and that he'd played with my dog, and, if Bilbo had allowed him into our house, I would have kept him myself. She looked at me, assessing the information she had just heard. Radja arrived, friendly but that bit more exasperated. 'And still it goes on, the flight, the return. You must have worn a path between your house and here by now.' He was speaking to me, but looked at his shoes. For the first time I suspected that Radja's upset had been intensified by this being part of a new experience for him – failure. He had probably never failed at anything in his life. I said that I needed to get home to fix some outdoor lights and left, aware I would never call to their house again.

Anger kept me warm all the way home. I remember dropping the door key. As I bent to pick it up, Mac nudged my hand. He was back and all I could do was close the door, leaving him outside. I spent most of Sunday morning digging in the back garden. Bilbo watched. The phone rang after lunch. It was Robert asking if the beagle had settled with his new family. I was sick of the saga but told him about my conversation with the doctor's wife. 'I have the solution,' announced Robert, speaking quickly. He lowered his voice and explained he was at the coast with a friend whose German Shepherd had been killed by a bus. The friend was very upset and Robert was intent on taking 'that Mac dog' over to him right away. He felt that it was obvious that the dog wouldn't settle with the doctor and he told me to bring him over to his house that night. 'This problem is solved,' he said. Robert to the rescue again. I laughed with relief.

*

It must have been shortly after nine o'clock and very dark when I opened the front door. Mac, who regarded the doorstep as his base, glanced up at me. 'Come on,' I said, as I looped a piece of curtain cord about his neck; but I didn't really need it, he always followed me. I arrived at Robert's and could hear the newsreader's voice. Robert said he would put him out in the garden for the night, with food and water and an old rug. 'It's secure – the walls are about ten feet high. In the morning I'll take him over to Andrew.' I was pleased, or I so I thought. Before I had reached Robert's gate I was crying and couldn't stop. Back at my house I looked at Bilbo, indolently sprawled king-like on his beanbag in the living room. I tossed the curtain cord at him. 'You're spoilt; you don't know how to share.' My voice was low, my tone was harsh and I went into the bedroom, crawling into bed still wearing my clothes, including my socks. A couple of minutes later I felt Bilbo lying down on my feet. I ignored him and drifted into an exhausted sleep, my eyes sore from crying.

Always a bad idea to cry yourself to sleep: you wake up looking as if you've been in a fight and lost. The knocking at the door was sharp and determined and prolonged – but I didn't answer it, I couldn't. It was a dreary morning. I stayed where I was, blankets over my head. About an hour later I went out, expecting to see a delivery note left by the mail man. There was a shadow against the glass panel at the side of the door. I opened it and Mac walked in, soaking wet, leaving a dry patch where he'd been sitting on the stone step. He shook his ears and drops of water flew across the hall, spraying the walls and floor. Bilbo didn't react. Mac kept on walking past both of us, straight into the kitchen and settled himself in front of the old dresser as if he had been sitting there every morning for years. Bilbo walked in and looked at him. Unlike Bilbo, I had seen Mac fight, so I filled a pan of water, ready to pour it over them if it came to that. I waited. Nothing happened. Bilbo looked at his own bowl, then glanced at the dog that would share his home, his life and me for twenty years; the companion who would survive him by twenty-seven days. I sat on the floor and watched them. It was time to give our new friend a name. 'You're Frodo and I bet you knew that before I did.'

That day was very important, not just because the quietly determined Frodo had won his place but because it proved Bilbo's depth of character. Dogs watch us, but, more than that, they read us. Bilbo knew I had wanted the situation resolved. I spent that day watching the pair of them, two very different dogs, both unique. They could teach me and I knew it. It was fascinating and intense; I was at the beginning of an adventure. Frodo was sufficiently confident to stay back and allow Bilbo to dictate their actions without being passive or subservient; he was benign but never weak. They both seemed to regard me as the leader. The hours passed quietly. I lit a fire and sat reading while Bilbo slept on his beanbag and Frodo lay on the rug.

Brisk footsteps stopped outside. It was about six o'clock that evening when someone knocked at the door. I braced myself. Had Radja found us? But it was Robert. 'I'm sorry, but that dog disappeared,' he announced, pausing to show his awareness of the gravity of what he was saying. He told me that the dog was gone, out over those high walls. 'Up and over. He must be spring-loaded,' he said and told me that he had called around about nine that morning – and I knew he had, I had heard the knocking – 'but there was no answer. I'm sorry, I wanted to help.' I waited until Robert had finished and took pleasure in telling him that the dog was in the kitchen with Bilbo and had been with us all day.

It had taken Bilbo two weeks to make up his mind, but he had tested Frodo's character and selected him even more carefully than he had chosen me.

7

Opposites Attract

Within hours it seemed as though Frodo had been with us
for ever, so subtle was his affection. I suddenly realised I had
been wooed for weeks unawares. Frodo was deliberate; the
entire Radja episode had been an elaborate plan, devised by
a canny, dignified original, astutely aware that his goal was
a home in which an intense relationship with a dominant
dog already existed. Bilbo had perfected the role of gifted
child, placing his front paws on my feet when I spoke on the
phone, appearing to nod in agreement with every opinion
I expressed, always ensuring that Frodo remained mindful
that, prior to his arrival, Bilbo and I had bonded. He stood
beside me not territorially but merely to assert his rightful
position as first dog in a hierarchy that Frodo would have
to respect.

Somehow Frodo indicated that he was aware of the
dynamics; he would look on, his long body relaxed, his back
legs stretched wide apart, as if he were a farmer just in from
the fields. He accepted that Bilbo inhabited a special place,
that he was fed first, and that Bilbo, only Bilbo, slept on
and/or in the bed, while he, initially at least, curled up on
the floor, never moving until we did. Frodo was a study in
patience. His face wore an expression of pragmatic content.
He was watchful but never wary; he had won and he knew
it. Yet he was too intelligent to become boastful or careless.
He sat in front of the old wooden dresser, framed between
its doors, and proudly gazed at his new family – us.

Up above Frodo's head, on the table top of the dresser, far too tall to occupy any of the three shelves, was the ceramic dog cookie-barrel that Trudi had presented to me in honour of Bilbo's arrival. Its vacant, painted brown eyes stared at me; the sweet, silly face with its splodge of yellow nose suggested good humour. Nowadays the Bilbo cookie jar is positioned on a wide windowsill in another kitchen, far from that one, always part of the view as I wash the dishes and look out across the fields, thinking, remembering, reliving. I can recall telling Frodo that I would have to find a companion dog for Bilbo's ceramic pot. That search would take some time. Finally, in a dusty country junk shop, I found a large Victorian beagle, made of heavy, painted clay. It was a traditional piece, rather more magisterial than Bilbo's painted dog, and far more life-like; the face was solemn, expressive. The eyes were particularly good. Frodo's dog, as it soon became known, now resides on a stack of art books, to the side of my flat open hearth.

Each winter now seems longer and darker than the one before, but that first one with the dogs was merely cold and often wet. Their outings went well, although now that I was being hauled by two dogs, each competitive and intent on being marginally ahead of the other, I had to balance between and behind them. I was Ben Hur, attempting to master a wayward chariot, and I began making jokes about how long my arms were becoming. You needed to be strong to hold them as they hurried along, heads low, their shoulders working at a brisk businesslike pace. By chance, I had learned of a hidden wood that could be approached from the opposite end of the small road that led to my cottage, off at an angle from the long, wind-blasted stretch. Few people knew of it; it was a relic of another time that had somehow eluded developers. Parts of the wood were dark, dense with old trees; many of them had stopped growing long ago and some were dead, but they stood, dried out and brittle, fragile effigies of the trees they had once been. The first time we went there the living trees were beginning to lose their foliage. Dry fallen leaves crackled beneath us. The wood seemed caught by a lingering autumn reluctant to yield to winter. Sunlight through the trees was bright although not yet with that sharp winter brilliance that seems to stab at the earth.

It was quite a discovery, that mysterious wood – an exclusive playground. We never met another human there; it was as if it were a secret. The further we went into the heart of the woods, the more certain I was that it was safe to allow the guys to run free off their leashes. It was very quiet; the only sound was the noise of the dogs as they raced through the eddying leaves. They seemed to enjoy the silvery, rustling sound, and were soon leaping and tumbling over each other, yapping manically. One moment they jogged together, then they would begin a mad chase: Bilbo showing off, with Frodo gamely in pursuit, his short legs moving in a scrambling, sideways action, nothing as fluid as Bilbo's graceful movement. On one of our earliest visits, all was going much as usual until I heard a scrambling sound, a crash and a blood-chilling squeal. I ran in the direction it came from, with an image already in my mind of Bilbo, always accident-prone, trapped by something that had caught his collar.

Suddenly, through the trees, I saw a flash of colour and heard Bilbo's short irritated bark, then nothing. I came up behind Bilbo; he trembled slightly, looked up at me and then back to where Frodo stood, aware of me and looking as if he had been caught in the act, his broad, flat paw on the heaving chest of a squirrel. I was shocked, but the fastidious Bilbo was disgusted. He peered at Frodo as if he were a degenerate. The squirrel was bleeding but still alive. I ordered Frodo to come to me and I pointed to a spot at my feet. He looked at me, affecting a demeanour of mournful obedience and carefully lifted his paw off his quarry. The squirrel lay still, it was dead. Bilbo had never killed anything, but, then, he had never had a chance. I had watched him so closely since he was a puppy.

We were all motionless, freeze-framed in a moment in time. I can see the scene before me as clear as it was that brisk winter's day. Then a twig snapped; the squirrel sprang back into life and ran up the nearest tree. Frodo honked emphatically. Within minutes there was another squeal, he came running up to me, and dropped a rat at my feet. Its dying expression indicated utter amazement, not terror. Frodo looked at me, shook his long ears, with that slapping, leathery sound that I have never forgotten, and then walked away from his kill, as if making a point. So Frodo could fight, clear a ten-foot wall on those short, powerful little legs and hunt. Bilbo, the fey, graceful dreamer, had bonded, as had I, with an extremely competent soulmate.

The sun was preparing to set, its light radiating splashes of pink, orange and red. It was magnificent, an evening sky that would have inspired Turner. Vibrant colour seeped away to purple and then to darkest blue and onwards to black. Day had ended and the houses were reduced to a series of shadows crouching in the distance. The guys pulled on as if they were huskies hauling a sledge over Arctic ice. I heard low growls and then Frodo lunged out to the left, snarling with intent. Something moved and that movement became a shape. It was the white dog, the one Frodo had been fighting the first time I had seen him. Bilbo moved in, both dogs united against an old enemy. I shook off my runner and threw it at the white dog, urging the guys to run on. We arrived back at the front door. There had been no real chase. Bilbo and Frodo pattered smugly into the hall, their nails tapping on the wood, the rattle of their leashes dragging behind them. On cue, the dogs, already life-companions, relaxed – Bilbo so much taller – each glanced at the other, anticipating food and padded into the kitchen. I closed the door after them and ran back for my shoe. There it was, on the ragged grass verge. The white dog had been banished, this time for good.

*

At meal times there was never tension; Frodo waited until Bilbo was eating and never displayed the slightest twitch of impatience. Bilbo remained confident, aware he was special. At just over a year old he was beautiful, muscular, yet still graceful and pretty, if somehow increasingly mature – a dog now, no longer a fluffy puppy and quite the German Shepherd in profile. He also retained his slightly dramatic approach to new events. Bilbo enjoyed drama. When the pipes froze and then burst, he danced around the edges of the puddles; he never liked water but barked, meaningfully, at the chaos – if always at a dry remove.

Yet again I was struck by how different Bilbo and Frodo were: Frodo was independent, a mature dog with, I was to notice as time went on, minimal interest in people. His loyalty to me was absolute, humbling. He had chosen me, just as Bilbo had. But Bilbo's selection had been straightforward; Frodo's the culmination of a complex plan played out before exasperated witnesses.

There was a problem. Frodo was accustomed to independence. Whereas Bilbo didn't seemed to think about the wider world until I was prepared to venture out into it, Frodo would wait in the hall urging me to open the door. Most of the material I read about dogs agreed that, unless they were intended for breeding purposes, male dogs were more settled and amenable, easier to handle if neutered. Anyone with an opinion on the subject also agreed. Bilbo's experience of standard canine birth control had been extreme and had left me suspicious of a 'routine' procedure that generations of dog owners have regarded, and continue to regard, as elementary.

The essential difference between the two of them was clear: Bilbo did not pine for the freedom of the roads but Frodo, self-contained and businesslike, was used to exploring, asserting his presence in the world. I couldn't have him coming and going, particularly once the local females came on heat; it would be confusing for Bilbo and, most importantly, roaming about greatly increased Frodo's risks of being injured or killed by a car.

Kneeling in the kitchen beside him as he gazed out the window, I wondered whether he was miserable or feeling trapped. Was this why he wouldn't settle at Radja's? But as I petted his dome-shaped hound's head, so different from Bilbo's, he hopped, stretching his short, strong little front legs and looked at me with his bright, liquid eyes, eager for adventure, but only if it was with me in tow. He was contented; it was just a different kind of life for him. The pads of his paws were so much thicker than Bilbo's. Instead of pink, they were a dusty grey-black. He had various scars here and there: a long one on the back of his left rear leg and a deep depression, an old wound, long since healed, that I discovered one day while grooming him. It was not visible, as the hair had grown back over it, but once my fingers felt it, I always found myself from then on going to the spot as if it were lucky, similar to the Prophet's thumb mark that appears on the necks of Arab horses but means something very special when it occurs on other breeds. My great mare, Kate, has one. It is more than a coincidence as she is like Frodo in many ways and shares that absolute loyalty to one human, while regarding the rest of mankind with Frodo's ironic detachment.

Weighing up the differences between Bilbo and Frodo, I tried to master my fear of having Frodo neutered by reasoning with myself. Bilbo had been very young when he had his close brush with death, and it seemed possible that his extreme reaction to a commonplace operation was connected to the distemper. It may also have meant that he would always be vulnerable to general anaesthetic. He was naturally nervy, a bit like a thoroughbred, although he was cross-bred, not a pedigree. He had a more delicate constitution. Frodo was older; a mature, experienced dog at least four years old. He was well developed and tough, not to mention blessed with nerves of steel and awesome determination. The more I studied him, the more I was convinced that this cute little character with the wonderful ears possessed a philosophical attitude: he *believed* in life. The two dogs had a rapport and I was aware that Frodo's presence would ensure that Bilbo did not become spoilt. They complemented each other. But Frodo's independence was a problem. In time Bilbo too might want to wander off into the night. The presence of a female in heat could start a dog fight even between friends.

My research revealed neutered male dogs were less

restless and less aggressive, and therefore less likely to fight. That caught my attention; I had already seen Frodo the warrior in action. It was important that both dogs lived by the same set of rules and Frodo, however capable, could not have a level of freedom denied Bilbo.

As Bilbo sprawled on his beanbag, his exclusive seat, a territory Frodo accepted as forbidden, the quasi-beagle inched closer to my chair through a series of elaborate circles, as if he wanted to appear far less intent than he actually was. As I stood up his eyes followed me, while Bilbo lazily cocked an ear and didn't feel the need to move his head. I went to fetch a phone book from my study, in reality a spare bedroom with an ugly old desk rescued from a skip. Settling back into the chair, I began to make a list of possible vets to approach about Frodo. All the uncertainties and the fears were returning to haunt me. One thing was already decided though: I would not be returning to the practice in which Bilbo's ordeal had begun.

*

It was a brief shortlist; each call began tentatively: the first two were answered by female voices that showed so little interest I may as well have been phoning about booking a car in for a service.

The next call went well. This vet listened as I gave a detailed account of what had happened to Bilbo. He described it all as highly unusual before suggesting that too much sedative had been used. His weight may have been estimated, whereas it is always safer to weigh an animal. He said that I had to decide if I wanted to go ahead with the second dog, and if I did, he would do it himself. He told me that there are always risks, but that it was a 'standard procedure'. Procedure: a cold, clinical word I had come to hate. The voice was kind, thoughtful. I imagined an older man with greying hair and corduroy pants.

This calm, understanding vet made sense, and had listened to an unedited account of Bilbo's crisis. If he thought I was odd, he gave no indication and remained as neutral as a judge, only far more human. To my reasoning, leaving Frodo as he was would give him a physical, maybe even a psychological, advantage over Bilbo, and that wasn't fair.

*

Arriving at that surgery, a brightly decorated place, was unsettling in an unexpected way. Its yellow walls were alive with paintings and drawings of cats and dogs. There were portraits and even group studies – it was more like an amateur gallery than a vet's clinic; none of the usual posters advertising products and services and intended to arouse mixed feelings of fear and guilt in an owner. Absent also were those gruesome giant-scale diagrams of the life cycle of the flea. There were only the paintings. The senior vet obviously had a hobby – art. All the paintings were his. Some of them were very good. But I was very nervous and felt I was trying to breathe underwater. A pulse was beating beneath my eye. Frodo hadn't eaten since the previous evening; I knew he was hungry and that he had forgotten what hunger was like, and so he was edgy. He had never seemed so irritated. The waiting room was empty, apart from us and all the painted dogs, looking down at us from the walls. The artist vet was good at depicting life-like eyes; I couldn't help noticing that. A door opened and I heard footsteps, followed by a man's voice. 'So this is the gentleman, a sturdy citizen. There's a lot of beagle there and dachshund and something else – interesting dog.'

('You can say that again,' I thought to myself, while only managing a bland half-smile.) 'He'll be fine.' Maybe so, I thought, maybe so.

It was shortly after nine in the morning. Frodo was uneasy, even as I patted him and assured him that I would be back. A shudder ran through me; I was told to phone 'just before six this evening' to collect him. I went out into the muted light of the street, so drab after the bright yellow of the clinic, took a few steps, then stopped and went to buy a paper. I had no plan and turned around in a circle, looking up and down the street and then hurried towards a coffee shop. Sitting down at one of the tables I ordered hot chocolate and a toasted cheese sandwich and then a second sandwich and I have never read a newspaper as closely as I did that day.

But two hours later another seven hours still stood between me and collecting Frodo. I thought of Bilbo, back at home, in the bedroom. I could imagine him, sitting on the bed, sighing; ears forward, staring at the bedroom door. After some haphazard shopping, I had gathered an odd collection of items, including a double packet of mouse traps. Still not yet noon – it made more sense to go home and wait. On cue, a sudden, cold rain began to fall; I headed back in the general direction of home, pausing a couple of times to hitch a ride. On my fourth attempt a car stopped and left me only a mile short of the house. I walked quickly, and was virtually jogging by the time I reached my gate. By two o'clock I was beginning to stare at the phone. I couldn't eat and didn't want to go out in case the vet phoned.

It was seven minutes after four by the old wall clock in the kitchen. I knew I could no longer wait, and dialled the number. As soon as I mentioned the dog, a litany of misdemeanours began. I was told that he had been awake for hours and had torn the blanket apart and had also attempted to climb through the bars of his kennel and had grabbed at food that had been prepared for the other patients. I asked the woman if we were speaking about the same dog. Frodo was calm and very patient. But the woman was not convinced and described him as 'very strong willed' and 'a handful' before grudgingly conceding that perhaps she was not seeing him at his best. She suggested I give some thought to consulting a behaviour specialist. On the other end of the line, I tried not to laugh and succeeded in making sympathetic sounds to the nurse, who finally told me to take him home as he was a nuisance and she was very busy.

*

At least I knew Frodo was alive. It was surprising to hear someone complaining about him, though, as he tended to be a quiet observer, while always maintaining a discreet distance. The nurse had described a hooligan I didn't recognise. I had heard the annoyance in her voice, her disapproving tone. She probably assumed I let him eat his food off the kitchen table.

Doubts began to creep into my thoughts. If he had physically come through well – and it sounded as if he had – was his temperament affected? Could his personality have changed? Perhaps it was different when a dog was older. Frodo had lived the life of an adult dog before I had met him; I knew nothing about his past. His exact age could only be guessed at. I would never know where he had come from or anything about his previous experience of humans, although I had already realised he was uninterested in people. Exactly what had happened at the vet's? A slow resentment began to simmer inside me; the nurse had sounded more like a put-upon childminder than a professional dealing with the post-operative situation for a procedure that would be paid for. 'Don't apologise,' I told myself; she wasn't doing me a favour, it was her job. Self-righteousness buoyed me up as I hurried back to the surgery and into the reception area which was resonating with Frodo's loud, honking barks.

The nurse looked up at me and sighed as if she had been wondering about the type of person who would own such a badly behaved dog, and I was that person. Frodo had made quite an impression. His ear-splitting honks were drowning any attempt at conversation. She stood up and glanced at the other owners in the waiting area, several of whom were laughing, speculating as to what breed of dog was making the noises. I wanted to laugh too as she turned primly, without further comment, and went to fetch Frodo. The nurse's re-entry was spectacular: Frodo, wearing a large plastic collar shaped like a megaphone, burst through the door, pulling the nurse off balance. She fell to her knees and the leash caught under the door as it swung back behind her.

Frodo's range of movement was limited by the leash; the megaphone kept wobbling and the door pivoted a few inches forward, a few inches back. I unclipped the leash from his collar, pulled it free of the door and placed it carefully on the desk. By now the nurse had regained her position behind it.

Pulling another leash from my pocket I bent down, aware that I would laugh if I met her eye. But I began laughing anyway as I tried to clip the leash to his collar. Frodo bounced up and down, appearing to be outraged. His anger was comic. I couldn't stop laughing; the more I laughed, the louder he honked. I was conscious that the nurse had already told me how much I owed but my mind had gone blank. I asked for the bill. She repeated the total, making it clear that she had had enough of me and my unruly dog, and in fact, asked me to leave because I was delaying everyone. As we left, Frodo, his nails scrabbling on the lino, was low to the ground and intent on escape, pulling me forward with all his might. Goodwill emanated from the waiting owners. I heard a man's voice; his tone was amused. 'He's a grand little man, a terrific hunting dog. There's a lot of power there. See the shoulders on him.'

8

Summoned by the Ancestors

Silence, all the way home. Frodo and I were sitting side by side in the back seat of the increasingly silent boyfriend's car. I felt very much like one of a pair of disgraced schoolchildren who had ruined a zoo outing. He, still indignant, shaking his ears, megaphone collar flapping, appeared deep in thought, too disgruntled to even bother barking at the motorbike that pulled up beside us at the traffic lights. At intervals, shivers of outrage rippled down Frodo's back, causing him to shuffle slightly, adjust his position, lift his paws and ensure his chest was thrust forward, his shoulders square. This was not a dog to be trifled with; humans were fools. Except, of course, me – or so I still hoped. He glanced up at me, his gaze softened, becoming benign and affectionate.

But I was worried for all that; there were doubts. Had his trust in me been damaged? On the final part of that desolate stretch of open road, I thought back to the day Bilbo had come home after his procedure, how he had lain suspended between life and death on a flat board. This time I was returning with a dog that appeared preoccupied with composing the letter of complaint he intended to send to the newspapers.

Eyes forward, he was looking at nothing in particular. I studied him, for the first time noticing the little shaven patch on his front leg for the anaesthetic, and imagined him wearing a waistcoat and a black fedora. Although I was watchful of any changes in his personality, I couldn't help smiling. Even in his fury, Frodo always made me smile – with or without a megaphone frill. He was stalwart; a self-contained individual. But that day there was something new, an unease. It was as if he was reconsidering his situation.

Once back at the house though, there was no hesitation; Frodo had marched righteously to the front door making it clear that he knew he was home from the wars. Relief took over. I went to the bedroom to fetch Bilbo, who jumped down off the bed, tail wagging, and greeted me. I was struck by how rarely I was away from him and he showed his excitement at my reappearance. He had been left alone while I had taken his companion on a mission. We had returned with a funny large plastic collar. Bilbo examined it at length before beginning to sniff Frodo in earnest. That distinct smell of vet's surgery and medication mingled with kennel disinfectant wafted strongly off his pal: it must have been overwhelming for Bilbo who would have had bad memories of that clinical scent. I wanted to have a bath to banish those odours of illness, and turned on the faucets. But Frodo honked. I looked at him. Was he in pain? Not at all, he was ravenous and led the way back towards the kitchen. For once, he pushed in ahead of Bilbo. Frodo was very hungry; this was no time for decorum.

*

It took several pieces of toast before Frodo settled down and drank some water. My guys relaxed and flopped down together on the wooden floor. The milk in the saucepan began to bubble and I reached for the hot chocolate, relieved to see three tins of it stored in the cupboard. At that point I thought of the bath and the water that had been left running while all attention had been redirected towards the kitchen. What mess was waiting? And I hurried to the bathroom, the guys as one at my heels. By a strange stroke of luck, or forgetfulness, the cold water had been running. Not for the first time I had forgotten that those faucets worked in reverse; for hot turn on cold and for cold, hot. The bathroom was particularly small; a pungent smell of vet surgery filled the damp space. I opened the window, pulling off various layers of clothes that were quickly claimed by the guys, each making a comfortable bed.

Steam rose up, clouding the room; the water was so hot it hurt. I waited, crouching on the thick rolled rim of the bath, until it was bearable. Frodo began to doze, tired by his adventures, temporarily indifferent to the plastic cone around his neck. Bilbo kept watch. He stood up and looked into the bath to see what I was staring at. As I tentatively slid into the tub, he seemed satisfied and settled down. Did other dog owners include their pets at bath time? Was I the adored object, or a figure of authority? Orders weren't needed, we just fell into step. It was a fellowship, I decided, our variation of *The Lord of the Rings*.

Just then a thrush landed on the windowsill and looked in. As a child I had a large picture book with the story of Thumbelina in it. There was a lovely full-page watercolour of the thrush that carried her away; it was kind-looking but powerful. I used to imagine being carried away by such a bird. I smiled at that old memory and then groaned: would there be an incident now that I was exhausted and sitting in the bath? Would there be frantic barking, yelping lunges at the window causing me to chase a bewildered bird flying overhead back out of the window? How would a dog, how would two dogs, react to such an intrusion? Bilbo was staring back at it, as was I, and I remember willing the bird not to fly into the room. Bilbo's reaction was interesting:

detached curiosity, no frenzy. It was as if he saw the bird as a thing of interest, not prey. But then, he had never hunted. The proven hunter, Frodo, sighed in his sleep. The thrush flew off and I reached up to close over the window.

I had never much liked baths, but the cottage had no shower. Being a shower person from California's shower culture, I had never seen the point of lounging in a bath. That day I changed my mind. Ease seeped into me; I could have remained in there for hours – at least, as long as the water stayed hot and comforting. Bilbo was awake, looking at me. His clean white paws were neatly side by side and he flexed his nails as if he were a cat. But he was happy; it was only then that I realised it was the first time that Frodo had joined Bilbo and me at bath time.

*

It was a small incursion; minor compared with the bed or the various beanbags and completely insignificant in the context of having gained entrance to the household, but would others follow? Was Frodo, in fact, the dominant dog? Yet later that evening, by the fire, he lay on the rug, content, while Bilbo looked down at him, from his throne, his beanbag. Frodo had made no attempt to climb on to any of the beanbags. He must have considered them to be forbidden territories. All was well, but even though I had initially noticed that Frodo was not overly fond of humans, it had become obvious that he actually didn't *like* people. Any visitor to the house was met with a low growl and a warning snarl; his snout rippled slightly and then lifted off his teeth – always surprising, those big white teeth. 'He's your dog,' Robert had said on that evening when he had called round to tell me that the little dog had escaped from his garden. 'Your dog; and your dog only. He's almost . . .

unfriendly,' Robert had ventured, tentatively, watching my face for a reaction. 'He's self-contained,' I had replied, aware he was mine, that Frodo had decided this even before I realised he was with us for life. What had happened to him that had left him with neither interest nor trust in the world at large? The more settled he was with us, the more protective he became; he lived happily with us, if at a remove from all else. People were not allowed casual entry into our world. Not a bad thing, I thought, already aware that he needed to be protected from his courage. Humans don't play fair; they abuse the heartbreaking trust that dogs offer so openly.

*

Three runners came into view; two of them, fit and sinewy, looked comfortable, at a steady pace, shoulder to shoulder, glancing at each other, discussing something. The third was under pressure, gasping, desperately trying to keep in touch with his companions. The gap between him and the others was perhaps ten metres or a little more. He was straining to keep it at that. His face was dangerously red and his breath rasped with a wheeze that caused the guys to pause and stare, while the veins of his thick legs bulged alarmingly. There was other activity; a small team of council workers had arrived with a truckload of young trees and were planting them in the green area; the no man's land appeared finally about to become something more specific than raw space. We hurried along, the guys tugging, heads down, intent, my arms flexed, stretched before me. I was tired from having run for an hour before breakfast. The morning had been spent in cycling into the city to collect a manuscript, a biography of a little-known eighteenth-century nobleman and patron of the arts. The task was to read it and compile an index. It was ridiculous: this was a highly specialised commission and way beyond me. All the way home, back along the windswept stretch of road, I had imagined climbing back into bed. The day was moving slowly towards a goal; that evening a new series was beginning, I wanted to follow it throughout the weeks of its run. Television barely featured in the house, as there was always too much to do: reading, running, working. But another small routine was about to begin, a weekly vigil to observe. The hours dribbled by.

It was time; the fire was lit; curtains that I had finally managed to make were drawn, the television was on, a plate of sandwiches ready – the phone rang. I answered it, only to say I couldn't speak, and hurried back to the living room where a low throbbing wail had begun. In silhouette against the light of the screen Bilbo was standing, head thrown back, howling, howling like a wolf. It was uncanny; something had caused him to revert back into a world of which he knew nothing, only instinct. Louder and louder, the noise was surreal, fantastic. Here was a pampered dog who ate toast, *expected* toast and slept in a bed, often under blankets; a dog who hated the rain and had his own beanbags, and he was howling for the wolf pack of the Russian steppe. Frodo had been watching, and as if on cue joined in. *Canis lupus familaris*, the domestic dog, descended from two defined species of wolf – *C. lupus* and *C. latrans*, as Darwin maintained – and yet, looking at most modern dogs, be they pedigree or mixed breed, it is difficult to see the connection. My boys howled on.

Admittedly Frodo was honking rather than howling. But still, it was a howl of sorts, a baying-at-the-moon kind of effort from a hound that bore no resemblance to

White Fang or any of his relatives. Bilbo, if only for a few moments, was pure wolf. It was the first time he had heard the haunting theme of *Brideshead Revisited*, as adapted for television from the classic English novel of the 1930s. Composer Geoffrey Burgon had captured the mood of lamentation that underlines Waugh's romantic story of yearning and regret for lost youth, forsaken innocence, the death of love. Bilbo's response was comic to see, yet also deeply moving. He howled for the ancestors as if his heart would break. Each time he heard that music, he replied by duty born of instinct.

For a few minutes, every week for eleven weeks, the plaintive sound of French horn and a high thin trumpet beckoned Bilbo into a sacred realm that was private and complex. There would be other pieces of music, particularly baroque concerti – Vivaldi, Bach, the Death March in Handel's *Saul*, Mozart's Great Mass in C – that also affected him: but the *Brideshead Revisited* theme became his. It was Bilbo, who, as if summoned by invisible masters, would position himself in front of the television and throw back his head. Whenever it is played, wherever I hear it issuing forth, plaintive and compelling – from a bookshop in Kensington or a cafe in Vienna, I see the young Bilbo, trembling in the flickering light of a small screen, acknowledging his origins.

*

During those brief interludes in front of the television, I felt as if a temporary wall had been erected between us; it was as if all the intimacy we shared was suddenly, if briefly, suspended. Bilbo, in common with all dogs, belonged to a community that is exclusive, one that no human can enter. Horses make no attempt to conceal the fact that, however close they choose to allow a human, a certain distance is maintained. As flight animals, horses know that in order for the human to get near, there is a price to be paid – the horse must concede its freedom: permit a rider on its back. An element of resentment at becoming a beast of burden is always there. The best horse must swallow its pride. We don't dream about dogs in the same ways we visualise horses. Horses are mysterious, iconic; their eyes appear to hold the secrets of the ages. A horse is a classical image, a symbol of enduring beauty. The horse is ethereal, majestic, and, above all, vulnerable; the warrior of old which has evolved into a sporting hero. From Eclipse to Sea Biscuit, to Nijinsky, or the incomparable Secretariat; from Arkle to Red Rum, to Best Mate or Sea the Stars, great champions emerge, are all-conquering, a Desert Orchid or a Milton. We cheer when they win and then, in time, weep as they are beaten by the next great champion. Yet the images that continue to dominate our dreams are often more romantic, scenes of uninhibited Arab stallions racing across the sand or the dependable cow ponies that carried ranchers out West to conquer a wilderness and banish the natives. There is nothing quite like growing up on Westerns. Forget about the cowboys: the true stars of those movies are the horses looking on with ironic stoicism as mere actors stare out across the landscape, attempting to give shape to the film-maker's version of America's destiny.

Horses are alluring yet elusive, they are invariably galloping *away from*, not *towards*, us. You have to work hard to win a horse's trust. Dogs are different; they forgive. They are also personal, specific to each of us. We may speak of 'the horse', but we are more likely to say 'my dog', because dogs are individual. Your dog sits beside you, eats beside you, shares your food, your home, your bed, your life, watches as you talk, as you work, as you laugh, cry and, at times, argue with people. He or she will witness your joy and sorrow and anger and will protect the home in a way a horse simply can't. There is a profound intimacy with a dog that even the most beloved horse is unable to fulfil because of its sheer physical size and flight instinct. Dogs understand and accept the trade-off, as the dog is the supreme diplomat, confident in the power of absolute affection. More than a horse, more than a cat, more than most humans, the dog has mastered the art of forgiveness. The dog can infiltrate the human world, is vital to it, but although humans expect that the one animal prepared to grant full access to the heart of its experience is the dog, we are wrong. Despite the intense bond between dog and man, some secrets endure. We watch them, we love them, we live with them but do we, can we, really know them?

The final bar of the *Brideshead* theme would fade, release Bilbo from its spell and he would shake himself free of this out-of-body experience, returning to his daily life and his reality as an individual, not as part of a continuum spanning countless millennia.

*

Frodo the experienced fighter and hunter had fended for himself after losing contact with whoever it was that had once placed the tartan collar around his neck. Although Bilbo the dreamer had had health problems, he had not had to deal with basic survival; he had never tasted a kill. As he ran through the leaves in the woods he looked to the sunlight, alert to the heat on his back. At times he would stand, his eyes closed, as if dreaming, or perhaps imagining those distant calls. Frodo, practical by nature, responded to the slightest sound. He watched the birds and the squirrels, willing himself not to move because his little family shunned hunting. In the open spaces Bilbo ran, he didn't chase; he was the leader. Delighting in his speed Bilbo zigzagged, changing direction in a stride, pursued by the robust, willing Frodo, whose splay-legged, sideways action contrasted with Bilbo's mercurial grace.

Beanbags, saggy, messy, barely worthy of being called furniture, are found on the floor of lowly student flats, frowned upon in most other places – bad for posture, indicative of laziness and tolerated only during a chronic shortage of chairs. But Bilbo's humble beanbags acquired lofty symbolism in our household, becoming territorial markers of profound significance. Few generals have scrutinised a map as solemnly as Frodo would gaze at the beanbag on which Bilbo was reclining. For Bilbo, it represented languor; for Frodo, it may have meant equality as much as a forbidden comfort. For several months each beanbag remained off limits. Should Bilbo happen to suspect that his associate was looking at an empty beanbag he uttered a low, lazy growl that amounted to a simple 'don't'. At intervals the beanbag covers would be washed; the frail cotton inner sack holding the filling seemed a miserable substitute for the outer corduroy covers; one was bright turquoise, another was a warm faded rose and the luxury one was a plush navy velvet. Bilbo liked to position himself with his tail draped over the side of his chosen bag. Sometimes he lay on his back. After he tired of contemplating life from an angle, head upside down, ears pulled into stiff points by the force of gravity, he would leap up and then down on to the floor, take several turns of the room, before jumping back on to his seat as if he had mounted a moving iceberg. Then he would walk around it in a circle and settle himself, eyes closed but alert, and, with a regal sigh, decide that all was well with the world.

Frodo watched, his head cocked thoughtfully. He would look to me, and then approach the beanbag, stopping as soon as Bilbo issued his muted warning growl. At times he would get very close, close to the point of lifting his paw off the floor, but before he could even touch the beanbag that cautionary rumble began deep in Bilbo's throat. Frodo, however, was a patient dog; he was prepared to wait. Sometimes I considered lifting him and placing him on the bag beside Bilbo, but that would have been unfair to both of them. They would settle this, if it was going to be settled. Until then, Bilbo endured the burden of privilege. Frodo was content with the hearth rug.

An interesting project materialised for me in the form of a late-night phone call. The entrepreneurial elder brother of one of my college friends had purchased an old canal cottage. He had several businesses and no time, so he wondered if I would sand and varnish the floor – he'd heard I was good at that. Perhaps one day someone would be interested in my views on Beethoven's string quartets or the nineteenth-century Russian novel? Meanwhile I would continue digging gardens and sanding wood. The canal cottage sounded charming. I could have cycled to it, but the dogs would enjoy the outing and so I pleaded my need of a lift. Besides, the tycoon would have to fetch the sander. But he was a man who didn't do fetching – the hire firm would collect me.

I waited, confident that an additional two passengers wouldn't matter. 'You'll have to stay, I suppose, for a night or two,' said the busy businessman, and he mentioned a shop nearby and that there was a kettle in the cottage and a mattress, adding that it was brand new – the wrapping was still on it. His patronising, half-amused tone did nothing for my self-esteem, but he was paying me well, and it would be a little adventure for the three of us. Best of all, far more important than the money, it meant that I could have some time away from my problematic relationship. I had already suspected that if I ever got married I would, in the interest of romance and sanity, advocate living in separate houses.

The equipment-hire man was perfect; he didn't speak. In fact, he didn't react to our presence in any way. I could have brought an entire team of huskies with me and he would have remained impassive. Asked to stop at a shop on the way, he just pulled over. The guys got out and stood to attention at the door of the shop while I went in for supplies. The minor routes and then the small dirt road leading down to the canal became increasingly attractive. It could have been Canada. There was a forest – admittedly, a conifer plantation – but sufficiently dense to seem more rugged than most blandly regimented commercial crops. The van bumped along, the driver silent, listening with a face full of sorrow to the sports programme on the radio.

Slow over an old stone bridge and down along the canal, the van rattled on; the road surface was severely potholed. A small lake was visible near the opposite bank. Here was a hidden wilderness, a gentle place without drama, yet neither empty nor boring. It was late spring but still cold and the first traces of colour, purples and blues, the dog violet, were appearing and there was the shabby white of the last of the wood anemones and wild garlic.

Then, the cottage appeared, freshly painted and partially surrounded with new fencing, the job not yet finished. There was a sense of purpose about the house; it had not been built as a holiday home. It had been lived in by generations of lock-keepers. The van driver gazed at it and then, slowly, his mouth opened. It was not the sight of the cottage that incited him to speech. 'Do you know how to work this?' he asked gesturing to the sander. 'Oh yes, I'm an experienced floor person,' I replied, the eager-to-please Girl Scout that I, at that time in my life, invariably sounded like. 'I'll collect it late afternoon, tomorrow,' and, looking about him, as if scanning the horizon for bandits, he added, 'It better not get robbed. If it does, you have to pay full price for a replacement.' I asked about the vacuum cleaner. 'No, don't have one. Oh, here it is,' he grunted, lifting the cleaner down with one hand and with the other tossing several belts of sandpaper on to the ground. Then he lowered the back ramp, so that he could wheel the sander down to me and then he was gone, leaving a faint trail of diesel fumes. The guys ran to the canal bank, and I followed. On a warmer day it might have been a pleasant place for swimming. But it was chilly, clouds had gathered and suddenly the water looked befouled and uninviting.

Slowly I eased the door open and, instead of the quaint interior I had expected, the door opened on to an unexpectedly large and bright open area that extended over the entire ground floor. The wood was old, although perhaps not the original timber. But there were hundreds of nails to be hammered down, and where could I leave the guys once I began the varnishing?

I remembered the soft bread that was in the bag by the door. I had cheddar cheese and milk. The original kitchen was still in use, if only temporarily. It was very small. But it was enclosed; the guys could stay here, I thought, and located the kettle. I wondered how often the owner would come here. The cheese sandwiches were quickly made and eaten with pleasure. Then we went for a walk, pausing only to drag the sander in through the front door. I was aware that hammering down the floorboard nails would take time. It was still weeks before the long summer evenings would make life so much kinder.

How many nails? Hundreds? A thousand? Horrible chore, on my knees, bending over, hammering – I smiled at the mindlessness of it. The best bit was the sanding. For some reason it was always an immensely satisfying task – except for the dust – because of the beauty of wood and the smell of it. I have always loved the character timber gives to a room and the way that over time sunlight alters the colour. Aside from the pleasure of the job, there was also the generous fee, and the guys were here with me. My labouring life was an interregnum, between the years studying and the exciting future that was supposed to beckon – only not yet. It was a useful injection of reality between all my running and the reading – I knew that what I wanted to do more than anything was read, just read the days away. No matter how many books I read, there were always so many more waiting, entire libraries, mountains of books, the world contained in carefully crafted words encased between so many covers.

About a mile down the canal bank, the foliage became thicker; willow and beech competed for dominance and large numbers of sturdy bog birch trees had grown. The long body of a heron unfolded and flew overhead, its weird shape startling against the sky. A strong breeze was blowing; I watched as it made a path down the backs of my dogs, particularly through Bilbo's thicker fur. Then back to work; Frodo sat square in the wide beam of sunlight, while Bilbo kept guard at the window, glancing over at me with concern each time I swore when I hit my thumb with the hammer.

Several of the planks were loose. And the overall levels were uneven; this would be a patchy sanding, but perhaps it would blend well with the rough rustic interior of the house. The daylight seeped away and soon I was feeling the nails by touch, not a sensible thing to do. It was time for more tea. I ate a banana while waiting for the squat little kettle to boil. The mattress upstairs was new, as were the blankets and a duvet with a Donald Duck cover. There was a packet of new sheets, silver-grey and expensive, purchased, I noticed with some surprise, from Harrods. I spread one of them over the plastic wrapping on the mattress, which I kept on to protect the bed from dog hairs. The sheets billowed out like a sail before falling on to the mattress. We would use the Donald Duck duvet, leaving the blankets neatly stacked. At first light the job would continue; the hammering was almost finished and the sanding would have to be completed before the grim-looking equipment-hire man returned.

The night was still; there was no moon as we huddled in the dark on the plastic surface. Each time any of us moved, the plastic squeaked. I had left the windows open, hoping to hear an owl hoot. The only sound that broke the early morning stillness was the cooing of the wood pigeons, and the sharp rasp of the hooded crows.

The shower had not been connected. Water flowed only from the cold faucet of the old clay sink in the small kitchen. Here I brushed my teeth and Bilbo stood on my foot, staring at me in bewilderment. Where was breakfast? Little remained of the bread and the cheese was gone. A quick run down along the canal bank to where the ridge of bog birch became denser and then back to the cottage would wake me up and calm the guys. Then it would be time to face the last, I hoped, of the nails. Outside, the air had a solid coldness that we could feel as we ran through it. Something was different; I realised there was no tension, no fear of cars, other dogs, people. Because it wasn't a wide open space, Bilbo didn't race off. He ran beside me, keeping a steady pace, Frodo at my heels. The sandy path was pleasant to run on. There was a slight bend, just at the point where the bog birch took over from the willow. We turned back; we were all hungry, but there was no other house in view. Even if there had been, I wouldn't have had the nerve to knock on anyone's door asking for food. How could I have forgotten to bring supplies?

The sanding machine bounced over the uneven surface made by the loose planks, but I pushed on, up and down, and the true grain of the timber was released as years of stains and dust were scoured away. The guys were sitting in the little kitchen; I could imagine their heads cocked at the roar of the sander. The machine kept catching, causing the belts of sandpaper to rip and then flap loosely. Finally, it was done. Then the vacuuming of the room, followed by a wiping down of the raw floorboards with white spirit; the room seemed surprisingly larger, cleansed. Light streamed across the floor as the clouds dispersed and the sky brightened.

This was not destined to be one of my best floors, but I worked on, careful not to create dips in the surface. It was done, not brilliantly, but efficiently. My college friend came to visit and brought much-needed food: gourmet sandwiches for lunch and a variety of chocolate, including three tubes of Rolos. Wiping a rag soaked in white spirit over the floor I noticed that, in spite of everything, the surface was smooth to the touch. It would be a good floor after all, and the light coming in from the three windows would help create a pleasing effect.

We went for a walk. Earlier than expected the hire van lurched into sight just as we returned from the canal. The driver had seen us coming down the path towards the house but he went directly to the sander and had it loaded before we reached the house. The guys barked at him and ran around. He didn't react and announced flatly, 'Hoover.' 'On the step,' I said, matching his monotone. 'How many sheets?' he asked, meaning how many I had used. 'All of them.' 'That's a lot,' he said, revealing the tiniest trace of interest. 'Timber was poor,' I responded in robot-speak. He turned, pulled open the driver's door and drove off without a goodbye, never mind even asking if I needed a lift home. 'Great,' I said aloud, looking at the guys. 'Now what do we do?' Well, I could begin varnishing but the first coat would take a day to dry properly.

One by one I carried the guys out of the kitchen where they had been waiting while I varnished. Leaving the fumes to clear, we went back up the track beyond the bog birches. By then the dark forest on the opposite side of the canal seemed far more interesting than our side, but we needed a safe crossing-point. On we walked. Around another bend the canal widened into an ideal swimming place with a stone bridge offering a diving spot, as well as access to the forest. We went on; I had my reasons for not wanting to rush back to my little house where the boyfriend's rock music bothered me as much as my reading annoyed him. Separate homes were indeed the ideal solution. I would need to become wealthy: my future peace of mind was a good incentive. The cottage was providing more than a project, it was a temporary sanctuary. The guys were enjoying themselves;

dogs are content with the familiar, and always seem to find something new in a place they know well. But this was new terrain, full of smells and animals that are rarely seen by day, their scents lingering. Frodo bounded over to a tree, and scratched at the trunk, before jogging back to us, content to leave whatever it was he had chased. We walked on, through the last of the bluebells, under tree cover so heavy that the sky all but disappeared from view.

The light rain had intensified, becoming determined hail, and we ran back. Carefully I lifted Bilbo into the kitchen, securing the door before bending down to scoop up Frodo into my arms. There would be another night on the plastic-covered mattress. I imagined the letters I could write if I had pen and paper, but recalled a comment an artist friend had once made to me on the subject of solitude and the need to empty one's mind. Bilbo's expression changed; his fur stiffened along his back. Both dogs stood and barked. The sound of a car engine upset the silence. It was my friend returning. Her brother had, apparently, at last remembered me, and realised that I was stranded. 'I'd hate to be out here, on my own,' she said, looking at me good-humouredly, but also with some concern. She paused before asking me if I was depressed or even scared. She admitted that if she found herself alone in such a place she would panic, and then most likely pray to be rescued.

Having grown up in a large family, I considered peace a wonderful thing. She had brought a pizza with her; we shared it and I drank a carton of apple juice as she told me the story of her latest romantic disaster, which sounded far more exciting than mine. *We* didn't have explosive arguments. Instead I had to deal with long silences, humming noises, complaints about dog hairs, the fact that animals should live outdoors, should not sleep on or in beds. Then there were the relentless questions on the theme of why I never got bored with reading and whether I ever suspected that reading was a waste of time. I envied my friend her dramatic angst and her colourful screaming matches with a succession of unsuitable cads. My situation was more of a stalemate that was increasingly leading to my spending hours sitting reading in the bathroom with the dogs while I was supposed to be having marathon baths to ease invented running injuries.

I suggested a walk, but she said her shoes would get dirty. Off she went in the car, driving in a wide arc instead of reversing. The car lights faded to tiny dots and we wandered off, me waving, in the opposite direction. She planned to come back the next morning, leaving me enough time to put on another coat of varnish. That night was singular, strangely endless – it was still and very cold, the moonlight bright as day, and there was a feeling that something was about to happen. I couldn't sleep; my mind was busy with disconnected thoughts. Yet I felt content, even if this was not the way to do any job properly.

After the morning run and breakfast I resumed varnishing. The fumes seeped up from the floor. It must have been near noon; we were sitting outside, using the duffel coat as a blanket. Bilbo was stretched out beside me, his head on his paws, and Frodo was curled in a ball, frowning slightly in his sleep. This time I heard the car and looked up. As it approached, I realised it was a different one: it moved differently, driven with confidence. It was the owner, the tycoon-in-a-hurry. 'Hi, I've come to fetch you. How'dya get on? Is it dry?' he called out before even getting out of the car. He ran up the steps to the house and opened the door. I warned him not to walk in as I had just applied another coat and I noticed the woman who had come with him. 'Have you been staying here alone?' she asked, more out of curiosity than concern, as she pushed her hands deeper into the pockets of her coat, a wonderful big coat. 'Keep them away from me, I don't like dogs.' She did not have to worry; they sensed her dislike and kept their distance. I was impressed by their aloof demeanour; Frodo's reserve was expected but Bilbo was still enough of a baby to expect to be fussed over. The owner bounded back down the steps, announcing distractedly that it looked great and that he was going to buy 'lots of rugs and stuff to make the place look old'. I wondered why he had modernised it if he had wanted it to look old. He seemed to see it as a stage set, not a retreat. 'Come and have a look,' he called to his far from enthusiastic companion. 'I'll wait', she said, 'until it's finished. You could get a boat and sail up and down on the water,' she added half-heartedly. 'Or a barge, but then, you wouldn't need the house, I mean, would you, if you had a barge?'

He offered me a lift home but his girlfriend objected, saying she'd be terrified in case the dogs attacked her. I laughed outright at that and she gave me a look that suggested she didn't want to be stuck with someone who had been crazy enough to live rough while painting a floor. He gave me more money than I had expected and said he'd send his sister back for me. Off they drove, leaving me to ponder yet again something that had long preoccupied me and always would. I was fascinated by Heathcliffian passion, romantic agony, the trials of eternal love, the pain, the grief, depths of devotion, particularly when unrequited; and to a lesser extent, I also believed in friendship, community and kinship. Unfortunately, most humans seemed incapable of either.

*

Time passed, perhaps an hour, maybe slightly more. I may have dozed. An entire night would often slip by with me staring at the ceiling or watching the stars, yet I could doze off abruptly in the middle of the day, for ten minutes or an hour, and then jump up and wonder where I was. The guys understood my sleep patterns. Perhaps they presumed I had acquired my habits from them? but I had always been like that. This time it was barking that woke me, and the sound of yet another car grew louder and louder, before it skidded to a halt. My friend had come back, excited with news of her brother's dilemma, confirming that, as I had concluded, the girlfriend had hated the cottage. 'She wants to holiday in Spain or the States, not on a canal. It was hilarious. He asked me to collect you. Just lock it up, you can leave. It's great – your work, I mean.' She told me to sit in the back with the guys; she had already covered the seats, faded and musty as they were, with an old decorator's sheet, to protect her car from dog hairs. It was the first time we travelled in that ancient jalopy. I smiled at her embarrassment: the unkempt interior was strewn with candy wrappers, clothes and old shoes, faded newspapers. But other than that one request, she made no complaint, and I sat in the middle, Bilbo on one side and Frodo on the other, while the cottage disappeared behind us in the rear-view mirror, leaving me to ponder my dirty face and my hair which, after almost three days of camping out, was matted and standing on end.

*

Although the cottage itself was not that important – I had no dreams of imitating Emerson or Thoreau there; my Walden would require a classically romantic woodland setting with a pond directly outside – the place was to become special in another way. We were to return, unexpectedly, within a few weeks, in the middle of May. It looked different then, more tangled, almost mysterious, with fresh greens and clouds of white and yellow. The trees had begun to wake; primroses were out in force and had been joined by marsh marigolds and yellow irises, so delicate yet so tough. The flowers rippled in the breeze. The road down to the house had become more defined thanks to the cow parsley along the ditches that flanked the hedges, heavy with hawthorn. It was warm and the car windows were open. We were again sitting in the back seat of my friend's slovenly old car; Frodo's ears swung back and he stared out at the world, his eyes creased into slits against the bright sunlight. Bilbo sat in close to me, alert, that funny half-smile of pleasure on his face, his black muzzle shining. He knew where we were going.

My friend had arranged a picnic, to celebrate her brother breaking up with his moody lover. I mourned that woman's coat – I had coveted it. The newly single tycoon had also lost enthusiasm for canal life. Operation Cottage was over; it would be abandoned and sold when he found the time to put it on the market. My pal was hugely amused and had decided that I would like a final look at my work. I knew the floor really needed a few more coats of varnish, but it wasn't my house. Now was the time for the swimming hole. But my unsporty hostess raised her eyebrows at the idea and spread a heavy cotton blanket on the ground. She informed me that she was going to sleep and I was not to disturb her, even if I was drowning, as she couldn't swim. The three of us jogged off; the place I had identified during my previous stay as an ideal pool was beyond a bend in the bank, near a stone bridge. It was perhaps a mile beyond the cottage so we ran on. Once more I was grateful for the lack of tension; no cars, no people, no other dogs. My guys free, no need of leashes. The summer growth made the swimming place seem more private, with the velvety brown of the bulrushes shielding it.

Water edged up to the soft bank: a step through a muddy wash brought us directly into the canal. I took off my trainers and socks, and walked in wearing shorts and a tee shirt. 'Just wait there, I'll be quick,' I said to the guys. Bilbo disliked water and sat back on his haunches, eyes closed against the sun and the flies. Frodo paused, but seemed interested. I waded out until the water was at waist height. It felt oddly tepid. The canal bed felt gravelly underfoot instead of slimy mud. I dived in and swam a few strokes under water before surfacing just as a splash alerted me to another swimmer. After running up and down the bank barking, Frodo had simply jumped in and paddled over to me. I felt such affection for the little trier as he battled to keep his head above the water. Most of his ears had disappeared below the surface. I swam over to him, intending to hold him up, noticing that Bilbo was very agitated. Suddenly I realised this was a bad idea, the one thing he hated was water and I had gone into it, leaving him behind.

Even worse, Frodo had joined me. I called out, trying to reassure Bilbo, but by sheer willpower he made himself charge forward and jumped in, disappearing under the water. Before I had located him, he had surfaced and was swimming. That same balance and grace that made him such an impressive runner enabled him to swim far better than any dog I had seen. He was a natural swimmer; Frodo was able, if awkward, but Bilbo, having never swum in his life, made a stylish debut and, with it, a signal of intent. Frodo's determination had been evident from the start. Bilbo had never had any reason to show his. That day I discovered something new about the dog I thought I knew so well. I was already aware of his reckless courage and that he would take on bigger dogs. But this was a different kind of bravery, and it was to prove vital.

I flipped over on my back to watch them. Bilbo swam on, deliberate, testing himself. Frodo was having fun. Back towards the bank, I stood up and walked out, and they followed. Frodo's sleeker fur dried quickly in the warm air. Bilbo looked like a teddy bear that had fallen into a washing machine. He shook himself furiously, happy to be out of the water. His coat was fluffed up, making his face seem smaller and his eyes enormous. I wondered whether Frodo's spontaneous leap into the canal had seemed like a deliberate challenge to him. Do dogs think like that? We jogged back.

That night at home, without any fuss or even a backward glance of either defiance or enquiry, Frodo, for the first time, jumped up on to the beanbag in the living room. Bilbo paused, and then leaped up beside him. They settled quickly, Frodo's head on Bilbo's hip. The final barrier had fallen.

9

Time for an Adventure

Rage, tears and accusations; a Greek tragedy in a modern setting was unfolding. The woman in the red vest was screaming. Her fists were clenched as she lay writhing on the ground, calling damnation down upon the fates. The younger woman, the timid-looking one with the face of a boy, seemed ready for death. There are times when innocence is not enough. Chance, misfortune, bad timing, all had contributed to a collision that would go down in track and field history. Both women were thin, ravaged, ultra-fit. The younger, a mere girl, slunk away but the older one considered her life over and was angry and distressed beyond measure. She was helped off, lifted bodily as if fatally wounded.

The women's 3,000 metres final at the Los Angeles Olympics in 1984 had not gone to plan. The much debated showdown between the home crowd's tragic darling, the gifted, if injury-prone, multi-world-record-holder Mary Decker-Slaney and her shy South African challenger, Zola Budd, running for Great Britain thanks to a technicality of ancestry and the support of an opportunistic Fleet Street newspaper, had not even developed into a proper race. Decker had collided with Budd and both fallen. It was an accident. Middle-distance athletes bunch in packs and often trip: Decker's foot had caught Budd's twice. Budd fell, pulling Decker down with her.

The American reigning world champion lay on the track,

her grief tinged with tantrum. The South African Briton had reacted in the only way she knew, and ran on to finish a valiant seventh. Few remember who actually won the race; Romanian Maricica Puica's achievement was overshadowed by the drama. All the hysteria certainly helped late-night viewers, watching thousands of miles away in Europe, to stay wide awake for the next event.

My own viewing had taken its toll. I was exhausted, and had been walking the dogs at odd times. They had become used to finding themselves back in the bedroom with me in the early afternoon for my snatches of impromptu sleep. It had been a divisive Olympics: the Eastern Bloc had boycotted them in response to the US withdrawal from Moscow four years earlier. Los Angeles, my birthplace, looked garish. The opening ceremony featured Gershwin's music and men in pale blue tuxedos, eighty-four grand pianos and multicoloured pastel ribbons. It was undiluted Hollywood. In those Technicolor games, nothing, not even Carl Lewis, seemed quite real. It had been in need of an unequivocally operatic moment – and, finally, it had one.

For a time the women's 3,000 metres final held centre stage. Medics and officials spoke to eager journalists. There was disbelief and the media had been suitably thorough in its relentless analysis. Re-runs of the collision from every angle dominated television screens across the world. But then the track was cleared for the race that really mattered: the men's 1,500 metres final featuring the uninhibited African middle-distance athletes and their main challengers. The absence of the Eastern Europeans would not affect the race. The defending champion, Sebastian Coe, the most fragile figure in the field, looked resigned following illness and injury. He personified the extremes of success and failure:

he had again failed to win the gold medal in the 800 metres, as he had in Moscow four years earlier, but then he had agonised for four days only to return and win the 1,500 metres. It was different now, his teammate Steve Cram, no longer a pretender, was on form. Younger, taller and tougher, he had also won the world title the previous season. The third player was Steve Ovett. Respiratory difficulties had weakened him, but he was sufficiently wily to appear still capable of a miracle. The rest were treated as mere bystanders in what was, as far as the British commentators were concerned, a very English battle of wits.

Bilbo was prepared for the frenzy that was bound to follow and had matched my intense attentiveness when watching European and World championship finals. He had observed my following of the McEnroe and Borg rivalry and seemed to approve of loud crowd participation, often barking as I shouted and groaned, roaring on my support. Familiar with the jumping up and down – I could never remain seated – and the wild waving of arms, the punching of fists, he was braced now for an imminent outburst. He had been at my side for many of Coe's great races; performances that had not only rewritten the records but had elevated athletics to the main evening news. The LA Olympic final was pitched for a different kind of drama; the once-invincible Coe had entered the twilight of his career and was known to be vulnerable. Cram was expected to win; still, any one of the Africans or the Spaniard José Abascal or either of the Americans Steve Scott or Jim Spivey could also settle it.

As my stomach began to heave with anxiety, Bilbo watched, poised, ready, his tail swinging. He could sense my mounting hysteria. I felt the emotion of being about to witness one of my heroes relinquish his crown in the most conclusive way, in an Olympic final. At the gun, the field set off; the home crowd was ecstatic at the early surge by Scott, attempting to run the speed out of the fast finishers. The central action concerned the three rival Britons. Coe was determined. Here was a champion prepared to go down fighting; defeat for a great athlete is far more decisive in its finality than death itself. For a brief moment, just as the race entered its final lap, off the bend at the beginning of the back straight, the three English athletes ran in a line across the track like a cross-country team of old.

Then Ovett dropped out just off the bend with a forlorn shrug of his shoulders as the pack raced on without him. Abascal looked comfortable and Cram seemed ready to take over. Yet Coe had stayed with them. With 200 metres to go, he looked across at Cram and then changed gear. The impossible seemed about to happen. I shrieked and jumped up and down, making that distinctive whooping chant perfected by Austrian ski fans. Coe sprinted faster and faster, as elegant as ever, while Cram began treading water and behind him the Spaniard held on for bronze. But it was Coe, running into history, the first man to retain an Olympic 1,500 metres title, who broke the field. I yelled, Bilbo barked and Frodo, wearing the expression of a concerned anthropologist, looked at us. It was 3.30 in the morning: I ran up the hall, opened the door, and the three of us ran out to do a lap of honour, more like a lap of relief, around the green space.

There would be yet another victory for us to celebrate. Two years later, in one of his finest performances, Coe, then aged thirty, and again returning from illness and injury, had been forsaken at last even by the once adoring British commentators. Cram was expected to decide the

European 800 metres final in Athens with another Briton, a new star, Tom McKean. Yet Coe defied all logic, and his current form. Having spent most of the race running in last position, he made a late challenge for the bronze, only to float effortlessly forward and away, sprinting to the gold, his face impassive. The only one involved or watching not to be surprised was Coe. As Coe began his victory lap, I jumped up and down, shouting in celebration; this time Frodo added his honk to Bilbo's excited barking. But we were by then in a different place, a different country.

*

It began with a book, strange and alluring, almost irritating in its artfulness. It was to open a door to the past and played with facts in the way that a story often does. On encountering the sprawling, murky Augustan London evoked by Peter Ackroyd in his novel, *Hawksmoor*, part-baroque pastiche and part-modern thriller. I felt a summons to action. A spell had been cast. The name, with its suggestion of a fierce, intelligent bird and a dark place, meant that there were layers of history to be peeled away. A man from another time stepped out of the shadows. Nicholas Hawksmoor (1661–1736) was an English architect; he had trained under Christopher Wren and was to work with Vanbrugh on Castle Howard in Yorkshire and later on Blenheim Palace. Castle Howard had come to be significant; it had provided the setting for the Marchmain home in the television adaptation of *Brideshead Revisited*, the theme music of which had so excited Bilbo. Quite unexpectedly, a vast, imposing Yorkshire mansion had become linked to my little dog.

Was it true that as a child Hawksmoor had watched both of his parents die in agony from the plague? I became fascinated by him and by the world he had inhabited.

I decided we should travel to Castle Howard. Now, as if superimposed upon the London of Dickens, a London I felt I knew from his and other nineteenth-century novels, an earlier, darker capital had emerged, one oppressed by the squalor of the Augustan age, the threat of plague and of malcontents schooled in the black arts patrolling dank alleys hunting for souls. Ackroyd had taken Hawksmoor's name and given it to a weary modern-day detective, bewildered by a series of ritualised murders, each committed on the site of a city church designed by the real Hawksmoor. Ackroyd had changed the name: his architect was called Dyer and his mind was replete with vicious images of disease, decay and death, but his work was Hawksmoor's. Our world seemed now to me too bright, too pristine. Those eighteenth-century churches would provide a set of keys. I had become drawn to the East End, a place I had read about but had never seen. The Limehouse that had been in Dickens's time the easternmost part of London, where ships were once built and kept at dock and where wandering sailors had finally settled, inspired mystery, dark intrigue and, above all, stories. Dickens knew this area well from walking it; he had visited his godfather there. The Grapes public house became the Six Jolly Fellowship Porters in *Our Mutual Friend*. And it was to the Limehouse dens that Wilde's Dorian Gray had gone in search of opium.

But before all of that, Hawksmoor had designed St Anne's, Limehouse, the finest of his six churches. The riverside community had gathered there to pray. Although badly damaged during the Blitz, the church survived and the clock on its tower remains higher than that of any other church in London. I needed to follow Hawksmoor's journey, and that also included Christ Church, Spitalfields, paid for by a coal tax, and initially used by the Huguenot silk weavers who had colonised the green fields of Spital. The English baroque, less extravagant than its French, Italian and German counterparts, but possessed of a stern opulence, also includes the Royal Naval College at Greenwich, where Hawksmoor had served as Wren's assistant. I thought we should go there and stand on the Greenwich Meridian of longitude, and wonder at the four directions of the compass and the men who had set sail to explore great seas.

Hawksmoor's presence and my notion of his London, mediated by Ackroyd's imagination, seeped into our lives. It was time for an adventure. Careful preparations began; a new urgency was in the air. Each walk became a stage in a formal farewell. In our woods we wandered, as if framing mental images to take with us. For once, the dogs didn't race about. There was no chasing: Bilbo stopped beside trees that he usually ran past. Now he looked at them as if measuring their dimensions. He sniffed and considered, paused, retraced his footsteps. He was not browsing; he was recording, leaving his mark. Frodo was even more intense, he was ensuring that no future dog could venture casually through this secluded haunt without being aware of the formidable partnership that had so conclusively traversed it. It was cold there on the evening of the final visit.

The removal team had been late; dusk was falling as the bicycle was hoisted up on to a rack inside the truck that was packed with boxes of books, a faded red kayak and the ugly old desk. A hollow echo followed us around the house. Empty, it looked like a stranger's dwelling, slightly bigger and shabbier than I had realised. No music, no light, no colour, only the ghostly shapes left by the pictures that had once hung on the walls. The fire had been set but not lit.

Others would sit before it now. We did a final tour of the green area, now less of a wasteland because of the young trees that had been planted. They were weak and bare, some seemed unlikely to survive. But trees often thrive when least expected. So many hours and days of walking in rain and sun; over frost-hardened earth and so many steps, taken at fast walk or run. That spot over there was where Frodo, then Mac but not yet Rusty, not yet our companion, had humiliated the white dog. There was the worn track to the local shop. Over there the abandoned car that Johannes had sheltered in. Further up the hill, the watery ditch which had become a spirited little dog's grave. Contemplated through detached eyes, this unremarkable place in what was left of the west County Dublin countryside with its scattering of houses might have been a struggling frontier settlement somewhere in Montana after the railroads had failed to push westwards. There had been high drama and contentment with the dogs; there had also been consolidation, perhaps even complacency, as Bilbo and Frodo had eased me through difficult episodes in my slowly ebbing human relationship, which had entered a phase of mutual acceptance. Now was the moment for us to move on.

Part 2

10

Walking in the Snow

Snow; thick and cold and lying everywhere, waiting to be made into snowmen. At first it was wonderful: it created a twenty-four-hour day, a surreal glow that illuminated the nights, while the sharp morning light cast dramatic shadows. Everyone seemed to be peering at each other and into the distance because of the alien brightness. The white coating suited the Kent countryside, with its tidy wooden fences and old-fashioned gates and stiles frequented by robins that resembled images in the engravings of Thomas Bewick. Old trees, tall and defiant, dominated the landscape; venerable oaks, beech and more willow than I had ever seen in one place. Broadleaf woodland had withstood war and development as well as time itself. The farms were modest but postcard pretty. On the way to the large parkland that had once belonged to a great estate – the bleak mansion house seemed deserted although I later discovered that the elderly lord still lived there alone with a tiny staff – I felt I was in not only a different country, but a different world, an older one. The dogs ran on, their paws setting off little explosions of icy powder. Frodo began licking the snow. I was worried about them falling through thin ice; the lake area was extensive and I didn't know where shallow surface water became the deeper levels of frozen lake or pond.

The initial reaction of the dogs to the snow had been comical. I had opened the door, and looked twice; the sudden snow had fallen without warning overnight. Bilbo stopped in mid-stride as he was about to step out into a garden that looked very different from that of the previous evening. Everything had been transformed. His right paw held high, with his head at an angle and wearing an expression of mild disbelief, he looked up at me for my reaction. It had been a long time since I had last seen snow, and then only on ski slopes in Colorado. Frodo dashed out, giving his characteristic hop every three or four strides, his quick movement causing snow to slide down off the hedge and on to his head. He shook his ears and ran back indoors pushing by me, surprised that the whiteness outside had left him wet, and he seemed none too pleased about it.

The fields stretched white into the distance. This was no gentle icing. It was beyond pleasure; this was real snow, heavy and consolidated, falling fast on to packed ice. Roads had become impassable, cars had been abandoned. Neighbours were asked to check on the elderly. The stoic English sighed and went to do battle. This was the reality of life in the countryside. Houses were cut off; power lines were down and people were panic-buying in the supermarkets. I watched a smartly dressed man in one shop reach for a can of black cherries and then take a second, before pausing to look around and claim the remaining seven. Common sense, or possibly guilt initially, made him replace one can on the shelf, then he shrugged and returned it to his trolley, which he pushed defiantly down the aisle, head high.

No such guilt troubled me. I took all the dog food I could carry, bringing two baskets up to the checkout and then returned with more. The assistant looked at me and suggested that I was feeding an army but immediately corrected herself, 'No, no, more like a team of those husky dogs.' I smiled and fetched more cans, as many as I could load into a rucksack and in the two large canvas carrier bags I had brought with me. My face was flushed with the effort as I staggered out of the shop and trudged back to the small rented cottage on the outskirts of the village. The cottage was tiny and dark, and very smelly. The exterior was quaint, with old sash windows. The frames were faded blue and matched the shutters; the paintwork was flaking and in need of attention. Ancient rose bushes dominated the small front garden. It looked like an illustration from a Victorian novel, no doubt a melodrama featuring a wronged maiden and possibly a ruthless mill owner. But inside the house was decidedly unromantic, damp and dreary with a slimy old sink that had required an entire bottle of bleach and several kettles of boiling water before it was fit for use. The toilet groaned and wheezed when flushed by pulling a long chain with a china handle.

Having often come across the word 'scullery' I finally saw one; it was the tiny space beside the kitchen at the back of the cottage, opening out on to an equally small cobbled yard, its walls draped in heavy swathes of dark green ivy. Inside the scullery, with its sagging shelves and collection of old jars and bottles, stood a washing machine that looked like a genuine museum piece, complete with a mangle. The grate was so packed with soot that there was no point in attempting to light a fire until the chimney had been swept. When the sweep arrived the dogs had danced about him, barking and snarling. He was very good-natured and admitted that he was seldom met by a wagging tail. That first snowfall came about a week after we arrived and it added to the novelty. Life in a 1980s English village seemed archaic; it was like stepping back half a century. Cars seemed out of place. I stood in the little village High Street feeling smugly responsible, having stepped down off the sidewalk as both dogs defecated simultaneously on the street. All very correct; I admired the large tubs and planters filled with conifers and cyclamens and a variety of other winter plants at the entrances of the little shops, their traditional facades painted in various shades of blue and red. Several were decorated in a smart dark green. Pink and grey were also popular. Heritage here was not something devised for the tourists; it was part of daily life. I heard a man's voice and smiled to myself as I turned, expecting to hear some friendly comment about the two mannerly dogs that knew better than to dirty the pavement.

The speaker was a middle-aged policeman, wearing that old-style helmet with its hint of fancy dress. He was not impressed. Instead he was gesturing towards the street, ordering me to pick up the mess and dispose of it, or else I would be fined. 'Be quick about it,' he said, probably because at first I thought he was kidding, I must have hesitated, but he expected prompt action. Sensing the tension, the dogs barked up into his face. He ignored them and I looked about for a bit of paper. There was none to be found on the litterless street so I looked into a bin, hoping to find a suitable wrapper or a take-away tray in it. My new life was not beginning all that well and the constable must have sensed my surprise. I was not aware there was a law banning dogs fouling the road. As if commenting on the weather he added in a studiedly neutral tone, 'That bigger dog there should be muzzled when walked in a public place.' He quoted the bye-law, and I was about to tell him that I was in fact new to England, but he turned away without further comment. No wonder the village was so tidy.

*

There were many places to explore. Whatever the official attitude to canine excrement, England loves dogs. We had arrived in a place where dogs were walked on leashes, even in the rain. Some wore shower coats. None ran loose. This was a society in which people really did gather their dog's dirt. The first time I saw an owner standing on a grass verge, leading into the village, holding a plastic scoop in one hand and a polythene bag in the other, I assumed the man was collecting botanical specimens.

Being discouraged from the High Street was not a problem, as I never felt comfortable about leaving the dogs tied outside shops. There was a far more interesting place to walk through: an abandoned churchyard with monuments and vaulted tombs dating back to the late sixteenth century. Most of the graves had subsided, causing the headstones to shift and lean, lurching at various angles like the final remnants of a forgotten army. Many of the inscriptions were weathered and illegible; yet it was possible to piece together fragments of clues about some of the lives. The majority of the women seemed to have died young, probably in childbirth. The derelict church itself was almost completely concealed by massive sentry-like yew trees. The double doors hung off long-rusted hinges. In common with the headstones, the doors had collapsed outwards and were standing only because they had jammed firm against the stone step. The little entrance porch was empty except for layers of old leaves, so dried out that they appeared to be a dullish grey. The door leading into the church, more of a chapel, opened easily on to a sight so forlorn it took me aback. The church was far more desolate than the ruined graves of the ancient dead outside. Layers of dirt covered the old wooden pews, not just bird droppings, but another darker mess, most likely left by bats. The roof showed clear sky in several places where slates were missing.

The churchyard was fascinating in daylight, but after dark it became terrifying. Here was a place to test one's nerve on Halloween night. 'Was it known to be haunted?' I asked. Most of the people replied with the same question, 'You don't believe in ghosts, do you?' It was disappointing: England seemed generously supplied with haunted castles and stately homes – Hampton Court, built by Cardinal Wolsey for his own use and later presented by him to Henry VIII in a desperate attempt to appease the monarch, is reputed to have about thirty restless souls who make regular nocturnal appearances – yet here was an atmospheric churchyard devoid of stories about broken-hearted girls, murdered gentry or notorious highwaymen. I returned alone to the church and took photographs of it. It was the afternoon, but I felt as if I was being watched. There was no one around, only birds who took control of the place by day, retreating by night in deference to the bats who may have been sleeping in the stone walls, preparing for the coming evening's hunt. I took the film to be developed but the prints could not be found when I went to collect them.

Despite the absence of supernatural happenings, the church interested me and I began making notes, beginning with details about the various graves, the type of memorial and what the respective headstones revealed about the social class of the departed. On other days I walked the guys through the grounds, always wondering about the stories that would never be told. One night, when I had returned late from London, we went for a quick walk. It was drizzling. I noticed a dark shape standing to the left of the path we were following. I felt cold and waited for the dogs to bark and lunge towards it. They didn't. There was nothing there. I remembered the words that were by then being constantly directed at me by the boyfriend – an initially casual remark, that I always lived in my head, had become a frequent accusation. The situation with him was worsening. It was no one's fault; he didn't like living with someone who wanted to read all the time, and I was not sociable. Our relationship was based largely on a shared interest in track and field – and little else. I could go running with him, but the dogs were mine, my companions. It was easier going for a walk with them than trying to make sense of a human relationship that never moved beyond that of being two friends with very different views on music.

*

The late walks on still nights were relaxing. Our route included the churchyard and various winding roads that undulated over the surrounding low hills. It had remained viciously cold for a couple of weeks after the last of the snow. Just when it seemed a shame that there would not be a White Christmas, there were further snowfalls. It took just one determined blizzard to return the village to its nineteenth-century aspect. The heavy snowfall created large drifts. The only vehicles abroad were tractors and jeeps, and that only by day. At night we saw shooting stars. The snow crunched under my boots while the dogs jogged on, convinced they were pulling me after them. Aside from their steady panting and the jingle of their leashes, or a cow lowing in the distance, it was silent. After a couple of these night walks I was enthralled. I wanted them to last forever and decided that the element of mystery made it far more exciting than walking on a hot summer's day. My face was burning from the cold, but I didn't mind; I felt so intensely awake.

On the fourth, or perhaps the fifth, of our secret walks, I realised we were almost home but didn't want to go back inside the cottage where the silences had become loud with tension. I wanted to walk all night. I turned up a lane. I wasn't sure where it led but it would be fun to try a different route. The alleyway opened on to a far wider road. There was a choice, left or right. The left was dominated by a huge hangar-like building, perhaps the local cattle mart. The right seemed more welcoming, less utilitarian; two or three cottages, set well back from the road, and a small row of little shops. A tall pole was barely visible beside what looked like a shelter; it was a bus stop. The snow on the road was clean and barely disturbed. No one was driving. A flurry of light flakes began to fall.

The closer we got to the bus stop, the more excited the dogs became, tugging, almost hauling me along. The pavement was slippery, as the area around the bus shelter was more ice than snow; the shelter appeared to have been somewhat protected from much of the fresh fall. The dogs had become frenzied, pulling me off balance. There was something there, a small mass or mound on the ground. Bilbo gave his short, rasping bark. My feet struck something that was soft yet solid. It was a body. The dogs recoiled and moved away as I knelt down. The moonlight reflected in the eyes of the woman lying there. She was small and stout, her bulky overcoat belted firmly around her middle. She was gazing at me yet seeing nothing. I took off my gloves, and touched her face, urging her to get up. I pulled her forward into a sitting position. It took an unexpected effort, she was astonishingly heavy. The back of her coat was soaked. There was no response. I realised she was dead. She had died alone in the snow. I ran back to the row of little houses and knocked at the door of the first one. Before the hall lights came on, a dog had begun barking. I could hear it bustling towards the door and a man's voice telling it to get back, then calling someone, asking them to take the dog. The man looked confused as I stood there, an upset stranger needing to shout above the noise of my barking dogs, and told him about the woman. He said he would phone the police, leaving me to run back to the bus stop.

My hands were freezing and I recalled taking off my gloves, and that I must have left them on the ground. Time seemed to have stopped in the stillness. I wondered if somewhere someone was waiting for the woman. She lay there, neat and orderly, dressed for a shopping expedition, her woollen hat still on her head. Lights came up the road; the car moved slowly towards us. The police arrived, followed by an ambulance. One of the ambulance staff knew the woman. The policemen listened; the taller one was holding her glasses and her handbag. I remember thinking how funny he looked, a large policeman clutching a ladies' bag. Having been told the woman's name, he didn't need to examine its contents for clues. I picked up her orange string shopping bag; it had been wound around her wrist but as they moved her it had fallen down. It held a box of scouring pads and a packet of fish fingers. The cardboard packaging of both was soggy. The policemen were very calm, resigned to the horrors of life, although I suspected perhaps not as hardened as their city counterparts. They kept referring to the dreadful cold, the freezing conditions, and seemed to be asking me the same question, over and over, something about walking in the snow.

Bilbo was pawing at me, demanding my attention; he held something in his mouth. I took the thing and stared at an object that made no sense. It was a dental plate. One of the policemen took it from me and they both spoke at once, saying that they would drive me home. My teeth were chattering, I had no control over the muscles of my face. The police officers agreed that I was probably in shock; it was as if they were speaking to me from some vast distance. I climbed into the squad car and felt disconnected and uncoordinated. I was surprised that the dogs were so wet as the snow had been hard and cold to the touch. One of the policemen said it was lucky that I had 'those chaps' with me, as it would have been easy to walk by her in the shadows. They reckoned she had been lying there for hours, having waited for a bus that never came.

11

Through the Window

One minute it was bright sunshine, the next heavy showers crashed down from under darkened skies. The train platform was crowded, but the intending passengers waited, as if resigned to yet another of life's daily trials. No sighing, no small talk. The exotic-looking man in the long, silken coat laughed and smiled. He didn't mind being barked at. He had long dreadlocks which he kept flicking back over his shoulders. His teeth were large and perfect and his surprisingly hearty laugh boomed out across the old-fashioned station with its dainty wooden trim which had been freshly repainted in contrasting shades of red and pink. I guessed that he was some kind of performer, most likely a dancer. He seemed confident and sublimely at peace with the world and himself. He waved his hands and then coaxed the dogs, beckoning them towards him. But Bilbo stood firm, barking from deep down in his throat. Frodo was silent, watching with his habitual expression of benign detachment. Bilbo ignored my embarrassed requests for silence and instead channelled even more energy into threatening the man who had walked over to us and was now standing with his arms folded, still smiling. Bilbo snarled and barked on; my face felt hot and I mumbled my apologies. The man considered it highly amusing and bent down as if to pat Bilbo. But first he crouched, rocking back on his heels and grinned knowingly: he knew what was bothering the dog. It was simple, he said, and raising his voice for everyone to hear announced, that 'this fine animal' had never seen a black man before and again he laughed as if it was all most amusing. Had this taken place in New York, there would have been a communal cheer and applause but we were in a country railway station in England and there was no reaction; the only sound was the rustle of newspapers.

Once Bilbo's head had been patted and he had sniffed at the pink palms of the man's long, narrow hands and at the edges of the silvery-grey garment that had fallen in, folds around the affable stranger, he stopped barking. The train arrived and the man strolled towards it, with his effortless dancer's walk, his coat drifting behind him. He turned to wave at us. I went to the back of the carriage and tried to make the dogs fit as neatly as possible down by my feet. I had an appointment in London to view a garden flat. A city would be more difficult for the dogs, yet they had become used to being on the leash and had probably long forgotten the secret woods where they had once run loose.

Things had changed since the night I had found the woman at the bus stop or, rather, the dogs had. Without them I would have walked right by her. I didn't even know her name. In the chaos of finding her body and running for help, I had never thought of asking. I knew nothing about her. That bothered me, but I didn't want to go back to the police in case they thought I was expecting to be thanked. Even after we had moved from the cottage to a house with a long, narrow garden, I kept reliving that night. One day I had sat on a chair by the window of the back bedroom and looked down on the garden, watching the dogs patrol the space so well ordered by a previous owner, a good, if conservative gardener. From that height, they had appeared very small, barely more than points of colour against the lawn. Small and, above all, trapped, as I was. What am I doing here? I wondered, realising that I wanted to leave the village, and my life of endlessly searching for a job. I continued to write book reviews, something I had begun doing while I was completing my thesis. The volume of reviews had increased but I needed to have steady work and had also begun reading manuscripts for publishers. Being able to cycle to the various offices would be more productive than always having to embark on lengthy train journeys or waiting for postal collections and deliveries. The boyfriend, on the other hand, was content in an office and enjoyed meeting his new colleagues in the local pub, a social scene into which I didn't fit.

During those restless months in the tall house I had begun to experience a panic that I later understood was caused by a fear of failure. Flight was on my mind, but I needed a place to which I could also bring the dogs. Now when I walked them, particularly at night, I dreaded that they would find another body. It was ironic, considering all the time that I had spent daydreaming in churchyards about ghosts. When I had actually stumbled upon real-life tragedy I had reacted like a mute sleepwalker, too shocked to respond.

A rural English train station barely prepared me for the desperate scrum of the London Underground where everyone appeared to be in a rush, as though fleeing a catastrophe, even if it was only a missed rail connection. It didn't take long to discover how easy it was to be on the correct line yet going in the wrong direction. The guys seemed to realise we were on a mission and watched me carefully. I crouched down by the sliding door of the carriage and they both stood in front of me. I had my arms around them. The only sound was the rumbling noise of the Tube train and the frequent explosions of air made by the braking system, but something had made me look up. An older woman was speaking to me. I couldn't hear her. She spoke again but I could only see her lips moving. I must have smiled blankly but she was determined that I would hear her. The train stopped and she bent down towards us, her face flushed with the effort of bending over and she complimented me on having such beautiful dogs with such 'lovely manners'. I was pleased but then she said something that at first I misheard. I thought she had said that they would bring me great joy. But that was not what she said. Her words were disturbing; she had said that they would cause me great grief, a great grief. For a moment I wondered if she was a clairvoyant who had seen some terrible disaster in our futures. Her words stayed in my mind, particularly because she had taken such care that I should hear them.

Rush hour on the Underground was wisely avoided, not only by dogs. It was only when travelling with them that I needed to use it, as I still could not drive. The rest of the time I cycled and avoided the Tube stations with their long, winding corridors and the sound of scurrying feet, like so many rats. Travelling around London by bike is the best way to explore the city and to learn something of both its geography and its layers of history. The Hawksmoor churches continued to intrigue me and one by one I investigated them all. The move to London had been relatively easy. The major difficulty was the contraction of space, not only within the rooms of the flat but outside, where we were now confined to narrow, congested sidewalks. Other dog walkers were physically closer and more of the dogs belonged to the larger breeds. Now I was aware of owners who had dogs that they had specifically requested from breeders. We were walking past dogs that had been purchased before birth on the basis of pedigree and the proven quality of a sire that they would never see. There were far more of these elite dogs than strays and rescue cases from animal shelters. As soon as Bilbo noticed a large dog approaching us he would prepare to lunge at them, snarling. At times it made walking an ordeal. On several occasions he pulled so hard that he broke the loop on his collar where it was attached to the leash. A couple walking an Afghan hound was taken by surprise but the man was quick and kicked Bilbo hard in the chest. He yelped with pain and fell over. As I bent down to lift him the man, acting as if I had planned the ambush, screamed at me, telling me to have my mad dog put down. The Afghan remained serene, taking no notice of the incident. I carried Bilbo home; he became heavier with every step, while Frodo walked calmly beside me.

But there were many pleasant expeditions to offset the worst episodes. The flat we had found was only metres from the Thames. The towpath was wide and it offered views across the river, beautiful and languid, particularly on the days when sunlight reflected off the pulsating water. The circuit from Putney to Hammersmith, on through Fulham, and back to Putney was an enjoyable run and in the early morning or on a quiet Bank Holiday became an ideal long outing for the dogs. Rowers outnumbered dog walkers. As the early spring weather improved I began to notice activity around various sheds, now revealed to be boathouses, that were usually locked. At certain times of day the doors were opened, revealing empty hangar-like structures with cradles for holding the racing boats. At first the sight of the oars cutting through the water, creating arcs of spray, alarmed the dogs but they eventually accepted the rowers as another part of our new life down by the river.

Fellow dog owners and people who just happened to walk by us often commented on the dogs but I soon noticed that for every enquiry about their names or their ages there were far more questions about their breeding, or rather their lack of it. I had by then come to terms with the revelation, courtesy of a literal-minded London vet, that Bilbo, until then described by me as a 'German shepherd-Collie cross' could also be classified as 'breed unknown'. I was increasingly hearing both of them being referred to as mongrels. This canine class system encouraged me to begin informing anyone who asked about Bilbo's origins that he was a Spirig, an Austrian sheepdog, a rare working breed prized for its intelligence and athleticism. People were invariably impressed, repeating 'Spirig' aloud and admitting that they had never heard of it. I had guessed, correctly that not many urban dog owners would know that Spirig was the name of a specialist Swiss saddlemaker. Frodo was more readily defined as a large dachshund, a badger dog, or increasingly, a beagle.

Genuine interest, not merely righteous curiosity, made me go to Cruft's Dog Show in order to see what was so special about the pedigree minority. No one could deny that the Irish setter, Dobermann pinscher, Rhodesian Ridgeback or German Shepherd or any one of several breeds of collie is as pleasing to the eye as a thoroughbred horse. But their cross-bred or mongrel counterparts are not only as attractive, they are constitutionally tougher, possessed, as the vet who had treated Bilbo for that near-fatal distemper had said, of 'hybrid vigour'. The mongrel is also more intelligent and resourceful, and, most important of all, has a kinder temperament and abundance of personality.

Then as now, the RSPCA was in dispute with the Kennel Club on the issue of breed specifications and the proven medical implications. The sight of thousands of dogs on view over the four day show is bewildering and it is not an occasion for the general dog lover. Cruft's is a trade fair at which the product is blood lines; everything you have ever half-heard about cloning comes flooding back. There is little fun to be had; the owners and handlers are understandably anxious and the dogs are glum. Most sit, slump or doze on open kennel benches. Their expressions range from resignation to boredom to downright depression. The pedigree show dogs don't respond to a greeting and they certainly don't wag their tails. To say that an individual is 'Best of Breed' does not mean that this is the dog you should take home to your family. The competitive note prevails: any dog competing at Cruft's has won its right to be there. If the prettiest dog seldom wins, it is because the Kennel Club has very specific demands. For the bloodhound the bigger the unsightly wrinkle hanging down over the forehead the better. As a breed, the bloodhound is suffering through trying to meet Kennel Club requirements. In order to see the third eyelid, one of the bloodhound's special features, it is necessary to peer very closely into the dog's blood-shot eyes. As a result of generations of in-breeding these splendid hounds are increasingly prone to epilepsy.

Founded in 1873 with serious aspirations to improve dog breeding, the Kennel Club is regarded by some of its critics as being closely involved with what has been described as 'genetic engineering'. Its stipulations have introduced radical physical changes; in some cases, actual distortions of physical features – and functions – that have serious medical implications. The Great Dane has been bred so big that its life expectancy has been reduced. The St Bernard is now too heavy to climb mountains. The quest for the perfect head has left the bulldog with a range of respiratory conditions. In common with other breeds with heavily folded skin, such as mastiffs and pekes, the bulldog also suffers from dermatitis. Red Cocker spaniels have periodic fits, while the Cavalier King Charles spaniel experiences a particularly distressing affliction known as 'collapsing syndrome' during which the dog goes rigid, faints as if dead and then gets up as if nothing has happened.

Enforced in-breeding has imposed hereditary diseases on most pedigree breeds. Hip dysplasia and degenerative joint problems affect the large dogs, while progressive retinal atrophy, now common to both large and small pedigree breeds, often results in complete blindness by the age of three.

There is no comparison between the formal show classes and the agility and obedience events where the clever working collies and sheepdogs upstage the fragile glamour of the show Borzoi hounds, themselves once fine hunting dogs favoured by the tsars of Russia. However funny it looks at first glance, the sight of Afghan hounds with their ears pinned up or wearing snoods is an appalling affront to the dignity of these dogs. I wondered about the Afghan hound that Bilbo had lunged at, the one that was being walked by the man who had kicked him. Had they been at the show?

Away from the spot-lit centre stage, where the shampooed if unhappy contestants await their moment in the show ring, is the reality that the RSPCA has to deal with: the plight of thousands of unwanted stray dogs and puppies, animals with great potential if no breeding. It puts the theatricality of shows such as Cruft's into perspective. For less ambitious pet owners, the most interesting aspect of this parade of selectively bred champions may well be to imagine how their dog would react if placed in the artificial environment of the show. Most, it is to be hoped, would rebel. Spirited cross-bred mongrels can usually be depended upon to riot and to conduct themselves like real dogs.

Aside from the strangeness of it all, and the unhappiness of the dogs, the most glaringly obvious fact to me was the lack of enjoyment apparent among the owners. Of the many qualities dogs bring to human life, pleasure is the most obvious and none of this was in evidence at Cruft's. I left the show content, confident that I was not only lucky with my ordinary dogs, but truly privileged. Perhaps I was also a bit relieved that Bilbo was not a German Shepherd. Owning a pedigree animal can involve an obsessive quest for perfection, which is ironic as the very thing that makes a dog, all dogs, unique, is that indefinable quality – personality.

12

The Runaway

Running along the towpath in the early morning mist was pleasant, although not without its occasional hazards, such as once running smack into an eights crew carrying out their boat from one of the larger boathouses. The rowers had reacted good-naturedly and thanked me as they realised that they too might collide with something unexpected on the river; they decided to wait until the dense fog had dispersed. I ran on. At times like this I felt that it was not so bad living in a city, the river creating a sense of freedom, albeit a false one. On other days the mist was more like a lazy haze. In the boathouses the fours and the eights radiated genuine camaraderie and team spirit, while the scullers, particularly the single sculls, appeared intense, introverted, more like the track and field athletes I knew. The individual scullers didn't waste energy on small talk. On weekend mornings the river was busy; more runners, appeared, as well as more people exercising dogs and there were many trainers and coaches holding stopwatches and shouting orders to the crews.

Two crews began to dominate the scene; the same faces became familiar as they arrived with their respective support staffs, their numbers increasing over the weeks. They were preparing for an event. The women were also noticeable, probably aspiring girlfriends, as no doubt the more established partners would have worked out that they didn't have to spend hours watching training sessions.

Among the tall, well-built rowers were smaller people to whom the crews deferred. These waif-like creatures were the all-powerful coxes. It dawned on me that these teams were the university crews preparing for the annual Boat Race. Life down by the river had become very interesting. The clash between the Blues, dark blue for Oxford, light blue for Cambridge, was about more than sport: honour and tradition were at stake. Since 1845 the course had been fixed from Putney Bridge to Mortlake, a distance of 4 miles and 387 yards. Only two World Wars and the occasional sinking of one or both of the boats had disrupted the race. A carnival mood was building in the background. For the rowers it would be tough – the course was marginally shorter than that of the Grand National – but the spectators would make a day of it. Some brewers had donated free beer.

On race day, the last Saturday in March, it was cold but bright and dry, and most importantly, it was still. Bunting had been strung across the bridge. Fast-food merchants with barrow stalls had appeared from nowhere and a band was playing the 1812 Overture and the theme from *Chariots of Fire*. A stout man wearing a Union Jack hat marched up and down, selling flags, and randomly declaring that everyone was barmy. I smiled at the word barmy: it was new to me then. I had been out early, walking the dogs without a person in sight, but now the scene was crowded. The BBC sports vans were parked in a group and cameras were carefully positioned. A man in a sporty suede jacket was holding a microphone and speaking to camera. The crews boarded to loud cheers, their respective boats shifting as each oarsman took his place. The river was calm, a powerful muscle ready to upend the boats if its mood changed. Thousands of flashes captured the moment. A ritual of which I had long been conscious was about to take place before me, a shiver of shared excitement went through the crowd. The dogs seemed calm, if possibly wondering why we were standing still. I wondered, how was the race started, was it by pistol shot? Then just as I remembered that sound so distinct at regattas, the raucous hoot of the klaxon signalled the off. Frodo yelped, darting away as if stung by a bee. He had slipped his collar and disappeared into the crowd.

Instead of watching the race I had to rush off after him, holding his collar and leash in one hand, as Bilbo pulled along beside me, dodging spectators who were not expecting to be jostled by someone charging through them. I could hear voices saying, 'Steady on there' and 'Oy, watch where you're going.' I barged by, wondering how he could have disappeared so completely, so quickly and why? Even more baffling was how a small dog could move through what must have seemed to him to be a wall of legs. Here and there I ran up against small groups of tall men, probably rowers. There were bikes that got in my way as cyclists attempted to follow the race along the crowded towpath. I looked up towards the side roads for cars, wondering whether Frodo would step out in front of one or if anyone would just lift him up to safety. Worst of all was the fear, knowing his fondness for swimming, that he would wander into the river – the currents would be far too strong for him.

There were too many possibilities. I needed help in the search; it was a Saturday and there was a rugby match so I was on my own. I stopped a constable. His response was predictable if not very helpful. 'You should have a well-fitting collar. I'd have thought that was basic common sense,' he said in a lecturing tone, but he agreed to keep a lookout for him – 'a weather eye', as he put it. I thanked him and ran off into another aimless circle. I didn't know where to look and felt that all too familiar panic beginning to surge through me. I followed the crowd up the river in the wake of the race, well aware that Frodo was unlikely to be drawn to crowds.

I began to wonder whether my insistence on bringing them everywhere with me was more about my needs than about theirs. What had seemed like a simple outing had turned into a disaster. Was this the 'great grief' that the old woman had mentioned in a comment that had come to feel more like a warning? Frodo was missing and Bilbo was exhausted from being dragged through the dense masses of excited people. I turned and walked back down the towpath. I was tired and shocked that no one else knew about the terrible thing that had just happened, no one except an indifferent policeman. I knew there were several animal shelters in the area. I would have to contact them. But Frodo was an appealing animal: perhaps in the chaos someone had got hold of him, and he, simply happy to be free from the crowd, had gone with them. Maybe he had already begun his next adventure? Perhaps we had been just another interlude for him? I looked down at Bilbo, who was walking alongside me. For once there was no tugging. We were on our own again, just the two of us. His companion had gone and I knew that the relationship with the boyfriend was also coming to an end. The move to London meant I had far more work and even less time for humans.

The river was empty now. The Boat Race celebrations were happening elsewhere. I didn't even know which team had won. There were other dogs being walked on the towpath. They looked normal; a human with a pet, no crisis surrounding them. But there was no trace of Frodo. I went back up to the bridge, and then turned down towards the side roads, scanning both directions, willing him to appear, jogging back to us, ears flapping in the wind. But he didn't. It seemed better to take Bilbo home, give him some water, and then continue the search alone. At each of the houses, so close together, I looked into the small London front gardens while hoping that I wouldn't find him lying on the road. My hands were numb and my face was stiff with dread. I stopped looking into the eyes of the people I passed; it seemed pointless to ask them if they had seen my dog. The effort of slowing my speech and carefully explaining what had happened to each person I met on the way had tired me out. I was babbling. Frodo had been so loyal. I couldn't believe that he had run away. This was my failure, though, not his. He must have hated living in the confinement of a city. I did. I could hear the voices of people – mainly men – with the irritable woman upstairs, make out the words of her various arguments, hear her television, her shower, even the sound of her toilet flushing. All of this must have driven Frodo away. That, and our token garden, and outside, the roads, the streets, the cars, the ever-flowing flood of people, moving, talking, filling all the space. He always looked annoyed when I went to carry my bike in from the garden, through the kitchen, out into our small hall, through the main hall and finally out on to the front path. It meant I was going into the city and that he and Bilbo would be left at home. We had come to a place in which every time they barked my heart raced for fear of complaints, and where two cats, who belonged to that brittle femme fatale woman upstairs with her ever-changing posse of suitors, sat on a windowsill staring down on the guys in the garden below, unintentionally inciting them, particularly Frodo, into relentless protest barking. The atmosphere in the flat was often fraught, and at times the rooms, small as they were, appeared to contract even further. No wonder Frodo had left. He was a great dog, but he was pragmatic.

All the noise emanating from the antics upstairs, the late-night comings and goings, must have disturbed him more than I had ever imagined. I knew I was going to cry. The next gate would be that of our little prison. I opened it and there on the doorstep sat Frodo. He got up, stretched and came to greet us. Whatever it was that had caused him to run off, it had not been enough for him to leave us.

*

Never had I heard so many police sirens. City life was hectic; so much was on offer, a wealth of distractions: galleries, theatre, music, amazing bookstores, cinema from all over the world, the excitement of being able to cycle to Wimbledon to watch the tennis live instead of on television. There was an endless buzz of activity, enough to keep any mind racing. But the basic noise was inescapable, a hum of voices, cars, buses, machines and always the sirens. They made me think of air raids but I knew they were connected with accidents and crimes, car crashes and muggings. People always seem angrier in a city. The only place that ever became quiet was the river. Nothing could overpower the noise of the streets, though; the movement was unending until the day a huge red fire engine raced down Putney High Street and everyone seemed to stop and look at it as if it were a sign from God. I watched until it had disappeared from view and then turned and walked the dogs home. Not for the first time I thought of how dull their lives had become, dodging pedestrians and other pet owners, out with their equally confined dogs. Sometimes they appeared to be as subdued as I was. Work had imposed a regimented structure on our lives. It felt as though I spent every waking hour reading and writing, cycling between various offices, collecting books and manuscripts. Regardless of what had to be done, the dogs had to be walked; sometimes now it was only a quick march in the drizzle. They seemed to be in a constant state of waiting, watching while I worked.

As for my human relationship, that too had been affected, for when I was at home I was working. A trial separation had been suggested. After the agreed month had elapsed, I waited. He did not call. When I phoned the temporary number I had been given I was told he had left; 'moved on' was the actual phrase used. Eventually a letter arrived. It was over. I was now officially on my own. Being a grown-up was proving to be a serious business. In the evenings after cycling home across the city, I would walk the dogs, at times forsaking the pleasures of the river and the tree-lined stretches of tow path that criss-crossed small parks and playing fields, to peer into front gardens and beyond, catching glimpses of elaborate kitchens and the elegant period drawing rooms of west London. Some of the lives seemed lavish and often included the expensively dressed children I saw being pushed in fine prams and strollers by nannies and young au pairs with high-cheekboned faces.

Trains are associated with freedom. Between London and the various places we visited lay a vast temptation, the British countryside. The seven-hour journey to Edinburgh in particular was difficult for the dogs, but that was when I learned that a dog can, if helped, manage to balance over a toilet in a moving train. On that trip the landscape was constantly changing from suburban to industrial to the wasteland approaches near the cities, but here and there were glimpses of the English pastoral, with fields of cattle and sheep and the always beautiful sight of horses. Now and again the train passed what looked like racing stables, and sometimes we saw jumping yards. A couple of places looked more like riding schools, with groups awaiting their turn in a lesson. When the view from the window became unexpectedly ugly and depressed, I thought of Orwell's poignant glimpses of other people's lives, such as when he sees the haggard young woman hanging out her washing and wonders about the bleakness of her future, or if she even has one, in *On the Road to Wigan Pier*. A mature stag had suddenly appeared, framed by the window, apparently staring at the train, with several females and their young grazing behind him. It was a small herd. The scene lasted an instant. Then it fragmented as he turned and they all ran off.

*

Once I took the dogs with me to Cambridge and I photographed the college buildings, passing students who were unaware that they might some day appear as extras in pictures illustrating tradition and privilege in a book I was thinking of writing about England. There in a pub I sat eating soup and sandwiches, while the friendly landlord presented the dogs with a bowl of water and recalled that he used to mind foxhound pups for the local hunt. In the corner I noticed a thin blond man in an immaculate well-faded blue shirt that matched his calculating eyes. His face was gaunt and his gestures erratic and mannered; he was holding court and it was apparent from his attitude that he was accustomed to being the centre of attention. It was the writer Bruce Chatwin.

York had a robust appeal. The walled settlement had a powerful ambiance, a confidence in its rich history. The people were direct and I enjoyed hearing their voices. I asked for unnecessary directions simply to hear more of that rich, emphatic accent. Dogs were popular, and mine attracted friendly salutes. I felt more of a newcomer than just another tourist. We followed the ancient walls and photographed the gates. I spent hours photographing the exterior of York Minster; the dogs waited patiently as if aware that, because they were with me, I couldn't go in. A woman with elaborately styled grey hair approached us; she was accompanied by a younger woman, her daughter. They offered to hold the dogs while I looked inside. The older woman, born in York, had lived for years in Paris but had come home after her husband had died. The sun began to feel warmer and it was pleasant to stand there and listen as she told the story of the cathedral, the long years of building it, its central role in the history of York and the way the mighty minster had withstood the wartime bombing.

Eventually we went to a small cafe, and the woman, Elizabeth, had no difficulty in convincing the owner, a friend of hers, to allow the dogs to sit under the table as we ate. She said that she had always loved the freedom dogs enjoyed in Paris; she felt that there they were properly recognised as a vital part of human life. When she began to speak about a dog she had had for almost fifteen years while her children had been growing up, her daughter stopped her, reminding her that every time she mentioned that beloved dog, they all began crying. That interlude of comfort, sitting in that tea shop as I listened to a detailed account of the care that was taken when the splendid medieval stained glass windows of the minster were removed during the war and stored elsewhere, was an episode I have never forgotten. On the train back to London I realised I still had not made the pilgrimage to Castle Howard. It didn't matter; I felt I would return to Yorkshire.

A horse brought me to Cheltenham, its faded Georgian grandeur cheek by jowl with ramshackle modernity; Desert Orchid, the peoples' champion, was bidding to win the Gold Cup and his fans wanted to be there, and will him on. He was a hero, a courageous front-runner who always gave his best and he loved the crowds. But the mud was his major challenge. Compounding the heavy rain was an unexpected snowfall. In contrast to Desert Orchid's famous dislike of mud was the known affection for it held by a rival named Yahoo. The pre-race talk that day was all about Desert Orchid; it was as if he was going to run solo over the three-mile and two-and-a-half-furlong course. It had been preordained. The other horses were barely relevant. It was the first time I ever took the guys to a place where no one seemed to notice them – it was as if they were invisible. Only Desert Orchid mattered. We walked about the famous racecourse and stood eating damp sandwiches in the rain at the statue of the great Arkle, who had reigned supreme more than twenty years earlier, a decade before Desert Orchid had been foaled. Self-consciously I reached up and patted the statue, hoping Arkle would help Desert Orchid. Most of the onlookers felt the same.

The race began. Desert Orchid went straight into the lead, attacking each jump and rising first. The grey horse seemed to shine, standing out from a field of bays. But by the sixteenth of the twenty-two fences and ditches, the expected script began to change: Desert Orchid came under pressure. Suddenly he was third and looked vulnerable. Despairing disbelief overwhelmed the crowd; Ten Plus had taken the lead. Four from home Ten Plus looked the winner; Dessie was tired and the mud-loving Yahoo was in contention. The agony was palpable, some people turned – they could no longer watch – and I squeezed the dogs' leashes. The crowd surged at an angle, my view was clear to the track. Ten Plus crashed to the ground and there were impulsive cheers, unsporting, yet, such was the love for Desert Orchid, it seemed almost forgivable. At the home turn it was Desert Orchid and Yahoo. With a jump to go, Dessie was the first to clear it but it demanded huge effort. He looked exhausted. Yahoo surged ahead, and the crowd groaned as one. There was just the final long, uphill stretch. Yahoo appeared to be flying, Desert Orchid was surely beaten, but still the fabulous grey fought on. It was a torment to watch, but Desert Orchid battled and battled, and at last pulled away, hating every inch of the mud. Desert Orchid, showing incredible courage, had won the Gold Cup. The roars of delight rang in my ears. Strangers hugged each other. I stepped clear of the crowds for fear the dogs would be trodden on. They looked up at me. Bilbo and Frodo were the only calm creatures at Prestbury Park, watching the human joy erupt all around them as Desert Orchid, a son of Grey Mirage out of Flower Child, ran into history.

That afternoon the world, at least the bit of it that surrounded Cheltenham, was heaven. Everyone was smiling. In the winners' enclosure a tall man with lank black hair, wearing a long brown coat, hugged his horse and wept. His name was Richard Burridge. His family had bred Dessie; he was a half-owner and the look on his face went beyond love. Desert Orchid posed for the cameras. Not for the first time I was struck by the self-contained awareness animals convey when they know they have touched the demanding, difficult and capricious human heart.

13

The Treacherous Teardrop

I have a photograph of Bilbo in which he is posing for the camera and appears to be smiling. He looks young, alert, happy and unfettered. The background is blandly formal; it is a cultivated, neatly mowed setting, most definitely a London park, not a private garden. It seems to have been an overcast day, but conditions appear dry, with a hint of haze. A close look will confirm that a leash is clipped to his collar. The longer we stayed in the city, the more I came to resent the leads. It seemed that everywhere that we went there were other people, all trying to snatch some space for their dogs on whatever available patch of grass could be found. The humans surged on, pushing their way through crowded streets, their dogs slightly ahead of them, aware that this was their exercise time, the brief interlude set aside for them in a busy day. Most of those city dogs seemed content with their lot: they had probably not had much, if any, experience of running loose. They had never known the excitement of careering about in wide, dizzy loops. Dogs adapt. My dogs hauled me along. At times their straining shoulders and bobbing heads made me smile; anyone watching must have thought we were training for an attempt at a speed endurance record. At night we walked at a more sedate pace, they browsed, sniffing at hedges and garden gates, marking territory while at times the sound of muffled barking could be heard coming from inside some of the houses. No challenge was ever mounted; very few dogs frequented the small front gardens of south London homes.

Each time I set off on my bike to deliver copy and collect books and manuscripts they both sighed. Bilbo developed a rather disturbing habit of lying down and stretching his front legs out towards me in a pleading gesture, his eyes bereft. Frodo would drop his head as if I had announced I was abandoning them. Yet when I was home and working they would lie down together and wait for me to move. The patience of a dog is a wonder – it is calm and serene. They wait because it is their way of giving support and comfort; it is also central to being part of their human's life.

Cycling down the mall and beneath the cool shade of Admiralty Arch on spring and summer mornings soon became a pleasant routine; I was enjoying being a commuter, if only one of the lucky ones, on a bike, gliding past the traffic jams. I preferred observing city life, though, and realised that I didn't want to enter it fully. Every time I went horse-back riding at a stables in Hyde Park, I felt slightly guilty, only too aware that my dogs were at home, waiting. Britain had beautiful countryside but we were not experiencing it. One evening on the Tube I noticed a poster fixed to the wall of the packed carriage, the Cornish coast. As the groaning train rocked and lurched along the tracks sounding as if it were ready to grind to a halt between stations, Cornwall's cliffs seemed to undulate with the labouring movement of the train. I thought of Du Maurier, of smugglers and wrecking crews and pirate coves, of the luminous images of the paintings of the St Ives School and of the robustly sensuous pottery crafted by Bernard Leach and his followers. I was in my usual position on the Tube train, crouching down with the dogs, my arms around them. I held them and we all swayed grimly with the motion. I knew Cornwall was in the extreme south-west, as far from London as Edinburgh, and was wondering how I could spare the time to explore the county in which the distinctive red campion flowers all year round. I wanted to draw them. While I was fantasising about a visit I looked at Frodo and noticed a piece of dirt stuck to his chest and went to brush it away with the side of my hand. But it didn't move. It was a hard little nub. I pulled it and realised it was fixed, and fleshy; it looked like a tiny pink raisin, barely visible through his fur. I wondered how long it had been there. It made me uneasy. But he seemed well and had not reacted when I touched it.

Later that evening I took him to the local vet, the one who had informed me that Bilbo was most definitely a German Shepherd crossed with 'rather more than collie'. He looked at Frodo and studied the growth, dismissing it as a harmless polyp. Dogs get these things, he said, 'As do humans; I shouldn't fret. They can be unsightly but usually fall off.' It had probably been there for a while, he decided, and told me that it was nothing to worry about.

It began to resemble a flattened wart. I waited for it to drop off. But it grew, developing a thin stem like a miniature umbilical cord. This stem became longer and the growth changed shape, elongating into a teardrop, trembling at the end of the stalk. The pink, fleshy quality had gone; it had become purple and red. I couldn't take my eyes off it. Frodo seemed fine but the nub was thriving and people had begun to comment on it. 'Have you not noticed?' I was asked, as if I alone could not see it. In time the texture coarsened, it became tougher. A cell-like pattern developed. The thing looked alive. I saw it as a parasite, feeding off Frodo. He seemed unaffected; I went to another vet who admitted it was odd and possibly viral in origin. He asked had we been in contact with strange plants. He was reluctant to touch it and advised keeping an eye on it. My fears deepened.

The stem grew longer and was less transparent; I imagined blood coursing through it. The rapid changes were disturbing. Now that it dangled freely there was a chance it could catch on something and tear. What if it bled? I returned to the first vet who now seemed alarmed. He commented on how ugly it had become but stressed the dangers of removing it. Tapping at it with his finger he remarked on the dramatic difference in its shape and appearance and said he would have to revise his initial comments. 'Meaning what?' I asked. He remained calm and said that he now considered it dangerous but that even attempting a biopsy could have serious results. He pointed out that it seemed to be attached to the blood supply and was feeding from it. I had already noticed this and again suggested removing it. He considered my question and explained that such a procedure could cause the dog to go into toxic shock and bleed to death. The consultation ended quickly. He again advised me to wait. Removing the growth would merely speed up whatever was happening. 'He's not in pain,' the vet concluded. 'Come back to me when he needs me.'

*

That was the problem. He was not in pain and he was very well, utterly oblivious to 'the thing'. He pulled on his leash and we hurried home to Bilbo, who sniffed the air delicately before moving in closer to Frodo for an intense examination. Although no medication had been administered to him, that distinct scent of vet's surgery clung to him. Bilbo sniffed Frodo's front paws and moved his nose slowly up both front legs. He then smelt his head, the back of his neck. Frodo did not react and instead sat as if he had expected this minute scrutiny. Dogs understand the tactile in ways that humans can't. Bilbo's extensive sniffing reassured his curiosity but it also seemed to comfort Frodo. I was less easy to assuage, my gaze drawn to the rogue appendage.

His coat shone, his eyes were bright. Frodo's appetite was the same, as was his happy, self-contained attitude to life. I began to avoid places with hedges or flower beds with gorse or anything with thorns. Even a rose bush was now suspect; if the polyp or its stem were caught or torn he might bleed uncontrollably. I watched it as it swung like a fleshy pendulum. The growth itself had retained something of its teardrop shape but the stem seemed weakened and stretched by its weight. By now when he walked it almost brushed the ground. Although it seemed safer in the open spaces by the river, the surface of the towpath was gritty. The risk of infection was increasing. There was also the possibility that he could snap the stem in the simple act of making himself comfortable on one of the beanbags. He could bleed in his sleep. The old woman's words about the grief that was destined for me played in my mind. It was as if nature itself had betrayed him, and a thing with a life of its own was invading his body.

*

My life had become unsettled in a different way. In the village in Kent I had lived in a state of panic, fearing that I would never secure work, either as a book reviewer or as an editor. But now I had made some progress, and I was reading manuscripts for various publishers who had received them unsolicited from aspiring authors desperate to be published. All the work, particularly the endless reading of novels and short stories, as well as regular reviewing, had earned enough money for me to slow down and spend more time at the flat. It became possible to walk two or three times a day down by the river. Then two things happened. The first was predictable enough: it was time to sell the flat. I had stayed on my own but the now former boyfriend judged at this moment, correctly, that it was a valuable investment, so he offered to buy me out. That didn't bother me. I had always known the dogs and I would have to move again. But the second occurrence was unexpected and proved to be a catalyst for yet more change.

It was a Sunday evening, cool and dry, near suppertime, and it was quiet down by the river. Both dogs were on their leads, with not another person or dog in sight. It had been weeks since they had been free to run. I looked around again, and realised that I was actually feeling as though I was defying some taboo. Had life become so restricted and regimented that the simple act of removing a leash from a dog's collar could seem subversive? City living, even so close to the great river, was becoming increasing repressive. Now the chance to run free was impossible to resist. There was an open stretch before us of about 300, possibly 400, metres, long enough for them to stretch themselves. There was a bright yellow 'Boats Crossing' sign. I rolled the leashes together and placed them down on the verge. We ran on; it was like the old days, the beginning that had started to seem far more idyllic than it probably had been. Daylight was fading. There was a burst of movement: two cyclists darted into view as if from nowhere. The leader stood up on the pedals and pulled away from the second rider. It looked as if he was cycling directly at Bilbo: he can't be, I reasoned, and yet he was. He crashed solidly and squarely right into Bilbo, causing him to yelp in pain. I remember the youth's white face and the smell of his sweat. He shrieked and then shouted, 'Fucking hell, fucking hell,' while Bilbo whimpered. The teenager kept going, his momentum appearing to carry him on against his will. Somehow Bilbo was caught under the bike behind the front wheel and the pedals. After about ten metres or so the bike pitched over and the boy fell off, but Bilbo was still trapped, blood shooting up out of his mouth, splattering the cyclist and me when I reached him. The second biker came up behind us, shouting, 'You plonker! You've killed the fucking dog!' He looked horrified and then began laughing hysterically. Bilbo's eyes were wild with pain, his teeth were bared and I thought he would bite me as I tried to pull him free. I stared at the youth and I remember asking him why on earth he had deliberately cycled over my dog. Hot tears splashed down my face and into my mouth. My eyes stung. I grabbed Frodo by the neck and held him between my shins. The thought that the boys might hit me never entered my mind. I needed to protect my dogs. The first boy was shivering – he had blood on his face. All it had taken was a few seconds for normality to explode into chaos. The boys were shouting at each other oblivious of me. The front wheel of the bike was buckled; it was new, an expensive sports bike, the kind I would have liked to own. I heard the boy gagging, he was saying it wasn't his fault, he hadn't meant to hurt my dog. 'I just wanted to scare you a bit,' he said. I went to lift Bilbo; his mouth was full of blood and his front leg had a deep cut. Beneath all the gravel and dirt and blood, the white of bone was visible. He would need stitches. The youth had calmed down and asked me for money to fix his bike. I told him to drop dead. My anger seemed to surprise him, and both youths immediately backed off.

Every step along the towpath Bilbo became heavier. My heart was pounding and the air was becoming damp. Frodo trotted beside me. He stopped and honked once, when we passed the spot where I had left the leashes. I had forgotten that I had dropped them. But I couldn't bend down for them. Bilbo was much quieter, a dead weight. I urged Frodo to follow me but I nodded towards the leashes, letting him know that I knew they were there.

*

Bilbo needed six stitches in his leg but most of the blood had come from his mouth, as he had bitten his tongue when the bike hit him. I watched as the vet shaved a large patch of fur off the area around the gash. He listened to my story and then mentioned that only the previous evening a man had been stabbed to death on the towpath. His body had been found by a couple out walking their dog. The world was changing, reflected the vet with a sigh as he gave me painkillers for Bilbo. I had become used to his world-weary comments, but that night he seemed more disappointed than usual in mankind. I knew he was from Malvern, as he had told me that once before. I remember saying yes, that's Elgar country, and the vet telling me that his father had known Elgar, not very well, but that he had a story or two about nights he had spent with the composer in the local pub. He said he had been a good singer and knew a lot of folk songs, but I didn't know if he meant his father or Elgar. The vet intended to move back to Worcester 'in time, all in good time'. He looked at Frodo and remarked that he still had his badge of honour. At first I didn't know what he meant, than I realised that he was referring to the polyp. It was the first time in weeks I had forgotten it.

I carried Bilbo back to the flat. His injured leg was bound

in a clean white bandage. Frodo tugged on my arm, on the leash the vet had lent me. After I got them home, I planned on running down to the river to collect our leads. But it was very dark and I decided to wait until morning. The garden gate was wide open, as was the front door, and the woman from upstairs was busily carrying in a number of cases and parcels, including a large crate of wine. A cab was pulling away. She looked at Bilbo's leg and casually mentioned that one of her cats had been killed on the road. It was the longest conversation I ever had with her. She had a deep voice, carefully modulated. 'Pets are such a nuisance in the city, I find,' she said, and mentioned something about giving 'the survivor', the other cat, to an aunt in Sussex.

Bilbo lay in the bed beside me, and Frodo curled up with us; I pulled the blankets up and listened to the sound of the television overhead. My neighbour stomped about. She sounded enormous, although I had noticed how small she was, like one of those thin girls who despise sport and seem to live on black coffee and wine. I lay in the dark, listening to her footsteps, the doors banging, the three-beat rhythm of her toilet flushing and I was glad that I had to leave. I was sick of noise and confined spaces and wanted more than anything to be in the countryside, but I needed to be near the publishing companies and the literary editors who gave me work. Bilbo whimpered in his sleep.

An alarm clock bleeped into life. It was not mine – I didn't own one. I could hear the radio news being read in a solemn BBC voice. Correct English received pronunciation filtered through the ceiling above me. The life of the woman upstairs was seeping into mine. It might have been doing so ever since I moved in but now I had begun to notice – and resent – it. Admittedly the smart wooden wine crate that she had left outside for the bin men was now on the floor of my kitchen by the table I worked at. I had retrieved it, and was using it as a shelf for some hefty dictionaries. It looked quite professional. But I was aware that it had belonged to her life of impromptu late-night parties that often ended in rows and shouting that started the dogs barking. The only reason I knew her name was that I had heard a man's angry voice declaring, 'It's my car, Amanda, and I'm having it back.'

Then one day the chance of a job on a national newspaper materialised. It meant returning to Ireland, and to Dublin, a city I didn't know all that well and with which I had no emotional connection. Back then, as now, the only cities I was powerfully drawn to were Vienna, Prague, Budapest, Warsaw and, in particular, Berlin and St Petersburg. But Dublin seemed a useful short-term solution. Any place I went, the dogs were coming too. For more than a week I spent entire days and most of the evenings on the phone, in lengthy telephone calls to prospective landlords, giving detailed descriptions of how well behaved my dogs were: how meticulously house-trained they were, how fastidious, how little hair they shed. I presented myself as an asthmatic who never sneezed, so clean, dust-free and flealess were my dogs. Each call ended with the respective landlord obviously impressed, at times, even moved, saying the same thing either sympathetically or more firmly – sorry, no pets allowed.

Finally I found a willing landlord. The woman said she quite liked dogs, at a distance. The flat was spacious and sunny, split-level, with a separate entrance and a garden. She dismissed the offer of references. It sounded good.

Packing didn't take long. The only things I wanted were my books, my music, the pots and pans, some framed exhibition posters, my bike and assorted beanbags. Again I watched, as the bike was loaded last. I wondered what had happened to the kayak. Then I remembered that it had been left behind by accident at the cottage in Kent. When I went back for it, it was gone, stolen. Humans always have too many things. Each time we move off, something is left behind.

My feelings about London were mixed. It was exciting but it was not a good place for dogs, although dogs were certainly popular in the city. It was too busy, there were too many people and too many cars. But places I had read about all my life had become real, from Hawksmoor's churches to the great galleries, museums and libraries. It was impossible to avoid the landmarks, buildings and statues, theatres and parks, and even streets, that had featured in my life, my imagination. Everywhere I looked there were blue plaques acknowledging the ghostly presence of Conrad, or Woolf, or Handel or Dickens, always Dickens. Highgate Cemetery and Westminster Abbey were filled with those that had defied death and whose names alone could spark off a sequence of stories. I had acquired a middling grasp of the Underground system and a sense of the city's geography, as well as a genuine liking for London, but I didn't like it enough to want to settle there.

*

Euston station was busy and far more appealing than any airport; the atmosphere was less fraught. The concourse was thronged by people scanning the electronic screens for information about their trains. The smell of coffee from the various stalls and cafes competed with the fumes from the waiting trains. Engines were running. Who would possibly prefer to fly if a train journey were an option? I imagined what it would be like to be setting off on the Orient Express to investigate eastern Europe and beyond, or beginning one of those long-distance rides across the United States or Canada that travel writers are always embarking on.

But my journey that day would be far less glamorous: a few hours in a train to Holyhead to catch a ferry. It was a journey that generations of Irish emigrants had undertaken. But I was not returning home, I wasn't an emigrant, just an exile from a relationship that had never developed into an enduring passion or even a romance. And now I had lost that person, who had been a much loved friend.

A woman with a small boy smiled at me: the child reached out with both hands to pet Bilbo and called him 'Big Dog'. They had no bags and were shabbily dressed. I wondered where they were headed. What was their story? Were they looking for something or someone or were they simply returning to the English or Welsh village in which they had a normal life? I soon lost sight of them. The platforms were crowded and, as always, the more anxious passengers were seen to be double-checking and triple-checking, asking every rail guard if they were on the right train. I went to board. I carried two bags and an electric typewriter. It was the only one I could use and I had become dependent on it.

People rushed past us. Backpackers jogged by. They appeared to be headless shapes on legs as the piles of gear on their backs were so high. Frodo walked beside me, eyes squinting tight with concentration. I thought how brave he looked, how he trusted me, the person with whom he had joined. A couple of strides ahead of us was Bilbo who glanced back, checking that we were following him. He had slipped his collar and leash, they were dangling empty from my hand. He looked purposeful and intent, leading the way. It seemed as if he knew where he was going – which was reassuring, because I didn't.

Part 3

14

Finding a Garden

My ambivalence about leaving England continued to bother me. I turned on the radio just as a recording of *The Lark Ascending* was playing. It was not that I had fallen in love with Britain, but the experience had left me with a sense of unfinished business. Somewhere in the English countryside, or more probably in Wales or Scotland, was the ideal home for me and the dogs. Instead, the promise of a job had brought me to back to a country in which I had never felt fully at ease and always an outsider. One of my father's more attractive dreams had brought my family to Ireland. He was scouting for a stud ranch and had met an Irishman at the races who was planned to settle in California, and so just happened to have a large cattle farm on the market. My family came over to see Ireland while dad returned to the US. His death there left my mother having to salvage the mess. Now circumstances were again dictating events, as just when I should have been making for Kiev or Berlin or Montana, I found myself heading to a newsroom in Dublin. The Irish appear to settle well anywhere, but most Americans confine their wanderings within North America, with occasional trips to Europe, invariably Paris – or so I believed, influenced as I was by reading US fiction and various biographies about the unhappy lives of American writers. No matter how often I reasoned that our stay in Dublin was merely a temporary detour in my master plan of finding an idyllic rural setting, and a future with children, several horses and all the space the dogs needed, our immediate world had contracted still further. We were living now on the top floor of an old house in Ranelagh, a village-like enclave well populated by academics and journalists. There was not even the consolation of a river nearby. The streets were indeed narrow. Within an hour of arriving at our new temporary accommodation, my bike was stolen in the time it took me to carry a box up the stairs. I noticed the removal men looking around, comparing the new house with the one I had left in London. The cheerful Londoners who brought my things all the way to Dublin seemed genuinely sympathetic. One of them remarked, 'You've come down in the world, luv.' I shrugged and pretended to be relaxed, hoping to convey an air of knowing confidence. 'It's only short-term; I'm here to do a job.'

Meanwhile the dogs were running around upstairs. I discovered with some trepidation that the flat was carpeted throughout. And the carpet was white. The kitchen had pink lino flooring, an aesthetic horror in normal circumstances but useful given our situation. I could see that we might have to live in the kitchen to protect the carpet. As for the garden, it was small and dense with vegetation, but we had no access to it. Yet the dogs looked at me with total trust. Bilbo's face wore that expression of polite concern as if he could read my thoughts, but Frodo appeared to be at ease with his new surroundings. He could adapt and he already had.

I had not expected the electric stove to be quite so old. I opened the oven and a foul odour escaped as if it had been waiting for some unsuspecting person. I closed the scuffed glass door and surveyed the kitchen. All it had to offer was a huge south-facing window. It was a sunny day, so I opened the window and looked out at my new view, a street scene.

The sill was made of granite and was wide, a good place to grow tomatoes. The sash looked worn and needed to be supported. Standing against the wall was a sturdy length of wood that looked as if it had been used to prop up the window. It fitted into place. I left the window open. There was a noticeable dip in the floor and it groaned underfoot. A few boxes were still in the hall. I decided to visit the local shop, a small supermarket with gourmet aspirations. I picked up the bike lock and then remembered that the bike was no more.

The shop stocked 'traditional' chocolate cake. I walked back down the street, not quite euphoric but anticipating the cake and pleased with the fresh cooked chicken I had bought for the dogs. It meant that I didn't have to start cleaning the fetid oven right away. Along the street I could detect the rich grass smell of mown lawns and a powerful scent of geranium coming from the planter boxes in the house next door. It would be a good idea to get a window box for the kitchen, I told myself, and, as I glanced up, I saw that Frodo was standing on the wide windowsill. If he jumped, the fall, never mind the impact of landing, would kill him. He saw me and began wagging his tail. The movement might cost him his balance. Would he try jumping into my arms? I knew his weight – about twenty-two pounds – would be increased by the speed of falling. 'Stay, stay,' I commanded, hoping he would not look down as I opened the front door and rushed up the stairs, two, three, at a time and flung open the door of our flat. I was shaking and fell over Bilbo, who had trotted over to greet me. Then I heard a thud in the kitchen and the sound of Frodo padding across the sagging floor. His nails tapped the lino. He pushed his paw around the kitchen door, which I had closed before going out, not realising he could open it. His coat felt hot from the sun. I held him so tightly he gasped. Climbing out on a window ledge some thirty feet above the road was the kind of madness I expected from the intelligent but absent-minded Bilbo, whose curiosity had often led him into danger. But Frodo was practical, streetwise and sensible. He had no intention of making a dash to freedom, but had been drawn to the heat of the natural suntrap. There was an old key in the kitchen door and I knew in future I would have to use it. I looked at Frodo and realised I had left the cake and the other shopping outside the downstairs door. He was unperturbed. As I went to fetch the chicken I noticed that there was something different about Frodo. His menacing teardrop, the growth that had changed shape and texture so many times and had swung from its ever-lengthening stem, was gone. It had vanished without a mark or even a trace of blood.

*

Never before had I noticed how much hair the dogs shed. Nor had I noticed how wet their paws could get in the rain. I had always dried them when they came in from a run in wet conditions, but we had never had to contend with white carpets before. The landlady was friendly but even her simple comment, 'You'd never know there are dogs here; they're so clean, there's just that doggy whiff about the place now,' was enough to have me fretfully spraying odour eliminators and opening windows. Before long I had a vast collection of sheets and towels – the girl at the laundrette asked if I worked at a guest house. It was impossible to relax. Every time the dogs drank water within minutes I was on my feet, leashes at the ready. They were tired from several walks a day.

One night I returned later than usual from the newspaper office to find the dogs sitting side by side on the bed. They were subdued, probably dreading that I would drag them out for yet another walk. I didn't feel like walking, having trudged back from work. The replacement bike I had bought had also been stolen. I had locked it to railings near the Abbey Theatre but the lock had been stolen along with the bike. Bilbo shifted slightly. That was when I noticed the mouse that had been sitting between them. The mouse stayed very still. As I slowly put my hand down to lift it, it scurried across the bed and disappeared. The dogs were quiet. The duvet was smooth with no sign of a chase or even of gentle play. The mouse must have sensed that these dogs were preoccupied and in no mood for games. It must have felt very safe. That was when I realised they were as depressed as I was.

On another evening as I walked them after a day spent at home reading, they seemed more like themselves and resumed their sled-dog antics, pulling me along in their wake. A police car pulled up beside me and asked me to stop. I wondered was it against some arcane Irish bye-law to be walking dogs in this part of Dublin as I had not seen any others, although there seemed to be any number of pampered cats slinking over walls. Had I noticed any suspicious persons, asked the policeman very formally, specifically a youth wearing a duffel coat and walking two dogs. Apparently there had been several reports of this individual and his canine accomplices, often very late at night, looking into gardens and through windows; the person had been observed stopping outside houses and was believed to be planning robberies. The policeman warned me to be careful.

We were really feeling the lack of a garden, and were getting used to spending our time in the kitchen with its drab pink lino in deference to the appalling white carpet, which remained clean. Then, by way of a reprieve, friends invited me to their cottage in Donegal. It sounded promising. We walked into the city to Busáras, the central bus station. All was fine until I went to board and the bus driver said, 'No dogs.' I explained that I had phoned the bus company and that these dogs were going back home to their owners who had been in Africa for two years. The human interest angle worked: my lies were acquiring plausibility. The driver became complicit, waving me to the back of the bus. 'And stay there,' he said. We did. It was a long journey. After a couple of hours there was a short break in Longford, I hurried up the aisle, Frodo in my arms and Bilbo in front of me, walking with that sense of purpose that suggested he really needed to go to the bathroom. Exclamations of surprise followed us; several people commented that the dogs had been so quiet they hadn't known that they were on the bus. We went down a side street and stopped behind a parked van. Both dogs sighed contentedly as they relieved themselves.

Back on the bus a couple were speaking with the bus man. The woman looked furious. The man at her side stood with his hands in his pockets, assuming indifference. As I got closer the driver was shaking his head and telling the woman that we were involved in a mercy mission and that he couldn't just abandon us. The woman turned and glared at me, accusing me of placing the health of all the passengers at risk by making them travel with filthy animals. She was agitated and accused me of being selfish. Conscious that the bus man was on my side, I assured her they were very clean, so clean that they slept in my bed. That really revolted her. The bus man was enjoying the dispute and advised the woman to wait for another bus. He told her that the dogs had been passed for travel at head office. I almost believed him as he reiterated my story: he began to elaborate about the poor people from Africa who were waiting for their pets and pointed out that none of the other passengers had objected. I was impressed with his defence: I had obviously convinced him, and the dogs had really been very quiet. He smiled at us and made a point of patting Bilbo's head. 'Nice girl, she's a great dog,' he said to him as I passed. It would have been ungrateful to correct him.

After the triumph of the bus journey, arrival at the house in Donegal was disappointing. Most of the guests were smoking pot, an alien activity to my nerd-like self which even now coughs within a mile of a cigarette. My host smiled pleasantly as he suggested, firmly, that the dogs be locked in the shed in which he kept a vintage car that he was intending, some day, to restore. Two, possibly, three minutes passed before the outraged honks started to attract attention. I realised that unless I slept in the shed with the dogs no one else would get any sleep. It was dark out there and the old car was only a shell; its seats were missing. We huddled down on an oily tarpaulin that looked as if it had once been used to cover a boat. It was a long night and the damp smell in the dusty old shack made me soon regret having talked our way on to the bus. Travelling with the dogs in Ireland was far more difficult than it had been in England, but then the English love dogs. Most of the conversations I had had with strangers during my period in Britain had begun because people made some remark about the guys. Not for the first time, I considered learning how to drive. But as my Californian childhood had been dominated by epic car journeys, including a two-hour commute over the mountains to school, I recoiled at the idea of it.

Even more important than a car, though, was a garden, preferably with a house attached to it. On the bookcase in the little sitting room of the flat was a postcard, propped up against the spines of hardback novels. It was a detail from a painting, *An Officer Dictating a Letter* by Gerard Ter Borch, which hangs in the National Gallery in London. But the postcard did not include the officer. Instead it had zoomed in on a dejected-looking spaniel, lying in the foreground in front of the table on which the letter rests. More and more, my dogs were beginning to resemble this unhappy seventeenth-century dog. They too were waiting for action, for freedom. I needed a house. One day a For Sale sign was being fixed to the railings of a modest terraced cottage near my flat. It had a garden. Swift action was required. It was run-down, cheap and ideal – at least for the moment. The bank acknowledged that I had a salary, but there was also the question of a deposit. It had to be found. In the absence of wealthy friends, I knew of only one way to acquire money legally – a day at the races.

As a child I had been to most of the major racetracks on the west coast, including Santa Anita, Hollywood Park and Del Mar. At Hollywood Park, an afternoon's card always began with the token pageantry of a man in a red hunting jacket trotting a horse down the track. I remembered the crowds in the stands, shaded from the hard bright sun and the eerie silence of the off, followed by shouts and cries of encouragement. I liked the smell of the stable areas, it was one I knew, that of horses. Most of all I remembered the frenzy of the punters, their desperation. The looks on faces engaged in silent prayer before the race, the hope. Then after the race, the same faces, defeated, sometimes angry, the ritual disgust as tickets were torn up and tossed to the ground. All that horse racing had ever meant to me was the courage of the horses and my feeling that the winning horses seemed to know they had done well, while the horses that had lost also understood what had happened to them. Failure seemed to make them look more tired, blow that bit harder. The losers always took longer to recover. But the winners stood tall, enjoying the attention. Their ears pricked towards the cameras.

The Curragh of Kildare, a great wide about thirty miles outside Dublin, was the obvious place to try my luck. The racetrack is surrounded by horse country, with an intense concentration of training yards. On the Curragh racing talk tends to overrule discussions about the weather. But it was too far to cycle. Leopardstown racecourse in the south Dublin suburbs was closer and there was the slight consolation of distant views of the Wicklow mountains. It was a stylish place, and had been modelled on Sandown Park in Surrey. Yet I felt shifty and mean-minded as I watched my chosen horses with calculating eyes and tried to justify my plan on the basis of urgent need. My dogs were suffering and I was asking other animals – race horses, professional athletes – to help.

Frodo had developed an allergy. In the course of one night he had stripped his hip of all its fur by tearing at his skin. The vet said he had been lucky: in some cases a dog could destroy most of his coat in a few hours. He had gone through a checklist of possibilities. Finally the cause was narrowed down to anxiety or, more likely, to the furnishings. The wool carpeting may have been cleaned with a harsh detergent. Or perhaps it harboured dust mites? It was a dense pile, and these dogs were used to wooden floors. Once again, Frodo left a vet's surgery wearing a plastic cone around his neck. The hair grew back but no dogs could be expected to endure such confinement for much longer. They had started out with me in a house with a garden and now were living in a few rooms and waiting to be taken on walks through a closely monitored residential area in which late-night dog walking attracted the attention of paranoid householders and the police. I needed to back some long-shot winners.

Many of the younger women at the races were well dressed, over-dressed, as if they had planned on attending a cocktail party but had lost their way. The men looked more serious. I too was on a mission. There wasn't time to study the race card and analyse the breeding and race histories of the horses. Instead I would rely on instinct and examine the competitors. Which of these horses wanted to win? Which ones had that unmistakable fire in their eyes? There is also something about the way a horse moves in the parade ring, a tension across the shoulders, an anticipation that says far more than words – it conveys intent. I made shrewd use of that pre-race parade, that's where it is sometimes possible to spot a winner. And it worked for me that day. By the end of the fifth race, I had won slightly more than I needed and I left. The lending officer at the bank would now take me seriously.

The estate agent, keen at the scent of a quick sale, came back with a further price reduction. The surveys had already discouraged previous potential buyers. Behind the plasterboard battened to the walls downstairs, the stone was wet. The dampness could be treated, though never with complete success, as a small underground river ran beneath the foundations of the house. I realised that only after the sale had been closed and I had received the deeds. But I hardly cared; the dogs would have a garden while I saved enough money to flee Dublin.

A previous owner had radically altered the upstairs rooms, creating an open-plan loft-like area with a kitchen, opening on to a crudely built veranda with shaky wooden steps leading down to the garden level. Downstairs the larger of the two bedrooms gave on to a patio and an unexpectedly large garden with an old potting shed. I had in fact bought a garden with a house attached to it. A small lane led up to the rear entrance into the garden, which would be useful for bringing in my new bike, my third since I had arrived in Dublin. It would also provide easy access for topsoil and plants I would need to create an adventure playground for the dogs. They had earned it. Even before the sale was complete, I bought some young trees and began gathering materials for the transformation of the garden.

My friends laughed at me for buying a house for my dogs. But I didn't care. The garden plan, complete with an undulating path running through it, had an element of mystery. For the first time in years Bilbo and Frodo ran about like puppies, playing in the topsoil, knocking over plants and seed trays. For once I wasn't scanning the horizon for cars, humans, other dogs, cyclists. I left some of the older plants that had survived in the wilderness condition of the existing garden.

Bilbo had a scab on his back that I assumed was from one of the thorny old roses. The wound developed into a nasty-looking lump. The vet explained that a sebaceous gland or hair follicle had become blocked, probably from all the soil

Bilbo had been playing in. The days had been hot; dirt and grease had caused the duct to become infected.

Of the many gardens I had worked on until then, this was by far the most enjoyable. The dogs loved it. But as always there was an unwelcome element of human intervention. The next-door neighbour was an elderly man who favoured two pairs of bifocal spectacles – one pair in the usual place, the other set on his head. They made his eyes appear enormous. He seemed deaf and could never hear what I was saying. Yet his hearing was sufficiently acute for him to complain, relentlessly, about the dogs barking.

After the third or fourth complaint he had threatened me with the police, informing me that the law laid down that dogs were not allowed to bark after six in the evening – what he was suggesting sounded like an unenforceable curfew on animal behaviour. Even so, as I closed the door I felt very sorry for myself. Frodo, it was true, had a particularly loud honk. That night I woke from a deep sleep. The dogs were jumping up and down on the bed, barking and growling, pulling at my pyjamas. I heard the thud of running steps followed by a crash of shattering glass and I ran out on to the patio just as figures were disappearing over the wall at the back of my garden. The frame with the now trampled tomato plants had been smashed. My name was being called. I walked over to the wall and hoisted myself up on it. My neighbour was standing there, thanking me, praising my dogs for saving him and his wife from a break-in. I was so relieved that he no longer minded the barking that I smiled back and said I was glad to help and slid slowly down the wall. The convenient back lane was also a useful access route, it now appeared, for burglars.

The next day, the guys barked again, this time far

less frantically. I opened the front door and my elderly neighbours stood there. I hadn't heard their knock. They had bought me a tree for the garden and the old lady held a blue pot. She had cooked what she called a 'thank you' chicken for the dogs. From then on she often gave us scraps of steak.

*

So many invitations began with the lure of sea views, wonderful food and great company, only to end invariably with 'but you can't take the dogs'. There was never any point in arguing. I didn't want to have to make a case for the existence of Bilbo and Frodo. Instead I offered thanks and excuses; there was always a good reason for not accepting. At one weekend house party in the countryside, when it did seem that the dogs were welcome, all appeared well until we arrived and I was told to leave them outside 'because that's where dogs live'. I invented an emergency and stayed in a small guest house, making my way home by train the next day, sitting on the floor of the guard's van, a closed carriage with only a tiny barred window in the door.

These train journeys could be exhausting. Although Frodo would curl up and sleep, Bilbo insisted on surveying everything, so I often stood the whole way, holding him up so that he could look out the window at the top of the door. I always bought a ticket, but became used to travelling like a box-car hobo. At every station, if there was any parcel to be collected, or a bike or a pram, the railway staff made a comment along the lines of, 'You're not supposed to be in there', 'No one is allowed to be in the van' or 'You'd better have a ticket', and I would be told about the likelihood of an inspector appearing who would order me off the train. That never happened; no inspector ever checked the guard's van.

I wondered about the possibility of free travel, but never risked not buying a ticket.

There was an exception; among all my dog-hating friends was a hospitable art critic whose philosophy of life was based on comfort for all, and the rationale that furniture was there to be sat upon. As a child she had been restricted, so now she made a point of putting everyone at their ease. She was a natural hostess, who drove her smart Saab all the way to Beara, a peninsula in the far south-west of Ireland, with my dogs sitting in style on the blanket I had spread over the leather upholstery. She said I had no need to cover the seat but I had insisted. Her car, she declared, was there to be used by all her guests, most particularly my 'gentlemen', as she called them. Among the many photographs of my dogs enjoying the welcome of her stone cottage is one of Frodo on the sofa, dozing in the glow of a sunbeam.

We discovered Connemara through many expeditions over the years, including once with a friend, a US academic who had hired a car at Dublin airport. She kept forgetting to drive on the left-hand side of the road, swore at the oncoming traffic and relentlessly chain-smoked as she presented a vivid account of her divorce – from a husband who was a top divorce attorney. The dogs sat quietly in the back, mesmerised by the smoke, which was making me car-sick. By far the most memorable journey was a helicopter ride that brought us across the country, landing in Clifden, the same small Connemara village near which the British airmen Alcock and Brown had ended their famous transatlantic flight in 1919. A friend had arranged it so that I could join up with other friends who were organising an archaeological conference.

We had arrived early in the morning at a small landing strip.

The pilot was doubtful that the dogs would board because of the noise of the blades rotating but they were unfazed by the whirling clatter. He was impressed and told me that only the previous week two experienced German Shepherd police dogs, required for a manhunt, had been terrified of the thudding roar and ended up being transported by van. Bilbo was fascinated, watching everything. Frodo looked around but soon settled on my coat and slept. Most of the floor was transparent, made of hardened glass-like plastic, offering panoramic views. Bilbo placed his paws firmly to either side for balance and leaned down to see. It was an amazing trip, not only for the dramatic views but because I could observe Bilbo's response to what he was seeing. He was very alert, appearing to notice everything, particularly the shadow of the helicopter as it passed over the changing landscape. For once he seemed entirely unaware of me. Frodo was in harmony with his world and content to keep it at a comfortable distance but Bilbo responded to it with an exciting, sometimes dangerous for him, intensity. I didn't like flying but a helicopter made me far more appreciative of the miracle of flight. It was like being suspended in a fragile bubble. The sky seemed vast and textured.

Later the same day we went by boat to Inishbofin, rich in archaeology and with a difficult, at times, violent, history. I was fascinated by the place and by Connemara. It was the closest Ireland had to a true wilderness. In the late afternoon the weather began to deteriorate, so the passage back from the island was choppy as the sea churned, angry and white. There was no helicopter waiting for us. The pilot had taken off earlier than planned because flying conditions were so bad. I ended up getting a lift to Dublin in the back of an old jeep. It was far less glamorous: the jeep didn't appear to have any suspension and bounced along through the landscape. I held the dogs, one on either side of me, but we were pitched about as the driver drove with alarming abandon over poor roads pitted with potholes. When the jeep eventually pulled up outside my little house, my balance had been temporarily affected. Both of the dogs had vomited during the journey. We sat on the stone steps, grateful to have stopped moving.

*

Again I gave thought to learning how to drive, if only to avoid another such experience. I realised how much easier it would be: I would be independent, the dogs would be more comfortable and I could stop feeling indebted to anyone willing to give us a lift. I felt I had reached an important stage and was now hovering on the fringe of a decision – doing something in which I had never had the slightest interest, driving. Then, completely unexpectedly, the news editor at work asked me what I knew about Liberia, and told me that I was going there to cover the civil war and famine. Several of my colleagues were amused at the notion of the book reviewer morphing into a foreign correspondent. 'At least you've read Graham Greene,' became a running gag.

I would be away for ten days: what would I do about the dogs? The only time the guys had been boarded in kennels neither of them had eaten. Instead of being sympathetic, the owner of the place had accused me of encouraging my dogs to develop chronic separation anxiety. All I could offer in my defence was that we were very close. The woman sighed and argued that it wasn't normal: they had each other. When I had collected them, they were weak and dehydrated. Remembering that experience, I decided not to go, but then a musician I was seeing at the time offered to stay at my house and 'dog sit' them; he said he would get some reading done. He knew they didn't like him but at least they would be in familiar surroundings. It seemed to make sense and I was curious, more than curious, to see what was happening in West Africa.

*

The history of Liberia, established as a republic in 1847 by freed US slaves, had become a vicious saga of brutality and corruption. Samuel Doe's coup in 1980 had ended more than a century of independence and prosperity, during which Liberia had been a major centre in handling the distribution of luxury goods throughout West Africa. Doe had held power for ten years before being overthrown then tortured and mutilated by Prince Johnson, a self-styled liberator, who had ordered that the ritual killing of Doe be filmed. It was screened everywhere, including in the schools. Famine had taken over while there was stalemate between Johnson, bunkered in a stronghold about three miles outside the devastated capital of Monrovia, and his rival Charles Taylor, who held the rest of the country.

Cholera, yellow fever, polio, typhoid – I am looking at a small booklet, an international certificate of vaccination, listing so many injections and all for me, not the dogs, for once. I must have used the card as a bookmark, and many years later, it tumbled out to remind me of that crazy African visit, a glimpse of hell. The experience began at four in the morning in the freezing cold at Dublin airport. I was to travel in an aircraft that had been chartered by the Irish aid agency, Concern. It was a huge Russian cargo plane, re-registered in Switzerland, but the three-man crew were Russian. All the seats had been removed to provide as much space as possible for the thirty-five tons of supplies the aircraft was carrying. The Russians argued among themselves for most of the journey. Their navigation equipment appeared to consist of a basic atlas, written in French and intended for use in secondary schools. Their voices rose from the open cockpit area and I could see their faces as I sat on a sack of rice eating chocolate biscuits. The night before I left I had written a review of the exceptional debut novel by the Indian writer Rohinton Mistry. The title, *Such a Long Journey*, struck me as ironic in the circumstances, but I also wondered if it would be the last book I would ever read, never mind review. Graham Greene had travelled to Liberia in the 1930s and had almost died there. The experience became the basis for his first travel book, which he called *Journey Without Maps*. I was hopeful, but felt equally bereft of guidance. If anything went wrong I had made a close friend solemnly promise to mind Bilbo and Frodo for the rest of their lives.

This arrangement was going through my thoughts as we suddenly lost altitude, and I feared the worst until I realised that the crew were preparing to land on an airstrip outside Monrovia. The pilots appeared to be in vigorous dispute with someone else, for a change. The Liberians were refusing to grant them landing permission as it was likely that the giant aircraft would break up the runway. We began to circle. One of the crew addressed me with the words, 'We not land, now to go back to Europe.' And the fuel tank was almost empty. Finally the senior Russian shouted 'Fuck you' to ground control and turned the plane around and executed a very bumpy landing. I fell off my sack of rice and scrambled to my feet, glad to be on the ground.

Once the hatch was open, it was like standing in front of an oven door after meat has been cooking in it for many hours. A wall of heat hit me. The intense light made it impossible to see at first. Then I noticed the tall grass, and it began to move. Gaunt soldiers carrying machine guns walked towards us out of the parting grass. Some of them seemed very young and nervous enough to shoot without asking any questions. It was the first time that my US passport earned me a smile instead of a scowl. The jumpy riflemen belonged to ECOMOG, a multinational West African peace-keeping force headed by the Nigerian army.

The sunlight was so harsh that everything seemed bleached of colour; the vegetation was brittle and snapped underfoot. The air was heavy without a trace of a breeze. The days were hot and airless and the nights were surprisingly dark and chilly. African fatalism as manifested in Liberia was both unnerving and impressive; people expected the worst and were prepared to endure it.

It seemed a good, if insane, idea to interview Prince Johnson, so I asked if I could meet him. The powerless interim government had set up base in a hotel, one of the few buildings in downtown Monrovia that had remained barely habitable and which consisted of stuffy, darkened corridors rank with the smell of sweat. On each of the eight floors security staff waited to search anyone that walked by. I remember glancing out of a window and noticing one of the many brightly coloured lizards scurrying across the faded blue floor of the hotel's drained swimming pool. I thought of Greene but also of J. G. Ballard.

I stood in a church in which the bodies of 700 murdered men, women and children had lain for months until they were finally removed a few weeks earlier. The tar-like substance sticking to the soles of my shoes was, explained my guide, a UN liaison officer, human remains. Dismembered corpses were strewn everywhere, near buildings, on the verges of the roads, in burnt-out cars. The only dogs I saw were dead and too diseased to have been eaten, which was apparently the fate of most of the other dogs and cats. There was no respite from the buzzing of flies. I remember a solemn-faced baby peeing on to the tray of small pats of butter its mother was attempting to sell. In contrast to the maverick gunmen in their rough fatigues were the ordinary citizens, starving and apathetic, huddled in small groups beside the rubble and debris that had once been their homes.

There was still a succession of unofficial advisors to deal with, dressed in scruffy bits and pieces of clothing yet maintaining all the while the standard self-importance of bored civil servants. It seemed that any hope of securing a meeting with Johnson would ultimately rest on finding some person who happened to be in a good mood. It became a game. To each enquiry of 'any developments?' or 'how much longer?' I was told everyone was busy. Soon a stock response emerged, a straight-faced, 'We cannot re-deploy our resources.' It began to preface every 'official' response delivered by whichever of the aides decided to answer me. There was a constantly changing staff, most of whom gave the impression of being there only because there was nothing better to do. Then an ECOMOG spokesman became involved; he seemed to think that the interview would happen. But the other men continued sighing, making remarks and staring into space. I was repeatedly informed that an armed guard was needed to accompany me, that there had been 'many, many attempts made on Prince Johnson's life'. I didn't present any danger, all I had was a camera – which was then confiscated as I did not have 'a passport' for it, presumably some form of clearance – and a pen and notebook.

After three days of waiting I was driven at gunpoint through the parched landscape of ruined buildings and burnt-out vehicles to his compound for an audience. The sun beat down and hurt my eyes as I accompanied the aid agency photographer to a long, narrow bungalow. The door was light, little more than a screen on a wire frame. The hall smelt of cooking and a rooster was crowing loudly. Another door opened into a long room that probably ran the length of the house and may have been intended as a lounge-style living room. The walls on each long side of the room were lined with men; there were no women. The smell of sweat was sickening. All conversation stopped. There, at the end of the room, sat Prince Johnson at a desk. Behind him on the wall hung a large and crudely executed painting of the Good Shepherd. There was also an amateurish portrait of Johnson himself as a determined-looking man in military fatigues. A US flag was hanging from the kind of flagpole this is standard furnishing in most American classrooms.

Prince Johnson was dressed in a smart black business suit with a red necktie and matching pocket handkerchief. He resembled Mohammed Ali in his prime and was affecting a statesman-like pose. At the mention of a photograph, he settled his tie and quickly removed two Budweiser beer cans that were on his desk. He was far more interested in being photographed than in answering any questions, most of which he reacted to with a crazed smirk. He was a killer who saw himself as a saviour. He waved his hands and asked me in an accusatory tone why I had waited so long to come. It was unexpected, considering the delays. 'Why did you take so long to come? You journalists don't care about Liberia.' He shouted and then grinned, playing to the audience of followers. He asked me where I came from and I remember saying, 'Ireland.' It was the only time in my life I ever answered the question without adding, by way of explaining my peculiar accent, 'Well, originally, California.' For Johnson, 'Ireland' meant only Belfast. 'Ah yes, Belfast, you kill each other there,' he said, and gave a loud guffaw. The gallery replied with the expected merriment. I felt ridiculous and wanted to laugh but was too aware of the rifle barrel pressing into the back of my head as I struggled to think up a question to ask him. But Johnson, buoyed up by bravado and delusion needed no prompting and believed his own lies. 'You people [he meant journalists] only care about the Gulf. We are very important too, even if we don't have oil.' He soon became bored with the questions and yawned loudly. His mood changed and the interview was over.

*

I travelled home via Sierra Leone, an even more corrupt place. Liberia had seemed acultural, with little sense of Africa; American brands like Coca-Cola and Nike had iconic status there. A tattered advertisement for Lone Star Insurances promising 'to protect you against injury and illness' seemed a bad joke. But Sierra Leone was beyond redemption, and appeared chaotic and utterly amoral. Sex was regarded as a commodity, and young boys were offering even younger children, possibly their sisters and brothers, for this purpose. I saw one woman having sex with a man in an alleyway off a busy street while two watching men patiently waited their turn. There were no rules. I waited three days in Freetown for a flight to London and then travelled on to Dublin, my mind racing with bizarre images such as a man squatting in the street with a collection of human skulls which he good-naturedly offered for sale. Nor had I forgotten the destitute man whose voice had been squeezed out of his throat, leaving him only a rasping whistle. He had been attacked by a hippo when he had worked as a keeper in Monrovia's zoo. But, by the time I met him, all the animals had been eaten and the zoo was deserted. The smell of rot clung to me; I smelt it off my rucksack, my hands.

After the intense brightness, everything in Dublin seemed under-lit and damp and so much smaller. I stood on my doorstep, scrabbling for my keys, suddenly irritated by the dirt of my letter box, which was smeared and greasy. I used to polish it regularly and couldn't understand how filthy it had become in less than two weeks. The dogs were barking, howling like wolves. My neighbour's door opened, he rushed up to me, horror on his face. Dreading, from the anguish on his face, that his wife might have died in my absence, I didn't know what to say. But all he could do was repeat over and over that he had tried to feed them, he had tried to feed them. No one had come and he couldn't get in. 'You should have left keys with me,' he said. He had tried to get in the back, but he was unable to climb over the wall. All he could do was push meat in through the letter box. 'But it is very narrow, the spring is so tight. It's like a trap.' On the other side of the door the dogs were crazed, they could hear my voice.

My neighbour must have been eighty years of age, and had seen so many things in his life and yet he stood that morning on the street, crying over the plight of two dogs that had been left to starve in the house next door while their human had been thousands of miles away, stepping over corpses and being told lies by killers and cowards. The guys jumped up on me, pulling at my clothes, whimpering and barking. The house stank of urine and dirt, and stained and torn cushions were everywhere. It looked as if it had been burgled, but the wide glass doors opening out on the veranda were still closed, smeared and dirty from their saliva. Both dogs had lost weight, particularly Bilbo; their eyes were huge. The only water they had been able to get at was the moisture they had got from licking the inside of the refrigerator, which they had managed to prise open. Because I had not expected my boyfriend to cook for them I had left a supply of dog food, mixers and treats – none of it had been touched. I gave them tepid water and a very small amount of food. They had eaten something; I could see that, as there were pieces of bone left from the meat my neighbour had pushed in to them through the letter box. But they must have gone a few days without food at all; it was the barking that had finally alerted the old man.

Stress and thirst and well as hunger had left the guys exhausted and weak. I phoned the vet and explained what had happened and arranged to bring them up for an examination. They needed something for their dehydration. As for the musician boyfriend, he claimed that the dogs wouldn't let him in and, when he had been offered a gig in London, he went. He thought I was making a fuss over nothing and said that they had been well fed all their lives and that a few days without food wouldn't hurt them. I never spoke to him again.

Small meals and brief sessions in the garden helped settle the dogs. Frodo recovered quickly. I was back and that was all he needed. But the always nervy Bilbo was more vulnerable; he was badly shaken and for the first few days home when I woke he was standing over me, staring and uneasy. I couldn't go out, not even to the shop, without him because he stood between me and the door, yapping and pulling at me. I kept thinking about what the vet had said; that it was the lack of water, not food, that would have killed them. Very few dogs, he had said, would have thought of opening a refrigerator. Their intelligence, not my kindly neighbour's bits of meat, had saved them.

Being accused of having married my dogs did not bother me. But I knew that I could not leave them with anyone ever again. We were all set in our ways: the dogs were obviously as eccentric as I was – and would remain so. Bilbo in particular was odd, hyper-sensitive and slightly obsessive. We belonged together.

*

It could no longer be ignored; now it really was time to learn to drive. True to the precedent set by bad drivers the world over, I acquired the car before I learned the skill. The vehicle had seen hard service and had been driven more than 200,000 miles. It was a Volkswagen, tough and reliable; a friend had found it for me. It roared into life at the first turn of the key. I pushed down my foot and immediately took off, crashing into the wall across the road. The left wing was dented; superficial damage, but enough to justify enrolment at the local driving school. The instructor had been open-minded about teaching me in my own car until he saw it, but then he refused, dismissing the vehicle as too old, obsolete even, and seemed surprised that I had succeeded in getting it insured. He insisted that we use one of the school's cars. The lessons went badly. Every time I made a mistake, which was often, the instructor sighed and mumbled. He refused to look at me and asked if I was dyslexic; he suggested that my coordination was impaired. My dreams of vacationing in Connemara with the dogs began to evaporate. Although I had paid for ten lessons, I gave up after six and took to sitting outside the house with the dogs in the stationary car. My neighbour warned that the battery would go flat.

A friend offered to help teach me. We had a few sessions in a vast, empty car park. Her patience was impressive. But she soon realised that she was not dealing with a natural driver. Aside from remarking that she had always assumed all Americans were born with the ability to drive, she was very kind and calm. On a Thursday morning I was told that I had to be in Sligo on the following Monday morning for a week-long literary conference exploring the work of W. B. Yeats. It was exciting. I saw it as my first challenge as a driver. The dogs would have to come with me; I knew I couldn't leave them and I would have to drive. There was no other way of getting there. It was not an unrealistic expectation; after all, many people far more stupid than me had mastered the mundane art of driving. But my progress was still slow. My lessons with my friend intensified. Early on the Saturday morning we drove for two hours and my friend showed no sign of ending the lesson until another car pulled into our car park. I felt I was improving. On Sunday afternoon we had another lengthy session. At the end of it, my friend sat back in the seat and advised me not to attempt the journey the next morning. She said it would be dangerous. She was encouraging and told me that I was certainly 'getting the hang of it' but that I was not quite ready, it would take more time.

Cautious by nature, I still cannot explain what madness made me set off early the next morning. Except, perhaps, that it was too late to make another plan and to back out would be embarrassing, and I was already very interested in Yeats. At four in the morning it was still dark, the world was asleep and the roads were silent and empty. Moving like a robot I packed the car, aware of the risk that I was taking but feeling that there was no choice. I had studied a map and decided to stay on minor roads and to drive along the margins. I would be alert and would not listen to any music in order to concentrate fully; my quick reflexes would help, that and the fact that there would be so little traffic. If anything happened we would all be together and the only thing in my favour, I felt, was that I would not be driving fast. I still remember the euphoria of pulling away from the kerb that morning. I can also recall the gnawing fear every time I changed gear, in case I accidentally reversed. I chugged on. But there was a problem; none of my driving sessions had taken place at night, so I had never discovered how to turn on the lights. Suddenly the car seemed to have far more buttons and switches than I had ever noticed. It even had heating and air conditioning. Somewhere hidden in the dash there must be a control switch for the lights. At least I found out, by chance, how to turn on the windshield wipers. That would be useful should it rain. I drove on, in first gear, the engine groaning. Perhaps I managed to get into second, I'm not sure. But on I drove, confident that I had also mastered the indicators and the hazard lights. The dogs, sensing my apprehension, stayed quietly in the back. Frodo sat on the floor behind the passenger seat, while Bilbo, always intent, studied the road ahead, breathing down my neck. We moved on, slowly and carefully. Finally after more than hour I saw a man unpacking trays of eggs in a little town. I slowed down and asked him how to operate the lights. He walked over and asked whether I had stolen the car. I said no, it was really mine. Was I running away then? He had become interested. I assured him that I wasn't but that I had committed myself to doing something and couldn't get out of it. That was why I was driving, or trying to drive, without knowing how to. He lectured me on the stupidity of the enterprise. I agreed with him and asked him again to put on the lights for me. 'Will the dogs bite?' he enquired, and then he switched on the lights, advising me to leave them on in case I became confused or, rather, more confused than I already was. He remarked thoughtfully that he should report me to the police, but that it was none of his business. 'I hope you get there,' he said before giving me a dozen eggs for luck. 'Mind you don't break them.'

Having the lights on made me feel suddenly more confident. Sunrise came, and with it day and a steadily increasing volume of traffic. As I drove along I realised I was now a motorist; most of the oncoming cars greeted me in what I thought was a kind of automotive solidarity. I honked back as I had not yet learned how to flash. Later I discovered that the drivers were only informing me that my lights were still on. Cars also began overtaking me, several with an emphatic flourish of speed, no doubt because I was travelling so slowly. But I did reach Sligo town, the eggs intact. I drove into the grounds of a church, and noticed that the clock in the tower was just about to strike nine. The bells chimed and it seemed symbolic, an acknowledgement of our triumph.

After driving across the country rigid with concentration, I was very stiff as I unfolded myself from the car. One of the conference lecturers was standing at the open boot of his vehicle, putting papers into folders. A kindly man, he was horrified when I told him what I had done but agreed to move my car for me, parking it in a shady spot under some trees. The dogs would have to wait while I attended the lecture. They would have more than an hour to recover from the daring jaunt that had got us there. There was no further driving for me that week. One of the lecturers in need of a lift to catch a flight to Berlin was pleased to drive us home while I sat contentedly in the back, again a passenger with my dogs, contemplating the landscape I had not noticed on the morning of my first solo drive.

15

The Clock Begins to Tick

Round and round; the circles made by the pen I was holding had sunk deep into the soft old pine of the table top. It was possible to lift the ink circle free of the rest of the sheet of paper. Bilbo glanced up at me. I called to him and he came over, wagging his tail. Frodo followed. I had brought Bilbo to the vet. Another sebaceous gland had become blocked. It was unexpected because his coat was clean and I brushed him almost every day. I could have dealt with it myself but he might have needed medication. The vet was a stern-looking older man I had not seen before. He was the senior partner and he was rarely there as he spent most of his time with his race horses. He was very formal, quite unlike his staff, and asked the reason for our visit. He stood back with his fingertips brushing the examination table and waited while I explained, hoping not to appear like a know-it-all. The vet looked at the lump and touched it carefully. He did not give the impression that he was about to squeeze it. Then he uttered the words I have never forgotten: 'That's a tumour.' I must have gasped; I stared at him, and he repeated what he had just said, adding that it was in a very awkward place. He asked me Bilbo's age and was surprised to learn that he was ten. 'I would have thought he was about five, perhaps six. He's in very good shape. But it's not going to help him.' The tumour was at the top of his shoulder in a nest of nerve and muscle. The vet studied Bilbo and began to ask if he was a stud animal but stopped, noticing that he wasn't.

The vet insisted that very little could be done and that the available treatments were costly and not very effective. Above all, he said with an almost campaigning zeal, he was opposed to radical surgery in cases such as this. 'He's had a good innings – he must have had or he wouldn't look so well at ten.' The growth had come out of nowhere, a cold, pointless blow. My legs felt weak. I needed to sit down. The vet had said what he had to say. He did allow a tiny element of hope by saying that it was not attached to a vital organ as it was on his shoulder, but crushed that crumb immediately by saying that, of course, he had not done an internal examination. He ended the consultation by saying that 'these things' move quickly or 'can take their time' and told me to go home and consider what he had said.

At home fear took over; fear and helplessness began to overwhelm the anger, although there was that too, and, as always, the voice of the woman on the Tube and the 'great grief' she had mentioned as if it were a gift, not a curse. Bilbo had endured several ordeals as a young dog, and now this. After all the careful feeding, being walked on a lead, finding a secure garden, nothing could protect him from cancer, just as nothing would stop time passing. I went downstairs. Both dogs followed me and I sat down on the bed, staring out into the garden. A grey cat that I had never seen before was grooming itself on the patio. Frodo noticed it and ran over to the glass door and began honking at it. The cat stopped, leg suspended in mid-air, listened and looked back at the door. I wondered if the cat could see into the room or if it was only staring at its reflection in the glass. Bilbo saw the cat but, unlike Frodo, he had seldom reacted to cats. He was a dog that could have lived in a house full of them. He ignored the tantrum taking place and sat beside me, leaning in against me. Frodo honked on, outraged at the audacity of the cat, which had resumed its grooming. I lay down and Bilbo stretched out across me. I forgot about the cat.

Unlike Frodo's strange appendage which had appeared, changed shape several times and then vanished, no mystery surrounded the growth on Bilbo's shoulder. At first it stayed static. Then it began to grow. I went to another surgery, believing that something could be done. I had to try. Meanwhile Bilbo was as active as ever, interested in everything, ears pricked at the slightest sound. The two vets at this surgery were in partnership. One of them had worked in Germany and had dealt with older dogs. He felt that the tumour could be removed without affecting Bilbo's mobility. He advised surgery as soon as possible before the tumour became more deep-rooted in the muscle. It was a high-risk operation and would require a general anaesthetic. I described his previous experience with one but the vet interrupted, pointing out that his exact weight would determine the sedation and that rough estimates were often dangerous. Bilbo's heart was strong. The vet said that his age was not on his side but that he was very fit. It was strange hearing Bilbo referred to as old. Time as well as the illness had crept up on us.

*

I had to make a decision based on the possibility that he might die during the operation or would certainly die when the tumour made it impossible for him to walk. I could let him go now while he was still able to run around, smell the plants in the garden, jog up and down the wooden steps of the veranda. The most serious dilemma any dog owner confronts is our own selfishness; our dependence, which causes us to force a beloved but weakened pet to endure – for us. Because we love a pet, we expect it to live on after life has been reduced to mere existence. A close friend who was terminally ill had not been allowed to die; instead she had had to suffer the horrors of bleeding out through her skin. The cancer had been insidious: it had rampaged through her entire body, killing her brain before it killed her. She had died a medieval death because the law insisted that she experience every last second of hell until nature, not her or her family, called a halt to her agony. But I could spare Bilbo that torment by letting him go. I sat on the patio, my back against the wall, watching the dogs patrol their garden. The sky cleared and it was hot. They trotted over to me and flopped down on either side of my legs. Within a couple of minutes Bilbo bounced up and thrust his front paws on my lap; he peered into my face and then lowered the front of his body, pushing his bum into the air, wagging his tail. He bounded down the garden and turned to me before running behind a thick bush. He ran back up and dropped a red ball at my feet and then spun around and raced down the garden again, Frodo following. Bilbo darted and swerved, showing off while Frodo cut corners, game in pursuit. I had to give Bilbo a chance that could save him or kill him while he was happy and full of fun, not weakened and depressed.

I remember standing in the vet's waiting room on the day of Bilbo's operation. The nurse handed me Bilbo's collar. I told her I considered it unlucky to have taken off his collar before the operation. It was a bad omen. She said, of course, it wasn't. She took it off because it would get in the way and it was better if I kept it safe. She was very encouraging and told me he had a great chance; he was strong and happy. She looked at the collar in my hands and said, 'You can put it back on him – you *will* put it back on him.' She said she would phone me later. I went back to the car and sat in it, too tired to think. Frodo was sitting on the back seat; I had insisted they always stayed in the back. It was a rule they had obeyed. The space I had driven into was now blocked by cars in front of me and behind me. I couldn't get out. I waited, staring at Bilbo's collar, running the leather through my fingers; I had not realised how worn it was, how soft. I felt that Frodo and I were inside a capsule, my car was invisible; no one knew I was there or what was going through my mind. A cyclist went by and swerved as a car knocked a bag off the back carrier. The bike fell over and the wheel kept spinning as the boy, probably a college student in a hurry, bent to pick up the saggy bag. It had been draped over the carrier, pinched in the middle by the spring. The bag had no handles, so he lifted it bodily as if it were a baby. Without my noticing, one of the drivers had returned and I could get out now. I slowly pulled away and drove back home. Frodo ran into the house and I sat down on the sofa with him, waiting. Hours passed before the phone rang. It was not the nurse, it was the vet. My mouth was dry as he asked me how I was. I felt he was preparing me for bad news but instead he said it had gone very well. Bilbo had been lucky: it had been possible to remove the tumour without compromising the shoulder and he was awake, very alert. I could collect him.

Gratitude more than relief took over: I thanked God, the vets, Bilbo's good luck, his courage. There were times when risks had to be taken. I had his collar around my wrist, pushed up over my sleeve. I decided to leave Frodo in the bedroom and collect Bilbo on my own. I knew he would have stitches and wanted to avoid any rough play in the back seat. Surgery hours were over, so I rang the bell. The nurse opened the door; she had her coat on and said she had waited for me and reminded me that she had predicted he would make it.

All feelings of joy faded on seeing Bilbo. He walked towards me like a ghost, so much smaller, so much older. The top half of his back was shaved; he seemed to be in a daze. Bandages bound both of his front legs. His tail waved half-heartedly. I bent down to him and he pushed his head in under my chin. The wound had been painted over with a silver substance, a type of iodine. I blurted out something about him looking like a crash victim. The vet said it was the effect of the painkillers, and that he would need more of them over the next three days. The silver paint was to prevent infection and the wound was better left open to the air. Stitches tracked through the silver. He warned me that the wound would swell. Bilbo must be kept quiet; he would have no appetite but would need water. 'Expect him to doze. Don't be alarmed.'

Words, directions, advice, encouragement, but I felt that familiar drowning sensation coming over me; it was as if sound had become muffled. Various packets of tablets were handed to me. Tears slid down my face. As I walked out, I noticed three other people in the waiting room. One of them told the nurse she had come for the two cats that had been spayed. I heard a woman's voice asking what had happened to my poor dog. I couldn't answer. After years of hearing people praise and admire him, a stranger was showing him pity.

*

I lifted him into the front seat so that I could reach over and hold him if I had to brake suddenly. He felt very light and smelt of medication and illness. The smell filled the car but I kept the windows closed. His skin was hot and his nose was dry, but his eyes were bright. He had always been intelligent, yet now he seemed wise, as though he had learned from pain and discomfort, and he looked at me as if he were gauging my capacity for dealing with this crisis. Down in the garden bedroom I pulled all the blankets off the mattress and put them on the floor. I didn't want him to fall off the bed. Frodo curled up beside him. The phone rang. It was the vet. He had seen how upset I was. I heard myself say that I should never have put Bilbo through this, that I had been selfish and that I should have let him be put to sleep. But the vet surprised me. He said that Bilbo was in a post-operative state and that normally after such a major operation a dog would be kept in the surgery for about three days. 'Owners don't normally see what you're looking at.' He said he had sent him home because he knew I would look after him, but that I had to accept that my dog had undergone a massive trauma. Then he went on to describe what he called 'the mass', and I noticed that the lump had indeed become a mass. The vet compared it to an iceberg. It was very big and Bilbo had lost a lot of blood, and he had to be given a transfusion. But at no time did his heart weaken. Listening to the vet was like hearing two sides of a medical case calmly argued out. Bilbo's age was a significant factor, yet his strength was an advantage. His intelligence would help; but his hyperactive personality could lead him to rip the stitches and damage the wound, possibly causing an infection. The vet said he had seen dogs younger than Bilbo die, while others recovered. It was, he stressed, the largest mass he had ever removed from a dog. He said he was optimistic, that he would expect Bilbo to live to fourteen or fifteen, but that the next two or three days were crucial and that he couldn't give any guarantees.

I looked at the dogs; Frodo was sleeping, his head on Bilbo's hip. But Bilbo was wide awake, watching me.

For two entire days he lay there, without drinking, without attempting to relieve himself, showing little interest in what was going on around him, barely even responding to my voice. I thought his body had begun to shut down and I waited. Then, about fifty hours into the vigil, he stood up, stretched cautiously and walked over to the glass door and out on to the patio. He slowly lifted his leg against a large ceramic planter and urinated at length. It looked normal; there was no blood in it. Then he walked back into the bedroom and drank some water, pausing to bark and look up at the ceiling in the direction of the kitchen. I ran upstairs and took a plate of chicken out of the refrigerator. I gave some to Frodo and left him in the kitchen area while I went back down to Bilbo. His ears were pricked as I came into the bedroom with the plate. He was hungry again.

*

Recovery is a strange ritual; the patient retreats into his or her body as if seeking refuge, albeit in a damaged shelter. The healing process is a different kind of growth. Instead of acquiring strength, it is about regaining something lost, an attempt to restore what has been stolen. Bilbo was relinquishing the ghostly aura left by the operation. For the first few days, each time he stretched he appeared to have mentally prepared for the effort, bracing his body for the discomfort. Then his natural ease of movement slowly returned, and these tentative pauses in which he tested himself ended. I watched while pretending to read. I had taken to bringing food down to the bedroom in which I had set up a messy camp. I drank bottles of water and kept Bilbo's bowl topped up with it. Frodo went outside only when he needed to relieve himself. He stayed beside Bilbo, usually with his head at Bilbo's hip. In his quiet, unfussy way, Frodo was also keeping watch. I kept my running shoes at the front door and went out for quick runs around the neighbourhood. When I returned I would climb back on the bed and resume reading. One of the books I read in those bleak hours was *The Tunnel* by the Argentinian writer Ernesto Sabato. It is a novel about obsession, in which an artist in prison for murder writes about his victim, the woman he loved. Sabato suggests that there is a point at which love degenerates into madness, that care can become a destructive mutual dependence. The book was brilliant and unsettling, a cautionary tract.

Along with waiting for signs of recovery was the dread anticipation of what the vet had predicted, that alarming but apparently necessary swelling. 'It will get a lot worse before it gets better.' By then I had stopped asking questions; I listened, braced for each piece of information that invariably shattered into fragments of hope and despair. The skin of my face felt stiff from being forced into the attentive, neutral expression of trying not to cry. Sometimes I suspected that for the vets Bilbo had become an engrossing test case to be discussed in conferences and journals; for me he represented an intense constant, a much loved part of my life.

I studied Bilbo and recalled the morning years earlier when I had been told that my father had been found dead. He had been alone. I did not mourn him. He was volatile, irrational, a dreamer, and had spent long periods away, travelling, only to reappear without warning. More of a house guest than a parent, he had delighted in initiating self-deprecating banter which would invariably explode into heated disputes. Aside from a shared interest in the

American Civil War and in Hitler's Operation Barbarossa and in horses, we had never been close. I could barely remember his face. That he had died alone was sad, yet I felt calm, detached. It was the absolute loneliness, not the solitary death, that had preoccupied me for months afterwards. Sitting in the silent sickroom with my dogs, I imagined that the world itself was empty and the only thing that remained were the peculiar thoughts spinning around in my mind.

Bilbo's wound did swell. Within a couple of days it looked like a box sitting under his skin. It rippled slightly as he moved, suggesting it might tip him off balance. I imagined the bruised ligaments and tendons regenerating after the violation of the surgery. Delicate stubble was beginning to cover the raw skin. I draped a scarf across his shoulders and photographed him, aware that it was a false image, showing Bilbo as he had been, not as he had become. But he seemed stronger and wanted to go out into the garden, so I slid open the glass door and walked out with him into the sun. Frodo followed. The sinister box appeared to swell as if an invisible pump were releasing air into it. The stitches had stretched and were ready to be removed. Somehow a week had passed. Back in the surgery we were greeted as survivors of a disaster. The nurses addressed Bilbo by name. The waiting pet owners examined us with interest. A man asked if my dog had been hit by a car.

*

Even as the swelling began to subside, I could see a noticeable difference between his two shoulders caused by muscle wastage, but the vet was confident that Bilbo would regain his muscular function. I monitored his exercise and for a few weeks let him wander about the garden as I worked in it. After about a month I took him out alone on the leash to help him build up his shoulder. It was unfair to Frodo, but it was vital that Bilbo did not begin pulling against my weight in his determination to stay fractionally ahead of Frodo. Each time we returned after our ten- or fifteen-minute walks Frodo was there waiting in the small hall. I could hear his nails against the door as I fiddled with the key on the other side of the door.

The local shop had a noticeboard. Among all the cards and crude slips of paper, some handwritten, others printed, advertising babysitting and flat-sharing and typing services, was a smart pale grey oblong. It stood out from all the white cards. FAITH HEALER was printed on it in bold capital letters. Just that: two words and a phone number. I thought of Brian Friel's great play, also simply called *Faith Healer*, with its complex theme exploring the ambiguity of memory and the ever-contrasting versions of the truth. I took the card over to the counter. The shop woman smiled at me – by then she regarded me as a local – and I asked her about this mysterious healer. She shrugged and admitted that she never bothered about anything on the noticeboard; people were always putting things up and taking them down. She said I could have the card. I went back to the house and dialled the number on it. There was no answer. It rang out for hours as I kept dialling the number. Soon I knew it off by heart.

Finally a male voice answered. He sounded wary and asked what I wanted. His tone was sharp. I was about to hang up but something stopped me, the chance that this person could help. He repeated his question and before I could finish saying that I had found the card on the shop noticeboard, he interrupted and said he didn't deal with pregnancies. 'It's not me, it's my dog.' The silence at the other end made me wonder if I had offended him by asking that he look at an animal. I could hear him breathing. He asked what was wrong and I told him the story. His first question was, why had I put an innocent animal through such an ordeal? He quickly followed this judgement with another question. Why hadn't I come to him first? All I could think of saying was that I had only just found the card. I felt foolish and awkward, uneasy about what I was doing. The truth was I hadn't ever thought of approaching a healer and I was not sure why I was resorting to one now. Bilbo was getting better but he was weakened, still diminished. The faith healer agreed to see him, but I had to go to his 'office', his house. 'Take down the address,' he commanded, and told me that I would have to bring a cash donation. When I asked him how much, he became irritated and said his clients – the word made me uncomfortable, was I a client? – gave him fifty pounds 'at least, but usually a bit more, about a hundred'. He paused as if considering what to say next. Healing, he said, was very demanding, it drained the healer. 'I might be able to invoke only one healing in a day. It tires me out. But you don't have to come if you don't want to,' he said, as if testing my sincerity. It felt as though he was asking if I really loved my dog.

Bilbo's 'donation' was still in the bank's envelope on the passenger seat beside me. The directions had taken me to a smart area near the sea just outside Dublin. The tall pink house was in the middle of a Victorian terrace. A woman answered the door, looked at me and glanced at the car. She told me to step back and then closed the door, leaving me on the doorstep, my face flushed. As I was walking down the path, I heard the man's voice. He was younger than I had expected, thin and sickly, and dressed in a ridiculous blazer, complete with nautical buttons. He called me back, gesturing to the house, but I said I needed to fetch Bilbo. 'Who's that?' Although I had told him that Bilbo was a dog, he seemed surprised and appeared to have forgotten our conversation. He motioned for me to put him back in the car. 'I can do him out here,' he said and he stood beside the car. He closed his eyes and seemed to be praying. After about a minute the healer announced that he was ready and asked for the money. 'But you never touched him,' I blurted out in surprise as much as indignation. 'You didn't even look at him.' He said he didn't need to touch him. But when I complained that the entire 'ritual', for want of a better word, had seemed very impersonal and asked why he hadn't just prayed over the phone, he told me to roll down the window and reached in to touch Bilbo's head, brushing it lightly with the tips of his fingers. As soon as he noticed the wound, which was still unsightly, he withdrew his hand. 'That'll do him, he's warm. That's a good sign. Have you the money now? The donation? It's an important part of the healing.' I watched as he tore open the envelope and tossed it to the ground. He counted the notes and walked back to his gate. I felt humiliated and angry. How stupid I had been. How many other desperate people, I wondered, had asked him for help? I drove away, conscious that if he had ever had a gift he was abusing it.

16

Like So Many Dragonflies

Bilbo looks attentive; he is sitting on wide stone steps beside a squat blue pot, from which thick white aubrietia tumbles over the sides. A small blonde child is reading to him. She is wearing *101 Dalmatians* shorts. But that was still years in the future. Images accumulate; memories, vivid and insistent like so many dragonflies, darting here and there. I remember these tableaux; they bring both comfort and sorrow. There is a moment when everything that matters slips further and further away, back into that place we call the past. But for a while, a time that can seem almost permanent, daily life allows us the illusion that it is constant and that little changes. I had reached a point at which I thought that Bilbo and Frodo would always be with me, and that this wouldn't change. People who didn't know my name referred to the dogs by theirs. We were a kind of family unit. Having the car made travel easy. There were no more exhausting treks from train stations or awkward inventive pleas to bus drivers, no more standing like minor criminals in a railway guard's carriage as the scenery flashed by through a small barred window. I no longer needed to accept rides from friends who later made comments about dog hairs and wondered aloud about boarding kennels. Our hygiene standards were sufficiently severe to intimidate fleas. I can't recall ever having seen the guys scratch, although I'm sure they must have done.

Once a reluctant driver, I was now committed to long-distance jaunts and enjoyed setting off early in the morning or late at night in order to drive into the dawn to the music of Bach or Handel. My childhood interest in classical Greece and Rome now extended to Irish archaeology, particularly the field monuments, such as hill forts and stone circles. Soon I had photographed every high cross in the country from every angle, trying to record the complex Biblical iconography that places them among the finest examples of medieval European sculpture. These photographs accompanied many of the articles on heritage that I wrote for my newspaper.

But long before I finally learned to drive, Connemara had become our favourite place, so compelling that I had begged and endured all manner of lifts in order to get beyond Galway into that extraordinary region of bog and mountain and coast. Now I was completely independent I could set off for the west every few weeks, if only for a day or two. Music made the journeys even more complete. Bilbo appeared to know Mozart's Great Mass in C Minor by heart; whenever he heard it, instant recognition registered on his face. And having our own car meant that, on the night we were camping on Omey Island, when the tent blew away in a ferocious sudden storm, we could take shelter in the car and watch as the sea lashed against the cliff while the ponies in the next field stood with their heads down and their backs to the wind.

Drivers are expected to see less than passengers, or so I'd been told, as the road demands full attention, but driving made me more aware of the dead foxes, badgers and the many cats littering the roads, all of them killed by cars. One summer's evening two cars ahead swerved suddenly as a van went out of control. It had hit a deer. The animal's body exploded in a shower of blood, the front of its torso staggered over to the ditch and collapsed, leaving the back legs writhing on the road. Parts of the stomach were still attached to this grotesque remnant. Several cars stopped. A man pushed the body parts away towards the verge, dragging blood with him. One car shot past the scene and quickly disappeared. But the drivers and passengers from the other cars waited with the man who had struck the deer, as if we had become mourners.

Another accident, far more terrible, happened on a dull late spring morning, approaching noon, only minutes before we arrived at the fringes of it. Two mangled cars, bodies thrown clear through the windshields, blocked the road. The victims were motionless on the ground, a man and two children, one woman; another person apparently still trapped behind the steering wheel. White-faced witnesses waved us on. Wandering about between the wreckage amid the chaos was a bewildered brown-and-white dog that must have been travelling in one of the crashed cars. Too many treacherous bends, too many roads that were hazardous, even for the sober, never mind the drunks, and there were always more than enough of them. One three-mile stretch of impossible road on the way to Galway had claimed so many lives that relatives had erected a series of white crosses draped in black ribbons along the verge. And for every hundred dead cats I would see a dead dog on a country road and somehow the sight seemed far more shocking.

The little car seemed indestructible; for all the madness on the roads, I clocked up thousands of miles and was now driving like a grown-up American – albeit not like a US tourist, as I knew how to drive on the left-hand side of the road, having only driven in Ireland. Each journey consolidated the liberation I had never known while trapped in the role of tolerated passenger. Bilbo's operation had become a distant memory. His fur had grown back, thicker than ever. He had regained the weight he had lost and had acquired slightly more muscle than he had previously had. Back on the open beaches of Connemara, Bilbo ran as well as ever, making wide dramatic circles through which Frodo took blatant short cuts. Frodo's muzzle had become very grey, but his dark eyes remained clear and bright. He had become more sedate and was more obviously the senior member of the duo – I had always reckoned that he was about four years older than Bilbo, perhaps more. Yet he showed no signs of stiffness.

*

Time passed and the number of our outings increased, producing boxes of photographs and true contentment. As a staff journalist I was able to specialise in the arts and review theatre as well as books, while also writing about archaeology and architectural history, and, when the opportunity arose, horses. I continued to dream of finding romance with a fellow amateur antiquarian or book-lover, preferably someone eccentric, but while I lived in hope I was happy to explore the landscape, most particularly ancient churchyards and deserted ruins. A chance remark had alerted me to an old photographic archive and the existence of a large classic doll's house in an eighteenth-century house near Ballina, in Mayo. We set off. It was a long drive, which the heavy rain made more difficult. The wipers couldn't deal with the volume of water falling from blackened skies on to the windshield. I peered into the darkness, the headlights creating blurred pools. A series of wrong turnings twice brought us back into the same village. Out in the countryside, driving through the flood, I found the gates at last. A long avenue opened on to a stately Georgian mansion. It was late, well after eleven o'clock. The owner offered to make me a sandwich. I had supplies for the dogs. She then remembered that she also had blackberry crumble and said she would make custard. Without any sign of weakening the rain simply stopped as if turned off, and the moon shone white. Off at an angle in front of the house was a lake and in the strange light I saw an owl swooping down silently over the water. We had time for a quick walk. Bilbo charged out into the night, full of energy after the long car journey. The woman laughed at his antics and said her dog had slowed down and was already asleep in the kitchen. She mentioned that he was ten years old and 'getting on'. I told her that Bilbo was fourteen and had survived cancer. She was surprised that he was so old, and I was too at that moment, because I realised that I seldom mentioned his age or even allowed myself to think about it. I usually avoided answering when I was asked how old he was. He still looked young and lively. Frodo walked to the door and glanced back at me. I opened it and was about to follow him out when the woman called me back to tell me where there was a wooded path that led down towards the lake and through the trees back up to the house. It would take about fifteen minutes, she said, and, when the dogs had stretched their legs, she would have my snack ready. I went out, calling their names. Bilbo came running up to me, but I couldn't find Frodo. I called again. Clouds gathered, masking the moon. There was no sign of him, no answering honk. I heard the woman's voice. I ran around the side of the house. Bilbo came racing back to me, jumped up and grabbed my sleeve, yapping. He ran off and yapped; I followed him.

There was a bank of short, thick foliage. Bilbo disappeared

into it. I could hear the rustling of his movements and I crashed after him; it wasn't very deep, only steep enough to make me lose my balance and skid slightly. Frodo was down there; I could just about see him, picked out by a light coming from a hallway inside the house that was reflected in his eyes. He didn't come to me. The clouds had dispersed and I could see him now in the moonlight. He didn't move. I lifted him; he did not respond – he was calm and very quiet. I took a run at the bank, with him in my arms scrambled up the slope and hurried back to the house. The woman was waiting in the hall. I said that something was wrong; I put Frodo on the floor. He didn't move, just lay limp, as if all the power had drained from his body. I was baffled and I remember how cold my face felt as a chill passed over me and I said to the woman that I thought he had had a stroke. It was the first time I had ever used that word, the word 'stroke' – stroke of what? misfortune? fate? – in a medical context in my life. I asked her if dogs suffered strokes and she said she was sure that they did. I remained there, crouched on the hall floor, the front door wide open behind me. She closed it and, nodding towards Bilbo, said that his friend looked very upset. Bilbo was sitting on his haunches, staring at us. I carried Frodo up to the room, Bilbo at my heels, while the woman said she would try to contact a vet but that it was very late and she said that my dog was probably better off alone with me. She said that it might pass. 'Dogs are very tough, they can take a nasty turn and then bounce back.'

But he didn't bounce back. He lay on the floor for the rest of the night. I stayed with him and, shortly after eight o'clock in the sharp, bright morning light, I drove through the countryside into the nearest town to find a vet. He was a stout, kindly man who smiled sympathetically and said he could do nothing except offer to take him for me. I understood what he meant and thanked him but said that I would bring him home with me. The vet said it might be difficult for me to drive home alone, that I'd be very upset. He told me that I was in shock, and that, when it hit me, I would be driving back alone to Dublin with my dead dog. But I kept saying I could do it: Frodo had been with me, with us, for a long time and I mentioned that his pal was waiting in the car. The vet looked at Frodo and remarked that he didn't appear to be in distress and that he was very calm. He asked me how old he was. I felt ridiculous saying 'about eighteen'; the vet was open-eyed and asked if I meant human years. No, dog years, in human years he would be, what, 126? Or something like that. I wasn't in the mood for stupid calculations. It was meaningless; I said that I reckoned the ratio of one dog year to seven human years was inane. I explained that I knew Bilbo was fourteen and that Frodo was at least four years older than him, possibly more. My mouth was dry; I hadn't eaten that morning and felt sick. Yet again I could hear the English woman's words, the 'great grief' always in my thoughts. I carried Frodo out to the car. His stillness might help him, I thought; perhaps it was somehow helping his body recover? I laid him down in the footwell of the passenger seat, in a nest-like bed fashioned from my coat. Bilbo stayed in the back; he knew they weren't allowed to sit in the front. I glanced in the rear-view mirror and could see his face, his eyes intent on Frodo.

We passed a small petrol station. A man was standing in the forecourt. I drove in and rolled down the window and asked him if he knew of any vets. He said the local fellows were all right, but that the best one was in another town;

about nine or ten miles further on. It was a modern surgery, he said, 'and dear'. Expensive, but it didn't matter, if the vet could help Frodo. I had to get him there. I kept feeling that this could not be the end. I drove back out into open countryside and saw a kestrel high in the sky, which might be a good omen.

*

The expensive vet was also sympathetic but offered no more hope than his colleague had. He admitted he had never seen anything like it. Frodo was still and quiet, composed and uncomplaining. The vet was wary of touching him too vigorously and we both kept remarking on Frodo's calmness. He did not appear to be in pain; his heart rate was not elevated. His eyes were clear and he was aware of us. The vet said he had no useful suggestions but believed that if Frodo was going to die that day, he would drift off quietly. I drove slowly back to Dublin. After another long night I phoned my vet and asked him if he had X-ray facilities. He didn't, but he could arrange something. In less than an hour I was standing in the university veterinary clinic. A huge black bull was being wheeled out of a theatre on a trolley manned by about eight people. Just as the bull trolley left the ramp area, rubber screening curtains parted and the little body of a bay-coloured dog, my Frodo, was pushed along by a young man in a white coat. I stood looking down into the X-ray area, numbed by the strangeness of it. Why were there so many people standing about in white lab coats? Students, of course. This was a teaching facility. Research was going on. Bilbo's front paws were on my foot. I moved away and waited outside with him.

Before the X-ray I had already been told about the possibilities and the risks. Frodo had not had a stroke. The professors had diagnosed the problem before radiography confirmed it. He had suffered a massive haemorrhage into his stomach; the probable cause was a major growth, a tumour. It was another impossible choice; the vets agreed that the next bleed would kill him. If the tumour was on his liver, there was no hope at all. But if it was positioned on the spleen, he might have a chance. He could live without his spleen. I looked at their faces and remembered years earlier how a classmate had died after a car accident in which her spleen had been ruptured. I was being asked to give my consent and I was unable to speak. Frodo had already been taken from me; it was unlikely that I would see him alive again. My last image of him as himself before he had entered this inert, passive state was when he had paused in the hall of the country house to glance back at me before walking into the darkness.

I had no real choice, and the vets seemed confident. One was a friendly, direct woman named MacAlister; I laughed abruptly, recalling that years before I had initially called Frodo 'Mac'. But that now seemed a lifetime ago. I walked out to the car and opened the back door for Bilbo. He jumped in and I sat beside him. At least I had been able to see the cancer that had attacked him; it had battened on his shoulder. But this was different; it was invisible and far more malign. I drove slowly home to wait for the phone call. I couldn't read; I didn't feel like eating. I had many boxes of unsorted photographs; I owned three cameras and had recorded most of the places we had visited. I began arranging the pictures; Frodo's story had developed into a singular narrative from that first sighting, his defeat of the white dog, to this. My eyes were burning. I had barely dozed since his collapse in Mayo and the exhausting drive during which I had stopped so many times to check if he was still alive. I must have fallen asleep and was dreaming.

There was no end to the railway track; it seemed to stretch for miles over the empty desert. How had a train raced into view without warning? It was such a relief because I was so tired. But it didn't stop; it must have run over me. Then the noise began and the scream, a feeble, defeated little sound. It was me. Then I heard the phone; I lunged at it and knocked it to the floor. A voice was calling my name. I answered, or tried to. The voice kept asking if I could hear. There was interference on the line. The first crossed line I had ever experienced. A woman said to hang up and she would call me back. She was from the university clinic and she sounded excited. She kept saying how lucky he was, it, the tumour, was on the spleen and that they had been able to remove it. He was lucky. I realised she was speaking about Frodo, calm, self-contained Frodo.

When I arrived to see him the room was crowded. A circle of people stood around the table. A young student announced that Frodo was older than she was; it seemed an odd thing to say. But it was true; her eighteenth birthday was still three weeks away. An older man, one of the lecturers, said that it was important to have given the dog a chance: while his age should have been a risk factor, nevertheless it hadn't been relevant. He said that Frodo had a beagle heart. Not for the first time I looked at Frodo with admiration. He gazed back at his audience as if he was wondering what the fuss was all about.

Within a couple of days he was back home, moving from beanbag to beanbag in his old routine with Bilbo. His wound healed very quickly. Unlike Bilbo, Frodo never seemed to spend any time recovering; he was sick and then he was simply better. Nervy, mercurial Bilbo had been drained by his operations, dazed. But Frodo was pragmatic, steadfast. He had been ill, now he was healed. He had made veterinary history. My ordinary dogs continued to surprise even me.

17

A Second Act of Faith

Bilbo's decision to attack the workman was apparently exactly that, a deliberate act, not a spontaneous reaction. He had been watching the man, staring at him, but not out of curiosity. He was monitoring his every move, while the man nervously made a few 'your dog doesn't seem to like me' comments. He was noisy as he worked and insisted on playing his radio while also sustaining a running dialogue – with himself. He kept scurrying out to his van. I remained in my basement study, trying to work. Looking back, I remember being surprised that Bilbo, rather than coming in to me, had stayed out in the lobby area adjoining my study with the man, who was laying parquet flooring throughout the small hall and into a large linen closet. The man kept revisiting his van, running up the stairs and out through the front door. The van doors opened with a metal creak, followed by the tinny judder as they were slammed and then the thud of his heavy footsteps running back up the stone steps, into the house and back down the stairs again – until the next dash out to the van and the relentless repetition of it all.

Every tool must have been carried in, one by one. He didn't look very organised. He told me that his wife was in hospital and that he had five children under six. Small wonder he was confused. Several of his workmen were off and he had had to begin taking on jobs himself, and he admitted to being out of practice. That didn't make sense, when I thought about it later; he had knocked on the door, asking if I wanted any jobs done. It was all very casual. But I chose not to question him about his qualifications. The old parquet floor had been salvaged from a church and it was beautiful. I wanted it relaid and fitted on my floor as soon as possible, as the stacked sheets of it were adding to the clutter amid which I lived. The noise continued. I needed a cup of tea but did not want to risk provoking more of his stories, so I remained in my study. I did hear low growling and smiled; Bilbo and Frodo did not like male visitors. They particularly did not like my new romance with a married man, who came and went as it suited him. The dogs were growling more than they had for years.

Then I heard the scream and the shouts. I ran out, closing the door behind me to keep Frodo from whatever was happening. Bilbo held the workman's arm, blood was already oozing through his jacket and drops were splashing on to the floor. The man was pinned to the wall and was terrified. Bilbo looked savage, his lips were curled back. His teeth were huge and still so white. I ordered him to release the man. He obeyed but his eyes were hot with anger. I was shocked and wondered had something erupted in his brain. Was this a seizure? What else could have caused such rage? Fear for him outweighed my initial concern about what he had actually done. The seriousness of the attack struck me. I might be forced to have Bilbo put down. But the workman was very good about it, and assured me that he had had worse bites and that he would rush down to the local A & E. My car was being serviced and I apologised, emphasising Bilbo's exemplary temperament, promised that he had never done anything like this and suggested that the electric drill must have upset him. All the while the workman said not to worry; he'd have no problem driving with one hand and that he wouldn't report us to the police. He'd be back to finish the job. And off he went, with me still abjectly begging forgiveness.

Bilbo had never turned on a human, not even on my married boyfriend. Any of his disputes with other dogs were territorial, and then only with animals that were larger than him. He was not a bully. I frowned at him, prepared to reprimand him for such misbehaviour, still concerned that the victim would alert the police. Bilbo looked righteous, not in the least contrite and jumped up and down, yapping at me, drawing my attention to a newly empty corner and the fact that the sound system was gone, along with the television and a small, but very good, portable CD player. Very little of the parquet flooring had been laid, because the workman had been systematically stealing sections of it. Not for the first time, Bilbo had proven a better judge of character than me. The workman was never seen again. I did not even have a phone number for him and the police merely smiled at my stupidity.

Humans tend to over-analyse words; animals respond to the tone of a voice more than to language and react to those sudden movements which they can anticipate before we begin to see them. That 'workman' had been clever enough to present himself as an irritating scatterbrain, without a trace of obvious menace. He had never threatened me or shouted at us, so I wondered why Bilbo had reacted to items being carried out of the house. Perhaps he had simply *smelt* the bad intent? The instinctive quality of a dog's intelligence can reason faster than the human equivalent. I had been given an impressive demonstration of canine intuition.

*

Not long afterwards we made the first of several expeditions to the Burren, a mysterious limestone landscape in north Clare famous for its variety of rare wild flowers and Alpine plants which co-exist with Mediterranean ferns and native hazel. Botanical wonders abound in its distinctive clint-and-gryke topography of fractured limestone pavements. Man has imposed himself on the stones and has farmed here for centuries, yet the ecosystem has survived despite the numerous environmental threats posed by development. The Aran Islands are a geological continuation of the Burren, and look from a distance like breakaway limestone fragments cast out into the Atlantic. As a landscape it is vast yet intimate; the animals grazing it sometimes resemble survivors of some secret disaster that has apparently reduced the earth to barren rock. Maidenhair spleenwort trembles in the breeze. The lunar surface of the Burren is fertile and enigmatic, rich in archaeology and ancient church sites. The light is clear and dramatic; there is a sense of limitless space and melancholy. We walked for miles and I filled notebooks with drawings of wild orchids and spring gentians, carefully pressing specimens between the pages, wishing the blue of the gentian would stay like that and never fade. The compact, tightly packed saxifrage felt springy, like moss. Outside a small pub a few musicians were playing German folk tunes. I ordered soup and one of the men introduced himself as 'a true Bavarian' and said he was from the Black Forest. He saluted Frodo as a big sausage dog and announced that 'this one', meaning Bilbo, looked very clever and was probably secretly writing a novel. It seemed a fitting tribute. Although my complicated and secretive current relationship often kept me waiting alone at home for hours, during which I discouraged my friends from calling in case the man I was involved with arrived by chance, at least the dogs were never neglected. They had both endured serous illnesses and had recovered against all the odds. Visiting the ruined churches in that extraordinary landscape was a pilgrimage of thanks.

*

Life was good, life was constant. But then Bilbo's malignant lump returned. It was still very small, but it was back on the same place on his shoulder, which meant back *in* his shoulder, festering beneath the surface. I remembered the vet's description of it as an iceberg. I felt it by chance as Bilbo lay down beside me in the dark and I patted him. The lump was like a pebble. I switched on the bedside lamp, desperately praying that it was only a burr caught in his coat. But it wasn't. I uttered a long, low groan and remember that as I stood that night on the bedroom floor, my fists clenched, the spine of one book of the many filed on the tall, wide bookcase, caught my eye. It was the bold blue and white lettering of *Judge on Trial*. It jumped out at me. Was it the word 'trial'? I don't know. But that night, having moved so abruptly between the dark and then the harsh electric light, and given the horror of the discovery, I saw the book so clearly, as often happens in times of stress when the most ordinary things acquire a bizarre clarity. For a split second that book was the only thing in the room.

The vet's reaction this time was far less optimistic. The most serious factor was his age. Bilbo was now fifteen. Time was really running out. Another major operation was asking far too much of an old dog. The only hope was that the growth would develop slowly and, possibly, be less invasive. I left the surgery and Bilbo looked up at me. I wondered if he could sense my despair yet he seemed fine, his character was unchanged as he continued to play Peter Pan to Frodo's serene sage.

Brooding and suitably troubled, my unpredictable married boyfriend would appear at my house, invariably later than arranged, and I would cook elaborate meals which were served on fine tableware. The guys sat watching these impromptu dinners, just about tolerating the guest. Eventually he would leave – he never once stayed the night – and I would wonder what I was doing with this man who was making no commitment of any kind. The dogs waited while I diligently washed the dishes, often to music of Schubert, particularly the melancholic *Winterreise*; it matched my mood. Most of all though, I found comfort in Bach's cello suites and the *Goldberg Variations*, and in Chopin's nocturnes and Beethoven's string quartets. Perhaps I was enjoying the torment of my situation as the doomed 'other woman'. Yet again I had taken to walking the dogs at strange hours, being careful not to linger at windows or garden gates for fear of being once more reported as a prowler. The great romance with a married man proved a testing experience; it taught me everything I would ever need to know about loneliness and being invisible. Most of all I learned what it is to be expected to accept a secondary role. The man's happiness is the priority; a mistress is a support system, no more. At no time is a dog's innate sense of irony more evident that when observing humans interact with each other. Dogs miss very little; they see the fundamental and detect the emotions that really matter.

This new tumour played cruel and sneaky games. It remained small, barely noticeable, now you see me, now you don't. At times it seemed to vanish. Then it would have a growth spurt, fall dormant and lose interest in its own malign life, only to wake with an evil abandon and bulge, extend, change shape, stretch, flatten, disappear. Snap, it was gone. Close your eyes with relief and then, snap, it was back, pulsating and vicious. I had an idea and called the guys. They jumped into the back seat and I drove to an imposing church that I had often passed. I had never been inside it, but I reckoned that it would have what I wanted. It did, just inside the porch: an incongruously humble metal font. I stuck my finger into it and felt a sponge. I took it up; it was heavy with water and I studied it. It was a small, ordinary sponge, more like something that would have seen service in an old post office, lying on the counter for people with an aversion to licking stamps. The sponge was tattered. It may have once been yellow but now it was a dirty mustard colour, so repellent in appearance that no one would have considered using such a thing to wash their feet. Yet there it was in a church ready for the fingers of the faithful. And for me. I glanced about, wondering what I would say if a priest or devout worshipper asked what I was doing. I expected a tolerant God to understand.

Bilbo jumped, startled by the sensation of water being squeezed over his back. I crushed the sponge dry and then rushed back into the church to replace it in the font before driving away, only to again submerge it fully and run back to the car, repeating my ritual. This time Bilbo was prepared and closed his eyes while tensing his body against the stream of sacred, if very cold, water. I ran back and left the sponge in the font. When I returned to the car both dogs were huddled in the passenger seat. I didn't react, and quietly watched them. They looked at each other as if agreeing that humans were not very bright. Outside my house, my usual parking space was gone, so I left the car at the end of the cul-de-sac and walked home. A few hours later the visiting car was gone and I went to move mine. The dogs came with me, and I was curious to see if they would climb on to the back seat. But an invisible line had been crossed; Bilbo jumped into the driver's seat, Frodo sat low on the passenger seat. It was the moment to begin issuing orders, reasserting my authority, but it was too funny, and they had obeyed me long enough. They had waited for the front seat and now they had established their claim. When I went to sit into the car, Bilbo made space for me, neatly stepping over the gear stick. After I had parked, I stepped out and closed the car door and made as if to go into the house. I turned back and once more Bilbo was in the driver's seat, resting his chin on the steering wheel, Frodo stretched out in the seat beside him.

*

I told no one about the holy water. By a strange coincidence, a few weeks later, the mother of a friend of mine made a suggestion. She said I should take Bilbo to Lourdes. She was a kind woman, an Austrian who loved dogs, never quite forgiving her husband, a pragmatic Scot, for hating pets and banning them from their home. She was a devout Catholic, yet hyper-sensitive and capable of becoming outraged with no warning. I debated telling her about the holy water I had taken from the church, and decided against it. Lourdes was, even for me, an impossibly long shot, rife with complications, including the quarantine regulations, and I wasn't sure how the guardians of the shrine would react to the appearance of a couple of pilgrim dogs.

Bilbo seemed well. I continued hoping that the vet was right, that the cancer might move very slowly. Perhaps it would exhaust itself? I clung to unreasonable hopes, and miracle cures. Weeks passed and then months, the seasons changed. I drove out to a place called the Meeting of the Waters in Wicklow, where two small rivers join together to form the Avoca, a beautiful stream polluted by nitrogen from a fertiliser factory. It was very peaceful until a tour bus loomed into view. I packed us up and drove further along the valley. In the narrower stream I noticed lovely rounded stones, and bent to examine them. They had been moulded by the water. But one of them was different, scoured flat and its shape reminded me of a romanticised heart. I took it up and splashed in the stream. Both dogs began to sniff the strange thing I had taken from the water. I put it in the back of the station wagon, intent on placing it in the garden.

One morning I noticed a crust on Bilbo's lump. Now it resembled the plug of a volcano, static but retaining its menace. I groomed around it. But at times I touched it with my fingers, very carefully, gauging its strength. Bilbo still bounced lightly up stairs. The thing was growing in him but had not begun to affect his movement. I recalled the days and nights spent watching Frodo's appendage as it grew longer and longer. But Bilbo's growth was far more dangerous and it was waiting to strike.

When it did, I wasn't ready. I had a flat tyre and no spare and was nursing the car along the busy motorway as it swivelled and lurched, an endless cavalcade of motorists overtaking us. I was returning from a seminar at which a poet had spoken about Synge's *Riders to the Sea* in a hushed voice. His theme was lamentation. The day was hot and the air was heavy, a heat haze made the road shimmer. Bilbo was beside me. The tumour burst with a wet sigh. I felt some of the discharge spray my face and a sticky fragment landed on my hand. Bilbo looked at me. Suddenly where there had been a hard surface was an open wound. The traffic made stopping too dangerous to attempt; I drove on, heading straight to the vet. A strong smell of blood quickly began to overpower the odour of decaying vegetation. My eyes were stinging, I was crying and the car seemed to be faltering, as if it too were about to collapse.

I nudged open the surgery door with my shoulder and carried Bilbo in. The nurse began to ask me the usual questions, my name, wanting to know if I been there before, but the vet came in behind me and simply took Bilbo from me, saying he would do his best but that this was probably the end. He smiled sympathetically and said that he would call me. Outside the car door was open but Frodo was sitting in the driver's seat. My heart was pounding and my legs felt as if I had run for miles on hard ground. The surgery door was closed but I felt I should be in there. I hadn't said goodbye. The days and years together ending just like this, with a closed door between us. I sat in the car. The nurse came out and I watched as she leaned over the door and told me to be calm, to go home, that she would call me. No decision, she said, would be made until they had spoken to me.

The house was cold, the dry heat of the day had receded and now I could feel a chill. It seemed appropriate; Bilbo's luck had run out. Our reprieve was over. I made tea I didn't drink and fed Frodo pieces of chicken by hand. He ate slowly. I tried to tidy my study. When the phone eventually rang, I picked it up and stood tight against the wall to brace myself. The vet addressed me by name and then paused, before telling me that he had expected Bilbo to die on the table but he had fought on, and they had been able to remove the tumour again. 'We almost lost him, I thought we had. But he just refused to go. This dog wants to live, it's . . .' He didn't say what it was. But I felt he had been touched or moved far beyond any strictly professional interest. I stood listening as the vet, a man not much older than I was at the time, spoke about Bilbo as if he was a hero, and described him as having clawed his way back to life. This was why people did not become vets, he reasoned, 'because dogs like Bilbo make it very hard'. It was more or less what my mother had said some years earlier when she told me to be a lawyer or a doctor, not a vet. She had said that I would get too involved and that my patients would break my heart.

Again I felt a sensation of guilt mixed with relief and gratitude. I didn't want Bilbo being forced to live for me. But when I came to collect him this time he looked much stronger than he had after the first operation five years earlier. He was older; he could no longer hide the fact that he was very old. But he did not have that dazed expression: he was composed, experience seemed to have helped him. We had been given more time, or rather Bilbo had grabbed it. Of course I loved him, but I also admired him. The vet had said things that I had always known but felt self-conscious about articulating. He had said that treating Bilbo was a privilege and that he was unique. I agreed: he had in so many ways opened me to life.

Not everyone wants to hear owners bragging about their pets. I remembered Robert and the insufferable Tessa. I tended to shield my dogs from people, protecting them from complaints about their barking, the dog hairs, the muddy paws. I had met too many people who were frightened of dogs, or who suffered from allergies. Some of them were smokers who carried nasty smells around with them yet remained oblivious to their own pollution, while emphatically dismissing well-cared-for pets as dirty. Several of the messiest houses I had ever visited had no animals at all. I had come to believe that to miss out on a relationship with dogs is to miss the experience of an intense bond that elevates us as humans. It initiates us into a rare kind of love, a real love that deserves to be recognised as such. Friendship between humans is wonderful but is often based on a mutual need, a yearning for convenience rather than affection. But when a human and a dog reach an understanding, it is a trust that articulates the full relevance of a promise to stay together 'till death do us part'.

Home from the wars again, Bilbo stayed close beside me. The post-operative swelling on his back this time was far less dramatic; the growth had been smaller but foul and nauseating. The vet could not explain why it had burst, but the same thing could have happened internally with devastating results. The wound had to be kept dry so I did not plan on returning to that church font. Instead an unexpected phone call led me down another track.

The mother of a girl to whom I was giving French lessons suffered from severe arthritis. At times it was so crippling that the woman, then barely fifty, could not get out of bed. They were a country family now living in the city, but still feeling displaced. A relative had put them in touch with a local man who helped with the harvesting back home and did odd jobs for various farmers but was now living in a small town near the border. My student was very shy and frail, but she was intent on training as a nurse. I couldn't imagine her having the strength to lift a patient. But she had a vocation and tried so hard, although she found exams difficult. The man they knew was a healer and her mother felt much better after seeing him; the girl believed that he had worked a miracle. I couldn't tell her about my previous experience with a fraudulent sham. I remembered the way that man had torn open the envelope to count his so-called donation, his reluctance even to touch Bilbo. But this girl's arthritic mother had recently cooked a meal for the first time in months and her daughter now urged me to take Bilbo to their healer. She said that he didn't pretend that he was 'a saint or something'. It was worth a chance, I thought; it might not help but it wouldn't hurt. My student had written his name on a page from her little notebook. The paper had a spray of pink flowers in the corner. Just a man's first name and a phone number; I promised my pupil that I would contact him.

The voice was encouraging. All he said was, 'I'm here, tell me your story.' He listened and said that he could pray with me over the phone but that he would rather I come to him. He wanted to hold the dog; he felt he would be better if he could touch him and talk to him, he'd get an idea of what the animal needed from him. It was simply said. The man sounded sincere and, as my student had promised, he gave himself no airs. There was no self-importance in the voice. I could hear a baby crying in the background. When he gave me directions, he told me not to worry, that I would find him. He said that his house was a bit of a mess, that I would lose myself in the garden. 'It's very wild out there at the moment,' he warned as if it was funny. I already liked him and then he said again that there was no chance I'd fail to find him. He had an old car and that something had made him paint it yellow. 'A bright, mad yellow, you'll find me.'

If he didn't cure my dog, he might at least help him. I felt that this was a way of arriving at an acceptance of what was about to happen to Bilbo. The healer had said something about three visits; that it would take three days. I wasn't sure. I set off the next morning. The yellow car was there, badly painted but unmistakable, a lurid shade that probably glowed in the dark. I patted the driver's seat of my car and told Frodo we would be back. I walked Bilbo up the unkempt path. A weary-looking man opened the door of the bungalow, holding a baby in his thick, tanned arms. The man could have been forty or fifty – I couldn't tell. He was heavy-set and wearing working clothes with a pair of brand-new white sports socks, no boots. His hair was wild and he had wonderful eyes, pale green and guileless, as if untouched by the hard living that had battered the rest of him. 'Hello, my man,' he said to Bilbo. 'You have seen the darkness,' then he looked at me and asked me to wait while he brought the baby, the babby, back to her mother. He asked if I'd like some tea. The little house was dark and cluttered, the lights were on. The curtains were closed, though it was only mid-morning.

When the man returned with a dainty china cup and saucer, and a slice of fruit cake, I felt as if I would cry. He said I should be patient, that the dog and nature would decide what to do. Bilbo and I had been many places, and now we were here.

'There, you sit there,' he said to me and I sank down into an old brown armchair. It was musty. The room was full, I felt like a conspirator. There were boxes, packing crates, and in the middle of all the male detritus stood an open carton of long-stemmed fake flowers. I realised I was panicking and needed to go to the bathroom, but didn't want to ask. As if he had read my thoughts the man looked away from Bilbo and said to me with some delicacy that I should go to the toilet, that it was at the end of the corridor and that we, meaning Bilbo and him, would begin.

When I returned to the sitting room, the man was holding Bilbo in his arms, cradling him as he had held his own baby. Bilbo looked smaller; the man's size diminished him. He was speaking to him. Then, pausing as if waiting for a reply, the man put his mouth to Bilbo's ear. He walked around, humming softly and then sat down, stroking Bilbo with his workman's hands. Huge hands with unexpectedly long fingers, strong fingers with blunt nails, one was black and misshapen. I noticed sweat running down the man's face in fat drops that were falling on to Bilbo's head. His eyes were closed, as were Bilbo's. The room felt hot. The man continued speaking softly and then the rhythm changed; he appeared to be reciting something. Perhaps he was praying, I could not tell. Bilbo's eyes were still closed, and he seemed very relaxed. The man crooned, Bilbo sighed. It was all very strange and somehow oddly comforting. I could hear the wood pigeons outside. Then the man looked at me with a start as if he had just woken up. 'Come back to me tomorrow, the same time and the morning after. Bilbo is deciding. He needs me to help him. And you're helping him, too. He is walking along a road.' He told me that Bilbo was 'searching for something'. I wasn't sure if he meant that Bilbo wanted to die and that he was ready. Perhaps by going to meet this healer, I would, as I had thought when my French student had first mentioned him to me, learn to accept that this was the end.

The next day when we arrived the man was waiting in his ruined garden. He lifted Bilbo up in his arms and we went inside. His wife had cooked me a breakfast, an omelette made of eggs from her own hens. She seemed much younger than her husband; she told me that they wanted to move 'so as to be near the sea'. I went into the sitting room. The healer and Bilbo were sitting on the old sofa; the man had his left arm around Bilbo but was leaning forward, his right hand cupping the side of his own head. Bilbo sat patiently, bending towards me, yet he stayed where he was. After a few minutes the man sat upright and then noticed me. He said he needed more time and asked me to fetch him a glass of water from the kitchen. I came back and handed the glass to him. He emptied it in a single vast swallow and returned to his meditation. I went outside to check on Frodo and came quietly back in to wait in the sitting room. The man stood up and smiled at me. He took Bilbo in his arms and walked out into the garden. About ten minutes later he came back, still with Bilbo held to his chest. He placed Bilbo on one of the larger crates and held his head, looking into his eyes. 'I'll see ye both tomorrow,' he said, by way of goodbye as he lifted Bilbo down and placed him on the floor. The man stood at the door, shoulders hunched, both of his arms wrapped around his body. Bilbo trotted to the car and then stopped, and glanced back towards the healer, who waved at us.

It was the final morning. I had withdrawn a hundred pounds from the bank; again it was in an official-looking envelope. But I thought it was cold and clinical. This healer had not mentioned money and had instead engaged with Bilbo as if they were old friends. Removing the cash from the bank envelope, I put it into a greeting card. It was a beautiful image; it had been reproduced from one of Stubbs's paintings, a study of mares and foals. Dandelions were out along the verges of the country roads, cheerful and vividly yellow. I decided to buy flowers for the healer, this large, physical, strangely gentle man, who had held my beloved dog as if he were a baby. As we neared the town I noticed a petrol station, and it had buckets of daffodils in the forecourt. I bought most of them and drove on. Again the healer was waiting outside. Bilbo walked into the room with him while I went back to the car to settle Frodo and to make sure that the flowers were still upright in the bucket of water I had borrowed, promising the man at the garage that I would return it on my way home.

The final session was very intense. I sat in on it for a while and watched the healer, struggling as though fighting with an invisible weight. Bilbo stood quite still with his eyes closed as if he too were concentrating. Once again the healer began to sweat. He held Bilbo so close to him I was worried he would crush him. His huge fingers met over Bilbo's head. The man spoke to himself, or to his gods, I don't know, but he chanted and quietly implored, asking for something in words I could not quite distinguish. Bilbo's eyes remained closed and then he opened them with a start. He looked surprised; it was as if he had returned from a strange place. He jumped down from the sofa and walked over to me, the man following. He told me to take Bilbo home. We began walking to the door; I remembered the flowers and said I'd be back. I felt awkward about the money and wondered if it was enough. The healer laughed at the giant bouquet and said it was wonderful. When I gave him the envelope, he said he only wanted the horses – he knew what was on the card although he had not opened the envelope, and dismissed the money as if it was something squalid. He said he hadn't paid for his power; it was a gift he could share and it had helped him in his life. His mother had had second sight and it had tormented her, he had not forgotten that. Flowers he could accept. 'I'm fierce fond of yellow,' he smiled at his shabby car and looked really young for a moment. Then he called gently to Bilbo. 'You're a very brave dog,' he whispered, 'and your journey's not over yet.'

18

Days of Sun

Bluebells and wild garlic dominated the woods, which were bordered by the gorse that had in places begun to come into yellow flower. It was overcast, and a weak, pallid light struggled to break through the clouds. Fermanagh is a melancholic archipelago of water, trees and shady lanes; the lakes are scattered with hundreds of small islands. On the way back from visiting Devenish, a monastic site founded by a saint named Molaise in the sixth century provided an appropriate moment to pay my respects to an ancient tree that stood in a demesne a few miles outside the town. It was only while gazing back at the round tower on the island as it retreated in the distance, and the little ferry chugged towards the landing area, that I had remembered the yew at Florence Court, once the home of Lord Enniskillen. I knew the tree was regarded as the mother of all Irish yews propagated throughout the world. A story dating from about 1760 tells of a tenant farmer who had found a pair of yews growing wild in the mountains nearby and had planted one on his smallholding. He had given the other young tree to his master, the then owner of Florence Court. The tenant's yew died but Lord Enniskillen's had flourished. Given the unexpected news that I was going to have a baby, the fertile old tree might also prove lucky. The dogs ran on, sniffing and marking territory among the trees along the short track, perhaps only about a half mile from the house that had been named in honour of a beloved young wife.

The yew tree stood in the parkland, surrounded by modest ash and laurel. It was not the most impressive of specimens, looking weary as if drained by its global fame, yet it was still upright and dignified. A good sign; at least, that is how I viewed it.

Impending motherhood is celebrated without embarrassment by everyone if you're part of a couple; the team effort is congratulated and all your friends seem pleased. But my boyfriend was not, and he had reminded me that he had an 'existing arrangement', namely a marriage, and that I would be on my own. The most frequent piece of advice that I received during the final months of what had until then been a secret pregnancy was that I should have the dogs put down. The reasoning was that they would be jealous and might attack my baby without warning. I listened respectfully, because listening was easier than arguing. But we carried on, the dogs and I, we continued exploring and I continued reading and writing, and I wondered if there was going to be a 'happy ever after'. I returned to the old yew tree about three years later. My daughter stood beside it with Bilbo and Frodo, by then very elderly, while she pointed out that the tree was not very pretty.

Babies, of course, introduce serious changes in any life and we needed a different, more suitable home, as the odd terraced house with its spiral staircase and wooden veranda was not safe for a child. It would also mean leaving the garden I had created for the dogs. We were, for the moment, still trapped in the city. A friend had recently married and had also inherited a large, elegant house in an exclusive part of Dublin and now had a smaller, and much older, house to sell. It would suit us for a while until we could finally move to the countryside, and it also had an old-fashioned garden.

In the months before the birth, my little house sold quickly and I bought my friend's house surprisingly cheaply. The first thing I did was to pull up all the carpets and prepare to sand the floors. I had not lost my touch. Yet again the dogs waited in the garden, more often in the car, while I stripped the impressively wide boards. The dust settled and the varnish dried, and our expeditions continued. Both dogs were well and were also taking various homeopathic supplements. But I was aware that one or both might die before my baby was born.

It was so important to me that they would still be with me, that somehow this child, already journeying towards us, would also come to know them. I was grateful that I had an archive of photographs recording the life I had spent with two unique characters yet wished that all of this had happened earlier when the dogs were young and that my child could have grown up with them, instead of just hearing stories or looking at snapshots. I already knew that he or she would have their own dog, I would make certain of that. I wanted this boy or this girl to experience as children what I had had to wait for until I was an adult. The weeks passed slowly; nothing passes as slowly as human pregnancy. My preparations were going well and I ticked off the days, only 117 to go, 116; time crawled, still 84 left and so it went on.

We set off for Omey again to stay in a house overlooking the sea, but now there was a fourth presence with us. I hoped that the baby would be a girl but always replied when asked that I didn't mind either way. On the way home I drove at a leisurely pace, as the back of the old station wagon was weighted down. I had become a collector of rounded stones. I made dramatic arrangements, small cairns of them in the corners of rooms and in the garden and I had returned to reading about the American Civil War, as I had years before with my father, although my fascination with history had nothing to do with him. It was more the comfort of something familiar that I felt I had known all my life. I often wondered how different my world with the dogs would become. The waiting was strange and exciting and unsettling.

*

At Maidenhall, the home of the celebrated Irish essayist, Hubert Butler, his formidable widow greeted us, her expression softening when she saw the dogs. She called Bilbo 'beautiful child' and told me about a collie she had had more than seventy years earlier. She said she had never forgotten that dog and, when he had died, she remembered telling her mother that she had wanted to die with him. Her story both charmed and upset me. The dogs explored the grounds, which overlooked a river. I took several rolls of film, with Bilbo standing in the sun, Frodo just behind him. Both dogs pottered about, completely at ease, without looking old or weakened by their respective illnesses. An ancient white bench was positioned against the back wall of the porch at the front entrance. It was ironwork, slightly ornate and quite long. Beside it, closer to the door stood a wooden chair. Just in front of the bench was a lower, far more modest wooden bench. Bilbo jumped up on it, and sat on his haunches, looking me. There was a stone pillar in the foreground; it seemed to frame the fine old double door, its turquoise colour faded by the sun. There were many scratch marks at the foot of the doors, made by generations of dogs. Bilbo turned towards the doors, one white paw slightly at an angle as if deep in thought. Then he stood, moving closer to the edge of the bench, poised to jump down. He heard the camera and paused, moving in stages, as if deliberately allowing me to photograph the sequence.

Inside the house, in a kitchen in which time appeared to have stood still, I helped our hostess prepare afternoon tea. She had insisted that the dogs sit on the rug that lay on the floor in front of the Aga stove. She said that the Aga only 'looked right' when a dog was stretched out before it, 'even better if there are two of them'. It was all redolent of an earlier, more civilised era. I could imagine living in a similar house; complete with its particular story and memories.

*

I remember the nights, the long nights of waiting. It was difficult to sleep. The move to our 'new' house, a very old building, tall and narrow with its now burnished floorboards, most of which creaked, was completed a couple of months before the birth. I was pleased with my handiwork; the floors were among the best I had prepared and varnished. Just as I finished sanding down the woodwork in the bathroom, I realised that an important appointment had finally become imminent. The guys were sitting on the bed when I reached for my small travel bag and they jumped down, expecting to accompany me. This time I had to go alone. When I returned about a day and half later, they acted as if I had been absent for months, although they had been lovingly minded by a friend who knew them and had stayed with them, playing a recording of Mozart's Great Mass in C as well as Chopin's nocturnes to ease Bilbo's anxiety. He always responded to music. The dogs welcomed me with such love. Then they noticed that I was not alone. Bilbo was intrigued and suddenly looked young again; he gazed at the baby and whimpered softly, pressing in against me. But Frodo was wary. It was ironic. Bilbo had been so reluctant all those years ago to allow his playmate to move in and yet here he was, content to have a dependent human enter his well-ordered domain. His reaction delighted me, whereas I was surprised that solid, reliable Frodo seemed confused and edgy. My daughter gave a loud cry. It took us all by surprise. I was still in a dream, but Frodo's reaction suggested that the walls of his kingdom had been breached by a usurper.

I thought about all the alarmist warnings I had been given about interspecies jealousy, but I also recalled the people who had decided I would be a great mother as I looked after my dogs so well. I held my daughter and couldn't help noticing that even a big baby weighed far less than either of my dogs. As soon as I sat down, Bilbo lay across my feet. He was keeping guard. Frodo then jumped up on the sofa beside me. I was ready for any sudden movement and knew that I could block him with my shoulder and arm if he came too close. But there was no need for concern. He looked down at the baby and then up at me, and then settled beside me. The dogs were very gentle. I had seen female cats attack kittens that were not their own, but these elderly male dogs showed no resentment. I knew how good older geldings were with mares and foals. It was about trust, and I had no reason to doubt my dogs, they knew me and they would get to know my daughter.

For months I sat up all night watching her sleep. Babies sleep so deeply, it was terrifying. Sharing my vigil were Bilbo and Frodo. Each time I stared at the baby, and glanced at them, they were looking at me. I have never read as much as I did during that time. Dickens helped keep me awake. It was the first time I had read *Our Mutual Friend*. Then immediately I re-read *Bleak House* and Tolstoy's *War and Peace*, and finally had the perfect reason for tackling Leon Edel's five-volume life of Henry James. I wondered was he lonely, this extraordinarily sensitive man, the ideal dinner guest who never found true love. Reading was the most effective way of staying awake. I sat up on the bed with my daughter in my arms, a dog on either side, and stayed more or less quiet until she woke at 6.30 a.m., as if set on a timer. We all went downstairs; the dogs ran out into the garden and then the ritual feeding began. Nothing much had changed, except that I now had a nocturnal life of reading, watching and listening. My girl began quietly, as if preparing us for the exuberance that would soon follow. She travelled in a kangaroo pouch when we went walking. We never had a pram. By the time I finally bought a stroller, when she was six months old, she pushed it out of the store. Back home she wheeled her soft toys and dolls about in it. She had begun walking at about five months thanks to the besotted Bilbo who was her support: she balanced against him, her hand on his back. When I think about it now, it must have looked funny, the four of us moving in a tightly packed group, even in the kitchen, as if we were tied together. The most consistent help I had with looking after that small baby came from my dogs. When I thought I knew everything about them and suspected that they could read my mind, they surprised me yet again.

Bright, clever Bilbo with his curiosity and intense intelligence displayed incredible patience when dealing with a personality as mercurial as his own. He would sit as she read him the stories that she imagined were contained in the pictures in her books. She conducted imaginary orchestras, he watched, and when she sang, he did too. Bilbo was the nanny, Frodo the guardian.

There was never any doubt about Bilbo's commitment, but Frodo was to prove his in an emphatic way. My friend Sophie invited us to her home; she owned several stridently manic cats which she admitted were beyond discipline. They were supposed to be denied access to her house while we were there. It was a very wet day and even the short walk from the car to her hall door left us drenched. Drops of rain bounced off Bilbo's tail as he shook himself. We went into the warm kitchen; the table was set as if for a celebration. My friend reached for the baby, then only a few weeks old, and Frodo launched himself at her, growling and forcing Sophie to retreat until she stood with her back to the wall. It was a striking display of loyalty. Frodo had decided that no one should touch our baby except me.

They had always been good watchdogs but now no one could get in the front door. Frodo planted himself solidly in the hall and was growling before a hand touched the knocker. I felt bad about having to lock the pair of them in a room when people came to the house. They made sure I could hear them sighing on the other side of the door – it was far more effective than barking. As soon as I released them from whatever room they had been locked in, usually the main bedroom, they ran over to investigate the baby. We were managing well; I read through the nights and seemed to forget that I had ever indulged in such a thing as sleep. I bought a large Winnie the Pooh play pen and I sat in there with her. It was a safe place to read while she drew and played with number blocks and letter cards. I had called her Nadia, Nadezhda, meaning hope, after the indefatigable wife of the poet Osip Mandelstam. Her first word was 'Bilbo', her first phrase 'mine dogs'. Whether this was motivated by her own feelings of ownership or from hearing me speak about them wasn't clear. But I didn't mind, she loved them. The disapproving comments continued and I often had to smile and be gracious while being reprimanded for having kept my dogs, and still I continued to be regaled with various versions of the dingo story about the woman in Australia whose child had allegedly been stolen by a wild dog during an ill-fated visit to Ayers Rock. Although I didn't attempt to defend myself, it was obvious that not only had the dogs sustained me, they were having a tremendous impact on my child's development. The dogs did not have to hunt to feed us but they gave me something of which many humans seemed incapable – emotional support.

*

If this was a lonely life, I didn't notice. It was simple, but it was also fun and it was real; I was grateful for every day that I could watch my child be happy with my dogs. But Christmas was a challenge. I decided to go to Connemara and arranged to stay, for the only time in my life, in a hotel at Christmas. The old seaside inn I chose had literary connections with Oliver St John Gogarty, a sometime associate of James Joyce and his inspiration for Buck Mulligan. More importantly, children and dogs were welcome. It was dry and bright, not particularly Christmas-like, but ideal for a walk on the beach. My daughter had insisted on bringing her giant Peter Rabbit, a soft toy large enough to fill a car seat. After I had settled the dogs in the hotel room with a bowl of water on the bathroom floor, I went back to fetch the rabbit. News of a gruesome murder was beginning to filter through; I had heard it in snatches, on a radio report in a petrol station, and later from the television news in the hotel lobby. On my return to the hotel room, I sat on the bed with my baby, and our dogs walked over to us. I turned on the television to find out what had happened. But the bulletin had ended.

There was to be a grand sitting of all the guests, sharing a communal Christmas supper. The dining room was very bright and too busy for me and I could see that my girl was becoming restless. Her face looked hot. Party hats were distributed, and although I took two paper crowns I realised that I could never join in. Already it seemed that the best part of our adventure was over: the early morning drive across Ireland, through deserted towns and villages, and the walk on the beach. What had seemed a good idea was appearing far less inspired, and the dogs were sitting in an unfamiliar room, no doubt wondering where I had gone, while I was feeling like a fool who had wandered on to a movie set. The manager was sympathetic and said he would have everything sent to our room and that he would send up scraps for the dogs.

As I was walking through the reception area, a small, dark-haired woman approached me and said how pleasant it was to come to a hotel that allowed dogs. Her eyes were bright and darted about. She barely looked at me. It was as if she was waiting for someone to walk in and was worried in case they might slip by. She spoke precise, elegantly accented English. I realised that she was French and I asked her why she had come away at Christmas. Her story involved her husband and his secretary. I said little in response. Then she mentioned the murder I had heard about; the victim was a woman from Paris, a well-known film-maker. Her family had understood that she was on her way home. But instead she had been found lying in her blood on the roadside in a remote part of County Cork. The horror of it seemed to add to the unreality of the overly bright hotel and the sight of someone else's Christmas tree while the one I had decorated with wooden toys and animals was standing miles away in the dark with no one to admire it.

The waiter delivered a vast amount of food to our room. The dogs enjoyed a surprising quantity of turkey and ate some of the vegetables. They dozed while the baby slept in her favourite pose, stretched out across me, her tiny arms folded back behind her head. I watched a movie in which Meryl Streep plays a former river guide, now bored with her life but intent on taking her son and mild-mannered husband on an adventure holiday through the rapids in the Grand Canyon. They meet two men who appear lost and bewildered; the Streep character agrees to help them and the men turn out to be killers. The mother battles to protect her family. They had been in the wrong place at the wrong time. It was an odd movie for Christmas night and although the situation it depicted was extreme, it was too formulaic to help make sense of the violent death of a woman on the road near her holiday house. Such were my thoughts as I watched my little family asleep in a bland hotel room when I knew we should have stayed at home.

*

Now there were three figures on the beach at Omey, a small child had joined the two dogs. The tide was so far out that only a thin ripple of water seeped across the faintly ridged sand. It was the baby's first birthday and she was discovering the place that the dogs had made their own. The evening sun was low in the sky but still bright. The three moved towards me, a close unit. There was barely any daylight between them. The sea had shaped a natural platform out of stone; it was pitted with small pools. Bilbo stood on the highest part of the formation, while the baby sat down with

Frodo at her shoulder. I knew I would always remember this moment; the sea birds were browsing through the seaweed. An oystercatcher used its long red bill to probe the sand. The rasping cry of the cormorant tore the silence. Each small movement was creating a photograph and I was there, in pursuit of a defining shot, intent on not missing a gesture, an expression. Bilbo ran over to me as I bent down and through the lens I watched the baby and Frodo as they stood shoulder to shoulder, looking at something along the beach: from that angle the sea could be seen in the distance. It was too late to drive out to the island; we might have become stranded as the tide sneaked in, as it always does.

The beach was completely deserted, except for us and the birds. The sun made a final line of brilliant yellow along the horizon and then it was gone. The sky was silver grey as it met the bleached beige of the damp sand. Bilbo, as if sensing we would soon be making our way back to the car, ran down the beach, and the baby and Frodo followed much more slowly. Frodo's unrushed amble, with its occasional hop, was sufficiently quick to keep pace with a baby, wearing a baseball cap, who was still learning how to run. It had been a wonderful day, one of so many.

Back at the cottage, I lit a fire and the smell of turf quickly filled the small room. I wanted this week to last forever. Bilbo stretched out in front of the hearth with Frodo on one side, and the baby leaning up against him, chattering away to him. He listened, one ear cocked as if he was hearing the outline of a daring tale. Nervy Bilbo had seldom seemed so relaxed. We had come to a perfect place. Children and dogs are good together; a child explores with the same intense curiosity and understands why the dog has little interest in linear forms of exploration and play. The dogs had waited as the baby collected pebbles and shells. They carefully sniffed at her discoveries. When she crouched to peer into the rock pools, they did the same. Bilbo gave a short bark as she reached to pick up a crab. She pulled her hand away, aware that he was warning her. The most exciting find of that afternoon was a sea urchin. Early the next morning we walked up the lane to watch the ponies in the field. The chill in the air reminded me that it was autumn, and that the days were getting shorter.

If there was to be an outing it had to begin in the morning because by mid-afternoon the light faded. There was also the pressure of work, so every day was not a holiday. But even a brief November day gave time enough to visit a churchyard a few miles beyond Drogheda to see the high crosses at Monasterboice, one of which is said to have been either built by or dedicated to Muiredach, possibly one of two abbots who had at different times presided over the monastery. Whoever he was, he had one eye firmly on eternity. The small church stands on the site of a monastery founded by Saint Buite of whom little is known. The round tower darts in and out of view on the approach. It is a beautiful place, very peaceful and secluded, while the cross remains a dense, powerful statement of belief. We had a picnic there and Frodo, true to his nature, chased a squirrel that ran up the nearest tall headstone before scrambling towards some trees. As we were leaving, a woman arrived to tend a grave. It expressed the continuity between the living and the dead. The surrounding landscape is working farmland, and life continues partly as it has for millennia. The baby dozed, as did Frodo, while Bilbo kept watch. Then he began to tense. Up ahead were flashing lights. I was not surprised – the romantic roads were a maze of sharp bends and were difficult to negotiate safely. But it was not an accident; it was a police road block. Two men in uniform motioned at me to stop. They peered into the car; I wondered would they object to the dogs sitting in the front seat. Bomb-making equipment had been discovered nearby. Irish political realities persisted, within miles of an ancient monastic site. Peace had not yet come, and back then the sinister guerrilla war seemed to have become endless.

*

Ironically, given the ongoing conflict in Northern Ireland, probably the most serene car journey we ever experienced was along the magnificent Antrim coast road one early morning, only a couple of hours after I had witnessed the impossible: Carl Lewis had won the Olympic long jump title for the fourth time. For all his gifts he had never become an American hero, but on that humid night in Atlanta, no one cared. It was remarkable. For me, watching thousands of miles away in Europe it was astonishing to see a thirty-five-year-old, who had only just made his national team by qualifying in the third and final place at the US trials, defy time and his younger rivals. Our destination that morning was a literary conference on the life and work of the Ulster poet John Hewitt at a school in the Antrim glens. Nadia insisted on carrying my briefcase, which I had emptied of everything except the text of my lecture, to make the bag lighter for her. I have a photograph of her walking ahead of me; the dogs were with me, on their leads. There were people about. I had wanted to make a discreet entrance and bring my entourage quietly to our accommodation, a small bedroom with a television and a view of the college quadrangle. On my way back to the car, I was met by one of the organisers. He seemed slightly disappointed as he said, 'Did you not bring your wee friends with you?' I said they were already in the room. His reaction pleased me. 'I'm glad, I want to meet them.' I often thought of the English writer J. R. Ackerley and his dog Tulip, a German Shepherd whose fraught personality irritated many people. Ackerley was devoted to her: she was the love of his life, the 'ideal friend' he had waited for and found in middle age. He had tried in vain to help her have a litter. He seemed completely unaware of the havoc she caused, or perhaps, more probably, he pretended not to notice. I did not share his indifference to criticism, nor his confidence in people's tolerance.

No matter how much you love your dog, or dogs, it is always vital to be alert to the slightest nuance in expression or tone in others' reaction to them. I was careful: I wanted my dogs with me and they needed me to mind them. But I knew not to force them on others; it's not fair to the dog, never mind the unwilling human.

19

Abandoned in the Dusk

Rathlin O'Birne is an Atlantic hermitage founded by Assicus, the favourite disciple of St Patrick, and it is he who is believed to have administered last rites to the dying saint. The island lies about three nautical miles off Malin Beg, on the south-west coast of County Donegal, just south of the historic pilgrimage route of Glencolmcille. Although situated sufficiently near the mainland to offer clear views of the sheep grazing on it, Rathlin O'Birne is difficult to reach by boat, though a lighthouse was built there in 1856. Even in calm conditions, the seas conceal vicious reefs and sinister undercurrents. On the day I was offered the chance to venture out in a modest powerboat, the sky was as grey as the sea. It was a tempting invitation and I knew that at no time would it have been safe to bring the dogs. We had visited many islands together aside from Omey; we had been to Aran and the smaller islands, as well as Sherkin off the Cork coast, Inismurray off Sligo and Clare Island and also Achill off the Mayo coast and Lombay off County Dublin, but Rathlin O'Birne was not welcoming. Many distinguished antiquarians and archaeologists and other scholars had been defeated by the conditions and had cancelled crossings. That so many had failed where sixth-century monks sailing in fragile, open currachs had succeeded is intriguing. But then, how can a modern mind hope to measure the determination of a devout hermit?

It needs a well-timed jump from the boat as it rises on

the swell to reach the slippery stone of the pier. But that morning's conditions asked for a wild leap that would test all but a marauding pirate. No, this was not a suitable expedition for a small girl and the dogs. They remained on shore with the boatman's wife and two wary archaeologists who declined to attempt the rough crossing. The wind tore across the island but it was an adventure locating the various pilgrim stations and again wondering about the solitary souls who had gone there to pray. The boatman was also a farmer and he kept sheep out there. As I wandered about in the rain I found an injured ewe caught up in barbed wire. The boatman was delighted and said that I had earned my passage as I carried her back to the tiny landing area. I sat in the boat with my face pressed down on the shivering animal's wet wool. On my return, slightly seasick after the violent pitching of the boat in worsening conditions, I was told by the boatman's wife that my daughter had eaten and slept well while I was exploring the island, but that the dogs had seemed worried and had stayed in the porch of the boatman's house, staring out to sea, 'looking very forlorn'. Bilbo pushed his head under my chin, always one of his most intense expressions of affection, glad I was back.

A few weeks earlier we had travelled through the Burren on our way to Connemara. It was late summer and the landscape looked noticeably different to me, as I was more familiar with its spring aspect, when it is rich in early season flowers. Convoys of Dormobiles driven by German and Dutch tourists snaked around the tight bends of the coastal roads. Finally we arrived at a small restaurant on the pier at Clarinbridge. The sun had come out and a fine morning had become a hot afternoon. There were several children playing among the tables and benches. My girl was standing on a chair, singing. She paused to remove her sweater and was struggling with it. I went over to help. Before I reached her, she had fallen. Blood splattered from her forehead. I could hear shouts, and several adults attempted to take control. I pushed her hair back and saw that she needed stitches. She was screaming. Too many people were speaking at once. A doctor was mentioned but the directions I was given seemed so complicated that a couple volunteered to drive us, and I asked the man to lead the dogs. He said he didn't want them in the car. As he was helping my child I couldn't argue, but asked if he would wait while I put them into my car. Perhaps he had not heard me, as he accelerated away, insisting that we had to hurry. The drive to the doctor seemed much longer than it actually was. When she saw us, she said the gash was too deep for her to stitch. We needed to get to a hospital. I suggested she tape the wound as it was long and narrow. She objected but soon changed her mind, possibly because my child had calmed down.

When we left the surgery, the couple who had driven us there were gone. It was several hours before we could get a lift back to the restaurant. It was deserted. The hot afternoon had faded into a dull and chilly evening. The large parasols on the tables had been closed and taken indoors. I could hear barking; they were over by the pier. Bilbo was tied to a post; a length of clothes line had been looped through his collar. Frodo was sitting beside him. They did look dejected, like two orphans. Did they think that I would have abandoned them? I hoped their trust in me was as strong as my mine in them.

None of the restaurant staff could tell me what had happened or who had tied Bilbo to the post instead of putting the dogs into my car, which was not locked. Despite my relief I couldn't help noticing how dangerously close the post was to the water. Had Bilbo panicked he could have fallen in and Frodo the swimmer would have gone in after him. I was aware of how close I had come to losing the dogs. My child's wound healed, and left no scar.

Within days we had discovered Ross Errilly, the ruins of a great late medieval Franciscan friary just off the Headford road in County Galway. In the distance it still looks as if it is a working complex inhabited by a busy community of monks, a labyrinth of cloisters and domestic dwellings built in grey limestone. The bell tower rises imposingly above the surrounding fields. I knew that there was a stone water tank in the kitchen building that had been used for holding fish. Ross Errilly lies not far from Lough Corrib. It is a serene, haunting place, dating from the mid-fourteenth century, now open to the heavens, the roofs having collapsed some time after the friars finally abandoned it in the early eighteenth century. We stayed there all day. My daughter pottered about, walking in and out among the stone rooms, following Bilbo. Frodo kept guard, checking on us all and barking at the hooded crows, now the chief residents. I photographed the windows, against the ever-changing light, aware that by sunset I would have a Monet-like series of pictures. Of all the images of the windows, it was the one taken of the great gable at dusk that I decided to have enlarged and framed. It hangs on the wall of my living room as a reminder not only of a beautiful place but of a wonderful day.

'Bare ruined choirs where late the sweet bird sang.' That line from Shakespeare's Sonnet 73 with its themes of death, time and loss, was now never far from my thoughts. While we wandered about in Ross Errilly I had watched the guys and wondered how much more time we would have together, how many more days like that one A few months later we set off for the ancient burial ground of Loughcrew in County Meath where a collection of passage tombs straddle two neighbouring rises on Slieve na Calligh, the Hill of the Witch. We had been there several times, but I had never noticed the steep gradient. I bent down as my daughter climbed up on my back and I also carried Frodo up to the cairn, telling Bilbo to wait for me to come back for him. But he fretted and walked along beside me. A hill that he had often run up had somehow become higher.

*

Many people have dogs, and there are as many poignant dog stories celebrating their devotion and courage, the places they make for themselves and the enormous gaps they leave in human lives. One of my close friends had a collie. I had known him well; he was a handsome sheepdog, sedate and given to taking life at a slow pace. He sighed often, long sonorous sighs that suggested he was aware of the effort that mere breathing, never mind movement, required. When we visited he would accompany us on walks through the fields, usually maintaining a steady pace for a while. Then he would select a spot where he could settle down and wait to join us as we returned from other fields, ones that my dogs investigated but that he had never felt the need to explore. He knew how to conserve his energy and spent hours lying in the family's kitchen, squeezed into a straw basket that had belonged to his predecessor, a much smaller dog. When he began to decline, he did so very quickly. He could not use his legs and often lay in his urine and faeces. I remember helping him out into the garden. He was completely helpless. My friend finally asked me to go with her when she took him to the vet; I sat in the back seat of her car with him prone across my lap as she drove to the same vet who had given him his first vaccinations many years earlier. The dog seemed indifferent to the fact that he was about to die. My friend's husband arrived just as the vet was preparing the final injection. The couple stood crying; they had been arguing, but now they were united in heartbreak. The dog had been a wedding present and was part of their history. The vet looked away as my friend wept. I carried the dog back out to their car and waited. The body was still warm but now it was limp and seemed heavier. It made me conscious of what was approaching for my guys.

But our story seemed set to continue for a while yet. I watched for signs of infirmity, for the apathy that overcame my friend's dog. On our return from a trip to a potter's studio in a mountain village, near Killybegs in County Donegal, we went to stay at an inn by the sea, but the few rooms had been taken. Another place was mentioned as a possibility, an old house that had been neglected for years but had been bought recently and was being restored. These new owners were referred to as being 'arty' and had begun replanting what had been a famous walled garden. I set off to find the house. I had been told to look for three horse chestnut trees by the entrance. I drove down a lane that gradually widened into a formal avenue. The rhododendrons became denser. At the back of a small clearing stood a lovely Regency villa. A man was standing at the open door. He was startled out of deep thought by the arrival of a car he had not been expecting.

A tiny, old dog appeared beside him; her yapping abruptly collapsed into wheezes and she stopped to catch her breath. He picked her up and invited us in, telling my dogs not to be frightened of her. He said with some irony that he had her under control and he brought us through to a bright, traditional kitchen full of new steel and glass appliances. A beautiful woman was making jam, pots of it, and she said the stuff one bought in shops was rubbish. She sounded very well-bred and was wearing a long dress. Her hair was piled haphazardly, if artfully, on top of her head. She smiled as if I were a long-lost friend and announced that she would 'ring the schoolhouse bell' when supper was ready. I wondered if there really was a schoolhouse bell or if it was their joke. Her husband gave us a tour of the house. 'You will love this,' he said, and led me through a stableyard into what seemed to be a groom's loft. Wooden steps led up to a small room, another door opened on to a dramatic space which ended with a large window overlooking a lake. He had created a concert hall in the woods. Pleased with my reaction, he said he had something else to show me.

We walked back down the stairs into a secluded section of the garden. Among trees and banks of flowers lay a grassed area, a formal grove, in which standing stones and monuments had been placed. It was a pets' cemetery. The man pointed to individual graves, the resting places of generations of the original family's animals, including a hunting horse. He said he felt like a custodian and remarked that for many people their dog or cat was the special loved one. I knew what he meant. He mentioned the fragile dog that had yapped at our arrival, and listed her various ailments and talked about the heart tablets that he struggled to give her twice a day. He said that she was the great-granddaughter of a dog he had loved so much that he had vowed never again to become so close to another dog. 'I've failed, of course,' he laughed.

20

The Coldest Sunlight

Luck or privilege or some divine generosity seemed to be sustaining us. Our little band endured. Experiences accumulated. It wasn't restlessness that kept us on the trail of adventure as much as the niggling sense of failure. I had not succeeded in finding our dream house in the countryside. Instead we were always visiting the homes of others, in search of an ideal way of life that had eluded us. There were increasing hints of time running out, some subtle, an occasional weariness discernible in the dogs. I monitored their exercise, often stopping a walk while the guys were still in mid-stride. I made sure that they rested. We were once sitting near a pond in a park, watching the ducks, when a woman stopped and complimented the dogs, remarking on how beautiful they were. Her son, who was about ten years old, peered at them and announced in a matter of fact voice, 'But they are old, aren't they?' It was the first time anyone had said that, apart from the vet. I felt that our situation had become precarious; we were clinging to something that was now under threat.

It had been cold and wet for what had seemed like a very long time. The winter was endless. Then the first signs of life brought some hope as the buds appeared. Quite unexpectedly an invitation arrived; a chance to stay at an unusual house, near Westport, in Mayo. It was part of a recently converted stableyard in the grounds of a Georgian mansion. We were to be the first guests; I felt privileged. I knew the area: the setting was serene, with views out over Clew Bay and beyond that the vastness of the Atlantic. A river ran through the estate. For once I had not had to plot and plan. All I had to do was drive there. I invited a friend to come with us; she was recovering from an emotional crisis that filled our conversations. Her moods moved between sorrow and rage. Within hours of our arrival the cottage became oppressive. I realised that I should not have asked her to come. But I listened, and as I listened, I became distracted. We had arrived during a rain storm and throughout the first night, gales tore across the sea. The roof shuddered. I began to realise that I could anticipate what she was going to say next. Her story moved in circles because the problems were impossible to resolve. I began to feel bone-weary.

The next morning was bright and warm, the earth was drying quickly. Steam rose up, creating a pulsing haze. Someone had told me that there was a lone corncrake in the area, among the last of a dying species, and to listen for its distinctive cry. I was hoping to photograph the rare bird. I opened the door for the dogs to step out briefly before we had breakfast. My friend had begun to weep and had snapped at my child as she had tried to comfort her by reading to her. She was not interested in hearing Nadia read about a boy who had too many teddies and had waved her away. I turned around quickly but stopped myself as I could see that my friend was not aware of how rude she had been to my daughter. Frodo was licking his paw. Everything in the kitchen was new; the toaster was still wrapped in plastic. I looked around for Bilbo to give him the ceremonial first piece of toast, but he wasn't there.

It was unlike him to go back to a bedroom, particularly a

room in a new place, without me. He wasn't in the bedroom or anywhere in the cottage, and the door was ajar. He must have gone out, which was also uncharacteristic of him. I looked around outside, then walked back into the cottage and my friend told me not to fuss, dogs were capable of independent action. No doubt, but not in this way, I thought, and turned to go out and heard the irritation in my friend's voice as I ran down the path out of the small garden. I hurried along the track into sunlight so intense that I couldn't see. I ran on, not knowing where to look. I could not guess where he might have gone. Frodo might have been lured by a squirrel or a cat, but Bilbo had not chased anything since the day years before during the seaweed expedition. And, as I hated admitting, his days of bursting into those exuberant runs were over. My boy was old and I knew his sight was failing. I could hear my own breathing, I was gasping, half sobbing as I called him. Then I became aware of the sound of water and ran towards the river. There was a narrow timber bridge over the stream, a modern replica of an older structure. I called his name, louder and louder, increasingly frantic. He answered. I saw a flash of colour, blue and brilliant orange, a kingfisher, then I saw fox-red, tawny, Bilbo, in the bright sunlight that was reflecting off the water, making it impossible to see clearly, except for the bird that had caught my eye.

Steam continued to rise off the drying earth around me. Bilbo was in the water and I could see he was in danger of being washed out to sea. I pulled off my fleece and my boots; I was still wearing pyjamas thanks to the chaos of the morning and my friend's relentless narrative of her woes, and crashed into the river, gagging as the cold hit me. I could see him, his head barely above water. I thrashed towards him, aware it had been ages since I had gone swimming; it had become difficult enough even to find time for a run. I reached him, but I needed both hands to support him. The current was strong, pushing against me like a great muscle. I could feel it driving us down river. Bilbo wasn't struggling; I could see the sun reflecting in his eyes. I forced myself to swim side on to the current and picked a point on the bank to head towards. The only way to get there was by rolling over on my back, holding Bilbo on my chest and kicking with legs strengthened from years of running. We got there. As I scrambled out of the river I noticed that the current had pulled my socks off. Bilbo looked like a skinned rabbit. He was soaked through and felt shockingly light and fragile in my arms. His coat was plastered to his body. I picked up my fleece, thankful I had taken it off; the wet weight of it would have dragged us to the bottom. I wrapped him in the jacket. The sun was already beginning to warm me up but he was shivering and seemed to be in shock.

All the way back to the cottage with its fairy-tale charm that now seemed ridiculous, I thanked God or whatever it was that had helped us get out of the water, and especially, the kingfisher, the tiny flash of colour that had guided me to Bilbo. He must have fallen off the bridge. Bilbo had never like swimming. Frodo met us at the door; he was very agitated but at least my friend, for all her depression, had been sufficiently alert to prevent him following me. My daughter sat with Bilbo as he dried out on the sofa, holding him, singing one of her songs. I was relieved when he showed interest in a piece of toast and went on to eat several slices. Yet again his recovery was astonishing, but I had begun to feel that each new ordeal was chipping away at his being, his very capacity to survive. It was as if he was now functioning on sheer intelligence and determination. They both were, but Frodo was hardy, still solid, defying time. His muzzle was no longer grey: it had turned white, yet his eyes remained clear, brighter than Bilbo's beautiful amber eyes which had begun to dim. It was only noticeable at times, but it was there, a slight veil clouding his gaze.

By the following morning Bilbo was ready to go walking. I went with him, feeling like a warden, prepared at any moment to lift him and carry him back into the house. He could have had a lonely end in the ocean a few miles away. There had been so many close calls over the years; Bilbo must by then have used up all of his nine lives, and a few extra as well. Still he fought on. I remembered the vet who had once said to me, 'This dog wants to live.' I had seen passive old dogs, weary of life, dying peacefully or indifferently, but Bilbo and Frodo were never passive. They retained their stubborn will to baffle the passing years.

*

A man had approached me, offering to buy my house. He had known the house as a boy some fifty years earlier. Now he was wealthy and wanted to buy it for his grown daughter. It seemed right; now we could at last move to the countryside. It was late. Bilbo and Frodo were very old and I had always felt guilty about not being able to create the life I had wanted for me and the dogs and now my child. My house was soon sold, but I needed to find another, and quickly. Each day I watched Bilbo, noting his irritation if he banged into something. He was good at concealing his blindness, it was our secret. I felt I could help him deal with a problem that would have been even more serious for a less cosseted dog. But I also began making preparations and, for a superstitious person like me, it was difficult. I made a phone call and explained the situation. I was lucky. The man who spoke with me was very kind and understood exactly what I needed. He made me a small coffin, of American oak. He said he would bring it to my house. Tears came to my eyes when I saw it. It was a beautiful thing, lined in white satin. I hid it in the spare bedroom. On the day of the move, it was still just another box to put in the removal van. I hoped it would not be needed for a while yet.

*

Dogs always know more, they sense things we miss. A few weeks before we moved, I had gone down to look over the house I had bought, the only one I had viewed. It was a run-down, late Georgian merchant-class house but it had a fine walled garden and some land attached to it. We had spent the summer's day in the garden and enjoyed a picnic. I began tidying up the old greenhouse first. It was a very peaceful day; the only sound I noticed was the bees among the flowers. The garden would be a safe playground for Nadia and the dogs. It was near the end of July, daylight lingered until late into the evening. I didn't want to return to the city. But reluctantly I began loading the car, placing my bits of cleaning equipment and gardening tools into the back of the station wagon. I had already settled my daughter into her seat. The dogs were waiting. Then Bilbo began barking and climbed over the seats and out through the open back of the car. He was angry and refused to get inside. When I went to lift him he shrugged out of my arms and stood his ground, staring into the darkness. At first I felt it was a sign that he wanted to move in right away. But it was the anger that bewildered me. The car clock read 10.55 and I was very tired. There he was, more than nineteen and a half years of age – what was that? about 135 in human years – yet still capable of becoming defiant and outraged. Eventually, he reluctantly obeyed me and climbed on to the passenger seat. I petted him and rubbed his shoulders and across his back. A line of fur stood up sharp, like a ridge, he was still annoyed, barking and fretting. Frodo joined in, but was slightly more composed than Bilbo. As I pulled away, it was Bilbo that jumped over the seat with his face to the glass of the rear window, sustaining his frenzied barking. I drove through the village and then pulled over; thinking he might have a heart attack. He looked at me, gave a sharp bark and sat hunched in the front seat, still bothered in a way I could not decipher.

It all became clear early the next morning. A phone call from a new neighbour explained Bilbo's fury. The house had been broken into and several of the pieces of abandoned furniture, wardrobes, sideboards and a three-legged armchair that had been left behind, were smashed shortly after eleven o'clock the previous night, within minutes of our driving away. A farmer driving by had noticed flashlights darting behind the windows. There were no curtains. The intruders must have been hiding in the bushes and behind the trees, waiting for us to leave. Bilbo had sensed that someone was there, but I hadn't noticed a thing.

*

The move was our final great adventure. We camped out in the big, old house. Problems with the antiquated wiring meant I had to use candles for weeks. Summer lasted into an unusually mild October. But when the winter arrived it came with an iron fist. Still I watched: the dogs were interested in their new world, they explored with a careful deliberation. They walked up and down the stairs. Where once they had run, they now jogged, or merely trotted. Most of all they favoured a sedate walk; the world for them was finally slowing down. Then the day of Bilbo's birthday dawned. It was not actually his birthday, of course, but the anniversary of the day we had met, the day he had selected me. I stood in the kitchen of this old house in which we had ended up, still together, after so many moves, so many journeys – spanning central England and up to Edinburgh, all over Ireland and many of its islands. Twenty years had passed. I was no longer young, and felt battered. But Bilbo, my Bilbo, was very old. The beautiful puppy had somehow become a very old dog. There had been so much time for us, wonderful years, an extended childhood of sorts; it had seemed that an inexhaustible supply of life was at hand. I may have been the leader but they had taught me, always helped me, and had often saved me. When my heart was broken they had healed it. But now it was coming to an end and I was watching for the signs that the moment had come. Bilbo gave me a message that stunned me with its simple eloquence. We were going upstairs to the bathroom, where I had to install a new fitting for the bath. It was the day after our twentieth anniversary. I didn't know many marriages that had lasted so well and smiled at the number of times I had been told that I was in fact married to my dogs.

Bilbo was walking ahead of me. He stopped so unexpectedly that I almost fell over him. He looked at me and gave me his paw. He had never done that. Despite all the hugs and the physical closeness, the way he lay down beside me, his habit of putting his head up under my chin, he had never, not once in twenty years, given me his paw. Instead of being touched and amused, I was devastated. It was my sign, the moment of our farewell. I bent down and hugged him. I felt a strange sensation, and finally understood what people meant when they said their blood ran cold.

We continued on up to the bathroom. He watched me as I replaced the fitting; I knew he couldn't see me very clearly but he was always inquisitive, even now. Frodo was standing by the door, watching us.

A couple of hours later, hours spent remembering, wondering, I recalled how that strange, gentle man, the second healer, who had been so kind, had said that the dog would decide for himself. I sat down in an armchair. Bilbo climbed into my lap. Frodo sat at my feet. I bent down and kissed Bilbo's head. He pushed it under my chin, that unique gesture, but without its usual force. I knew he was going, I could feel him drifting away. It felt right, he had decided. After all his battles the one burden he could not accept was being blind. He died in my arms a few moments later and as I looked at the old dog, I could see the puppy he had been. Frodo came with me as I carried Bilbo up to the bedroom to wrap him in my patchwork quilt, the only one I had ever made, when he had been a puppy pulling at the fabric and had given me a fright because I thought he had eaten some pins. I placed him in the coffin that had been ready for so many months. Bilbo's eyes were closed tight; when he was sleeping he always looked as if he felt he had to keep them shut tight, in case they opened before he was quite ready to wake. Frodo sat down beside the polished wood side of Bilbo's coffin, and dropped his head. Suddenly he seemed ancient and utterly defeated. His grief matched mine. The old woman on the London Tube all those years earlier had been so right, the grief was great. It had to be, because the love had been that and more.

*

Bilbo lay in his coffin in my bedroom. It was freezing outside, the ground was solid with the cold and all the surface water had turned to ice. Frodo lost interest in eating and would take food only if I fed him from a spoon. The two of us were like ghosts. The brief cold days of winter dragged on. It was a strange Christmas. Friends who regarded the countryside as alien territory best left to the wolves filled the house. I cooked a lot of food and spent hours washing dishes.

*

That New Year's Eve was the third day of continuous rain. I told Frodo we would go out into the garden for a little walk as soon as it stopped. The night before I couldn't sleep but wanted to stay still as Frodo had settled beside me and seemed so weary. I watched a video about Otto Dix, and about halfway though the film, Frodo had begun to yelp in his sleep. He seemed very distressed and I stopped the tape and was never able to resume watching it. Perhaps Frodo had been dreaming. I wondered what kind of dreams dogs have and wondered if he had dreamt about Bilbo. Each time my daughter or I mentioned Bilbo, Frodo's face would fill with hope. It was agonising to watch. Twenty-seven days had passed since Bilbo had died, almost to the minute, eleven o'clock in the morning, in the same room, and Frodo was bereft. I knew I was keeping vigil with him; I wanted to be there for him as I had been with Bilbo, whose death had been as graceful as his entire life had been. But, although I had been so vigilant, Frodo took me by surprise. The rain lashed against the windows in a final squall. I felt it would soon stop and clear and I told him we would go out into the garden in a while.

Frodo sat bolt up right and barked as if he had been stabbed. He fell forward and I dropped to my knees and took one of his broad, flat paws in each of my hands and stared at him. I would like to say that it was peaceful and gentle; and that I was comforting and eased his way. But I didn't. I cried and sobbed and begged him not to leave me and I looked into his eyes until the life was gone. Sunlight streamed into the room, the sky had brightened and the rain had finally stopped. Only now it didn't matter.